KU-598-960

Beckett Matters

Beckett Matters

Essays on Beckett's Late Modernism

S. E. Gontarski

EDINBURGH
University Press

Edinburgh University Press is one of the leading university
presses in the UK. We publish academic books and journals
in our selected subject areas across the humanities and social
sciences, combining cutting-edge scholarship with high
editorial and production values to produce academic works
of lasting importance. For more information visit our website:
edinburghuniversitypress.com

© S. E. Gontarski, 2017

Edinburgh University Press Ltd
The Tun – Holyrood Road
12(2f) Jackson's Entry
Edinburgh EH8 8PJ

Typeset in 11/13 Adobe Sabon by
Servis Filmsetting Ltd, Stockport, Cheshire,
and printed and bound in Great Britain by
CPI Group (UK) Ltd, Croydon CR0 4YY

A CIP record for this book is available from the British Library

ISBN 978 1 4744 1440 1 (hardback)
ISBN 978 1 4744 1441 8 (webready PDF)
ISBN 978 1 4744 1442 5 (epub)

The right of S. E. Gontarski to be identified as the author of
this work has been asserted in accordance with the Copyright,
Designs and Patents Act 1988, and the Copyright and Related
Rights Regulations 2003 (SI No. 2498).

Contents

Acknowledgements

I am grateful to the organizers of three events, literary conferences and performance festivals, for inviting me to deliver Keynote or Plenary Addresses and so to present portions of this volume's Introduction to gatherings of literary scholars, performers and philosophers. In particular I should like to thank department chair, Professor Petr Kotatki, and colloquium coordinator, Tomas Koblizek, of the Department of Analytic Philosophy, Institute of Philosophy, Czech Academy of Sciences, Charles University, and the Theatre Faculty of the Academy of Performing Arts in Prague, Czech Republic, for inviting me to address the 'Chaos and Form: Echoes of Beckett in Literature, Theatre and The Arts' gathering on 11 April 2016 and for their gracious hospitality. 'Chaos and Form' was the 11th Prague Interpretation Colloquium.

I am equally grateful to the organizers of the 'Beckett and World Literature' conference at the University of Kent in Canterbury, UK, for inviting me to address the gathering on 4 May 2016. The conference organizer, Thirthankar Chakraborty, assistant lecturer in comparative literature, and fellow organizers, Selvin Yaltir and Rosanne Bezerra de Araujo, have earned my gratitude for their timely invitation and their hospitality. The Kent conference was offered in conjunction with and made possible by the support of the Centre for Modern European Literature, the School of European Languages and Culture, and the Humanities Faculty Research Fund of the University of Kent.

Finally, my thanks to the organizers and conveners of the University of Gdańsk Samuel Beckett Seminar, Dr Tomasz Wiśniewski, Dr Monika Szuba and Professor David Malcolm, for inviting me to deliver a Plenary Lecture on the topic 'Experimental Beckett': 'Samuel Beckett's Elsewhere: The Remains of the Modern and the Exhaustion of Thematics'. The Gdańsk Beckett Seminar was held in conjunction with 'BETWEEN.POMIĘDZY 2016: An International Literary and Theatrical Festival/Conference' in Sopot, Gdańsk, and Gdynia, 19–21 May 2016. In addition, the conference offered me the opportunity to discuss my previous book, *Creative Involution: Bergson, Beckett, Deleuze* (EUP 2015) in a public conversation with poet Jacek Gutorow (University of Opole, Poland), to engage in a forum after the screening of 'NOTFILM: a documentary on the making of *Film* by Samuel Beckett', a discussion between me and Ross Lipman (the director) conducted by Tomasz Wiśniewski, an evening held in conjunction with the DOCS AGAINST GRAVITY film festival, Gdynia, and the opportunity to offer a performance workshop on *Ohio Impromptu* with London actor Jon McKenna, Polish actor Ryszard Ronczewski and filmmaker Elvin Flamingo. Such lectures, public discussions and cross-disciplinary engagements have enhanced my scholarship, research and theater work immeasurably.

Unless otherwise noted all letters to and from Barney Rosset and the Grove Press staff are in the Barney Rosset/Grove Press Archives now at the George Arents Research Library at Syracuse University, the John J. Burns Library, Boston College, the Wilson Library, University of North Carolina, Chapel Hill, and the Stanley E. Gontarski Grove Press Research Materials at Florida State University, Special Collections. All material is used with the permission of the principals.

Earlier versions of the essays revised and collected as *Beckett Matters* appeared in the following publications. My thanks to the editors and publishers of the books and journals for permission to reprint.

Chapter 1: 'Beckett and the Voice of Modernism', in Dirk van Hulle (ed.) *Beckett the European* (Tallahassee, FL: Journal of Beckett Studies Books, 2005), pp. 150–63.

Chapter 2: 'From Unabandoned Works: Samuel Beckett's Short Prose', in *Samuel Beckett: The Complete Short Prose, 1928–1989*, edited and with an Introduction and Notes by S. E. Gontarski (New York: Grove Press, 1996), pp. xi–xxxii; and 'That white speck lost in whiteness: Imagining the Death of Imagination',

Introduction to Samuel Beckett, *Imagination Dead Imagine*, 50th Anniversary Edition (Dublin: The Salvage Press, 2015).

Chapter 3: 'The Conjuring of Something Out of Nothing: Samuel Beckett's "Closed Space" Novels', Introduction to Samuel Beckett, *Nohow On: Company, Ill Seen Ill Said, Worstward Ho* (New York: Grove Press, 1995, paperback only), pp. vii–xxviii.

Chapter 4: 'Samuel Beckett's "Imbedded" Poetry and the Critique of Genre', *Fulcrum: An Annual of Poetry and Aesthetics*, No. 6 (2008), pp. 478–83.

Chapter 5: 'Art and Commodity: Samuel Beckett's Commerce with Grove Press', in Mark Nixon (ed.) *Publishing Samuel Beckett* (London: British Library Publications, 2011), pp. 139–51.

Chapter 6: 'Editing Beckett', *Twentieth Century Literature: A Scholarly and Critical Journal*, 41, No. 2 (1995), pp. 190–207.

Chapter 7: 'A Centenary of Missed Opportunities: Assembling an Accurate Volume of Samuel Beckett's Dramatic "Shorts"', *Modern Drama*, LIV, No. 3 (2011), pp. 357–82.

Chapter 8: 'Still at Issue After All These Years: The Beckettian Text, Printed and Performed', *Journal of Beckett Studies*, 24, No. 1 (2015), pp. 105–15.

Chapter 9: 'Beckett and Performance', in Lois Oppenheim (ed.), *The Palgrave Advances to Samuel Beckett Studies* (New York: St Martin's Press; London: Macmillan Press, 2004), pp. 194–208.

Chapter 10: 'Reinventing Beckett', *Modern Drama* (Special issue: Samuel Beckett at 100), XLIX, No. 4 (2006), pp. 427–50.

Chapter 11: '*Company* for Company: Androgyny and Theatricality in Samuel Beckett's Prose', in James Acheson and Kateryna Arthur (eds), *Beckett's Later Fiction and Drama: Texts for Company* (London: Macmillan, 1987), pp. 193–202.

Chapter 12: 'Samuel Beckett and the "Idea" of Theatre: Performance Through Artaud and Deleuze', in Dirk Van Hulle (ed.), *The New Cambridge Companion to Samuel Beckett*, 2nd edn (Cambridge: Cambridge University Press, 2014), pp. 126–41.

Chapter 13: 'Greying the Canon: Beckett in Performance, Beckett Performing', in S. E. Gontarski and Anthony Uhlmann (eds), *Beckett After Beckett* (Gainesville: University Press of Florida, 2006), pp. 141–57.

Chapter 14: '"I think this does call for a firm stand": Beckett at the Royal Court', in David Tucker and Trish McTighe (eds), *Staging Beckett in Great Britain* (London: Bloomsbury Methuen Drama, 2016), pp. 23–40.

Abbreviations

CDW	*The Complete Dramatic Works* (London: Faber & Faber, 1986)
Company	*Company* (New York: Grove Press, 1981)
CP	*The Collected Poems of Samuel Beckett*, ed. Seán Lawlor and John Pilling (London: Faber & Faber, 2012)
CSP	*The Complete Short Prose, 1929–1989*, ed. S. E. Gontarski (New York: Grove Press, 1995)
Disjecta	*Disjecta: Miscellaneous Writings and a Dramatic Fragment by Samuel Beckett*, ed. Ruby Cohn (New York: Grove, 1983)
Dream	*Dream of Fair to Middling Women*, ed. Eoin O'Brien and Edith Fournier (Dublin: Black Cat Press, 1992; New York: Arcade Publishing, 1993)
Endgame	*Endgame* (New York: Grove, 1958)
Letters 1	*The Letters of Samuel Beckett, Volume 1, 1929–1940*, ed. Martha Dow Fehsenfeld and Lois More Overbeck (Cambridge: Cambridge University Press, 2009)
Letters 2	*The Letters of Samuel Beckett, Volume 2, 1941–1956*, ed. George Craig, Martha Dow Fehsenfeld, Dan Gunn and Lois More Overbeck (Cambridge: Cambridge University Press, 2011)
Letters 3	*The Letters of Samuel Beckett, Volume 3, 1957–65*, ed. George Craig, Martha Dow Fehsenfeld, Dan Gunn and Lois More Overbeck (Cambridge: Cambridge University Press, 2014)
Nohow	*Nohow On: Company, Ill Seen Il Said, Worstward Ho*, ed. S. E. Gontarski (New York: Grove Press, 2011)

TN 2   *The Theatrical Notebooks of Samuel Beckett,*
               Volume 2, Endgame, ed. S. E. Gontarski (London:
               Faber & Faber; New York: Grove Press, 1992)
TN 4   *The Theatrical Notebooks of Samuel Beckett, Vol.*
               4, The Shorter Plays, ed. S. E. Gontarski (London:
               Faber & Faber; New York: Grove Press, 1999)
Three Novels *Three Novels: Molloy, Malone Dies, The*
               Unnamable (New York: Grove Press, 1955)
Watt   *Watt* (New York: Grove, 1959)

For Marsha,
For all she has said and says,
For all she has thought and thinks,
For all she has done and does,
For all she has been and is,
For all,
Again.

The Remains of the Modern and the Exhaustion of Thematics: An Introduction

ὁδὸς ἄνω κάτω μία καὶ ὠυτή [The way upward and the way downward is one and the same.[1]] (Heraclitus, fragment 60 (Diels), epigraph to T. S. Eliot's 'Burnt Norton', *Four Quartets*)

> The words were spoken as if there was no book,
> Except that the reader leaned above the page,
>
> Wanted to lean, wanted much most to be
> The scholar to whom his book is true, to whom
>
> The summer night is like a perfection of thought.
> The house was quiet because it had to be.
>
> The quiet was part of the meaning, part of the mind:
> The access of perfection to the page.
>
> And the world was calm. The truth in a calm world,
> In which there is no other meaning, itself
>
> Is calm, itself is summer and night, itself
> Is the reader leaning late and reading there.
> > (Wallace Stevens, 'The House Was Quiet and the World Was Calm')

When I found myself, with students, reading some Beckett texts, I would take three lines, I would spend three hours on them, then I would give up because it would not have been possible, or honest, or even interesting to extract a few 'significant' lines from a Beckett text. The composition, the rhetoric, the construction and rhythm of his works, even the ones that seem most 'decomposed', that's what 'remains' finally the most 'interesting', that's the work, that's the signature, this remainder which remains when the thematics is exhausted [. . .]. (Jacques Derrida, 'This Strange Institution We Call Literature'[2])

Samuel Beckett's 'Work in Process'

Samuel Beckett seemed, almost from the first, simultaneously here and there, within and without, of his time and beyond it, always somehow elsewhere, or rather between there and elsewhere, simultaneously rooted and rootless, historical and ahistorical. His *oeuvre* was the product of an artist who underwent serial re-conceptions, transformations and reinventions over his long writing career, and so his work is not easily classifiable, characterised as it is by change, movement, denials, rejections and negations. Thus, Beckett pushed his work beyond limits, restrictions, boundaries, and then pushed beyond yet again, to the exhaustion of the possible. The youthful poet could engage, embrace, emulate and ridicule the cult of difficulty among his Modernist peers and elders – as in his first published poem of 1930, *Whoroscope*, with its clumsily punning title, its formal echoes of T. S. Eliot's *The Waste Land*, its travesty of Descartes's personal predilections and peccadilloes, the poem complete with the requisite, signature footnotes, yet avoiding, if not ridiculing, Eliot's grandiose thematics. Even amid such parody, Beckett was simultaneously elsewhere, playing the don and professional scholar, building a career, dutifully filling commissions, explicating James Joyce's *Work in Progress* to readers 'too decadent to receive it', as he declared in his mentored essay 'Dante... Bruno. Vico.. Joyce' (*Disjecta* 27). The Joyce essay first appeared in what was something of an avant-garde club, the literary journal *transition*, and was almost immediately republished as the lead essay in the 1929 volume called 'The Exag' by those involved, the essay composed as he was struggling to complete, in the summer of 1930, another commission, a shortish monograph on Marcel Proust.[3]

Shortly after the publication of the Joyce essay, Philippe Soupault generated yet another commission when he suggested to Joyce that, along with Alfred Peron, Beckett translate into French segments of what was still called *Work in Progress* but would finally appear in 1939 as *Finnegans Wake*.[4] The translation was rushed for its scheduled appearance in *Bifur*.[5] A deferential, even diffident Beckett wrote to Soupault from the *École normale* on 5 August 1930, including 'Two copies [of the translation]. In case *Bifur* wanted one', noting further, 'But I would not wish to publish this, not even a fragment, without permission from Mr Joyce himself, who very well might find it all really too badly done and too far from the original' (*Letters 1* 39). French bookseller Adrienne

Monnier described the commission in her 1976 memoir, *The Very Rich Hours of Adrienne Monnier*:

> Beckett's and Peron's work went to the stage of being set in type (I have the *Bifur* proofs which are covered in corrections), but it did not go to the stage of being approved for printing, for while Joyce was very satisfied with the result when he was consulted, he got it into his head to team seven persons together under his guidance (five in addition to the two promoters). That was to have the pleasure of saying my 'Septuagint' [. . .] [or 'LXX', the translation of the Tora or Pentateuch from Hebrew to Greek by seventy-two scholars for inclusion in the Library of Alexandria]. In my opinion, Joyce's revision was very desirable, considering his genius for language and his knowledge of French, but it did not appear to me either useful or just to add to those who had done almost all the work – and magnificently, I assure you – five people of whom some, myself for example, were there only as supernumeraries. (Monnier 1976: 167)[6]

Despite his deferential note to Soupault, Beckett took umbrage at Joyce's shift in strategy and returned piqued to Trinity College in September of 1930 to resume his Fellowship, and so also his (short-lived) teaching duties for Michaelmas term, about which he was at least as conflicted as he was about his Modernist peers. Steven Connor sees something of an additional slight from Joyce towards his callow acolyte in the final sentence of the *Anna Livia* excerpt (although more than one critic has associated the slur with Joyce's Dublin arch-rival, Oliver St John Gogarty):[7]

> If we are to judge by the final sentences of *Anna Livia Plurabelle*, the figure cut by the young Samuel Beckett in the Joyce circle was that of a brilliant, if slightly bumptious scholar. The putdown of the uppity young Protestant swot that suddenly appears in Joyce's text – 'Latin me that, my trinity scholar [*recte*, scholard], out of eure sanscreed into oure eryan!' [*FW* 215, 26–7] – is given its sting by the fact that Beckett had been involved in translating part of this section of the *Wake* into French: Beckett in fact quoted the sentences that immediately precede this one in his 'Dante... Bruno. Vico.. Joyce', but broke the quotation off just before it. (Connor 2009)

We might question Connor's chronology some, but Beckett would indeed have been sensitive to such matters. Further insult may have been added with the play on scholar, the word 'scholard', ending with a 'd', might have suggested the word 'dunce', a word etymologically neutral for a time as it was linked to followers of Duns Scotus who were considered enemies of learning. Yet further, *A Dictionary of Hiberno-English: The Irish Use of English* suggests that the term 'scholar' was generally used for 'primary school children' in Ireland, hence connoting a callow student. Returning to Trinity chastened, perhaps, Beckett stopped off in London just long enough to deliver the *Proust* typescript to Charles Prentice personally, writing formally to request an appointment on 15 September (*Letters 1* 48). To his confidant, Thomas MacGreevy, two days later, Beckett would admit to something less than confidence with this project as well: 'I saw Prentice this morning and handed over *Proust*. He was charming, but I have a feeling he won't touch it for Chatto & Windus, that it isn't scholarly and primo secundo enough. However there it is and off my hands at last' (letter only excerpted in *Letters 1* 48n1).

Beckett did return to Paris in March of 1931 for the launch of the revised translation, now published in *La Nouvelle Revue Française*, his work receiving little attention and so little acknowledgment at the celebration *séance* even as the product bore, as Monnier suggests, striking resemblance to his and Peron's original draft, the duo credited only in the work's appearance in *NRF*. By 1934, however, sidelined from the *Finnegans Wake* translation, Beckett would begin to release something of a Modernist countercurrent, to recoil from, and to suggest a certain embarrassment with, displays of acrobatic prose, of esoteric knowledge and arcane forms. He would begin to distance himself from such efforts (and from Joyce himself, for that matter) in his very personal, even confessional 1931 (quasi-) love poem that appeared prominently in *The European Caravan: An Anthology of New Spirit in Literature*, edited by Samuel Putnam et al. (1931), under the title 'Casket of Pralinen for the Daughter of a Dissipated Mandarin', in which, after an ostentatious display of Joycean erudition, the unnamed narrator notes a revulsion for the act of representation itself –

Oh I am ashamed
of all clumsy artistry
I am ashamed of presuming to
arrange words

of everything but the ingenuous fibers
that suffer honestly

– returning here perhaps to what he called, in the 'Dante... Bruno. Vico.. Joyce' essay, Joyce's 'direct expression' (*Disjecta* 27). He returned to such stuttering hesitancy again in his 1934 quatrain 'Gnome', with its qualified attack on at least 'a world politely turning / From the loutishness of learning', although the prose arabesques of *Watt*, and the 'loutishness of learning' on display therein, lay before him still. The quatrain in toto gives as follows:

Spend the years of learning squandering
Courage for the years of wandering
Through a world politely turning
From the loutishness of learning.

Deirdre Bair, moreover, cites a dismissive note Beckett wrote in a copy of the Proust monograph that turned up in a Dublin bookshop: 'I have written my book in a cheap flashy philosophical jargon' (Bair 1978: 109).

Such bouts of recoil and distancing – his rejection of what will become a championing of the necessity of difficulty in poetry offered in T. S. Eliot's 1933 Harvard lectures, 'The Use of Poetry and the Use of Criticism' – suggest, however, a Beckett on his way to affirming refusals, the 'No', and a different sort of 'unintelligibility' in his own work. At Harvard, Eliot would proclaim that

something should be said about the vexed question of obscurity and unintelligibility. The difficulty of poetry (and modern poetry is supposed to be difficult) may be due to several reasons. First, there may be personal causes which make it impossible for a poet to express himself in any but an obscure way; while this may be regrettable we should be glad, I think, that the man [the poet, we would say today] should be able to express himself at all. Or difficulty may be due to novelty. [... Finally,] there is the difficulty of the author's having left out something which the reader is used to finding; so that the reader, bewildered, gropes about for what is absent, and puzzles his head for a kind of 'meaning' which is not there and is not meant to be there. (Eliot 1986: 143–4)

Unlike, say, William Carlos Williams's rejection of Eliot, claiming that the latter had 'returned us to the classroom', the nature of Beckett's rejections simultaneously reinscribe the difficulty that Eliot *et alia* celebrated, that is, they create a tie to and thus may constitute one of the shifting points of Beckett's betweenness – Beckett, like Eliot, being preoccupied with the intersection of worldly chaos and the promise of aesthetic, principally poetic, order, in Beckett's case amid linguistic failures. Subsequently, Beckett would, on occasion, reject his rejections, refusing to allow both 'Casket of Pralinen' and 'Gnome' to be reissued in various collected editions and allowing the *Proust* monograph to be reprinted only reluctantly, at the insistence of his English publisher.

However, if not an embrace of at least a conversation with Rimbaud's 'Il faut être absolument modern' ('One must be absolutely modern') from *A Season in Hell* (1873), and with Pound's Chinese borrowing and redrafting of 'Renew thyself daily' as the anthem of Modernism, 'Make it new'[8] (as something more than a celebration of novelty) remains in Beckett's work as trace, that is, as remnant, remainder, ruin, the way that the ghost of Eliot's dramatic monologues remains, or the spirit of Apollinaire's walking poem 'Zone' remains, the long poem celebrating the new, the narrator walking across, through and beyond time zones. Beckett translated the poem, following Apollinaire's use of couplets, in March of 1949 as he was retyping *En attendant Godot* and just before beginning to write out, in June, his colloquy on art as 'Three Dialogues: Samuel Beckett and Georges Duthuit' (*Letters* 2 109). 'Three Dialogues' was published post-war in *Transition Forty-Nine*, No. 5 (December 1949: 97–103); 'Zone', translation unsigned, in the following issue, *Transition-Fifty*, No. 6 (October 1950: 126–31), the latter of which John Pilling rightly calls 'perhaps the most successful [translation] he ever attempted' (Beckett 2012: 414). The translation, then, forms something of a bridge between 1949 and 1913, the year of the original poem's publication and one of the miraculous years of Modernism, only three years after Virginia Woolf's proclamation that 'human character has changed'. Apollinaire's poem appeared in the same year that Stravinsky's *Rites of Spring* premiered, a year that Jean-Michel Rabaté (2007) has called 'The Cradle of Modernism'. By 1917, Apollinaire's manifesto praising innovation, 'The New Spirit and the Poets', would be published, along with his edition of Baudelaire's poems; Beckett's translation would thus link the earlier poets and him to a new age of innovation and renewal: post-war Paris in the midst of its post-Nazi recovery.

*Our
Exagmination
Round His
Factification
For Incamination
Of Work
In Progress*
Samuel Beckett
& others

Even with diminished eyesight, from 1922 to 1939 Joyce saw, or rather oversaw, the production of what would be his final novel as a constantly accumulating, encyclopaedic *Work in Progress*. Beckett's own literary output, if rather less than encyclopaedic, might productively be thought of and read as a single, sustained 'work', as John Updike suggested in his 1961 *New Yorker* review of *How It Is*.[9] Beckett's enterprise, however, is more a 'work in process', the *oeuvre* a developing, continuously connected process rather than a series of discrete and so more or less static and complete products; not a linear, progressive, or even regressive continuity, but a disparate, digressive, erratic, rhizomatic process, which in its ambition and in its own way is as grand as Joyce's, a continuous and contiguous rethinking of the nature, function and impact of art in the twentieth century, and equally, or relatedly, of the philosophical, aesthetic, epistemological and ontological crises of the artist producing it. Engagements with Beckett's *oeuvre* thus become extended meditations, themselves 'works in process' on Beckett's 'Work in Process', 'appearing in transitions', as Sylvia Beach punningly said in her Preface to the 1961 Faber reissue of 'The Exag' – which, moreover, now featured Beckett prominently as lead author on the dust cover and on the book's spine (some compensation, perhaps, for the credit originally denied his and Peron's translation of 'Anna Livia Plurabelle' as 'Anna Lyvia

Pluratself'). Little wonder then, as Beckett turned his attention to theatre, that in his staging of his works in print, as well as, in some cases, new works, the process continued – could not but continue, his theatre productions becoming part of and not apart from the process of artistic creation, and thus his performances in themselves becoming *new* works, even as the published texts (or typescripts in some cases) on which those productions could be said to be based had been in print for some time. Such a process continues, as it should, among contemporary theatre directors on a global stage, that is, elsewhere, at least among directors who see theatre as a living institution of which Beckett remains an integral part.

Samuel Beckett's Elsewhere

The milieu of experimental, modern, or avant-garde art in which Beckett worked in the early part of the twentieth century was, then, what has come to be called Modernist, even as he was a late or belated arrival on that scene, and thus a second wave or second generation Modernist, that is, one born in the twentieth rather than the nineteenth century. His guiding of his friends' reading into the post-war years reflects his continued immersion in that milieu, his taste and interests decidedly leaning towards experimental, anti-bourgeois art, to Modernism itself, if late. Writing to Morris Sinclair from the rubble that was the city of Saint-Lô on 21 October 1945, for instance, Beckett accepted the role of at least erstwhile don, offering some tutelage, suggestions about his cousin's PhD aspirations, and offering personal contacts: 'I should be very glad to help you and could introduce you to Sartre & his world. [...] If you don't know any Sartre and can't get him in Dublin, let me know & I'll have you sent from Paris anything I have' (*Letters* 2 22–3). On 27 May 1946, now writing from Ireland of his French story 'Suite' – which would be published, at least in part, as 'La Fin'[10] – he tells his sometime-agent George Reavey that, at 45,000 words, it might make a stand-alone volume, noting that 'Camus's *Etranger* is not any longer'. Of Camus's novel he continues, 'Try and read it, I think it is important' (*Letters* 2 32). In a letter to Georges Duthuit of 1 September 1946, furthermore, Beckett announced that, 'The first part of my story, *Suite*, has appeared in the July number of the *Temps Modern* and the second and last part will appear in October' (*Letters* 2 39). It did not, and

Beckett took the failure to complete the publication personally, as a slight from Sartre and de Beauvoir.

Furthermore, writing from Dublin to former lover Pamela Mitchell, on 19 August 1956, Beckett continued to play the role of Modernist tutor, recommending as 'books you could read' a list that lays out a certain tradition in contemporary French literature, including Sartre's *La Nausée*, Malraux's *La Condition Humaine*, Julien Green's *Léviathan*, Céline's *Voyage au Bout de la Nuit*, Jules Renard's *Journal* and Camus's *L'Etranger* (*Letters* 2 493). The suggestions themselves detail Beckett's debt to his age and to a literary spirit of experiment, Beckett very much a product of a liminal culture, a culture in transition, which change he would help foster and accelerate; that is, he was a writer shaped by and a shaper of his age, even as he exceeded it. Asked about the literary influences on him and his work by Hans Naumann on 17 February 1954, Beckett was, as usual, reserved, circumspect, if not evasive. Of Kafka, Beckett would admit to having read only parts of *The Castle*:

and then in German, that is losing a great deal. I felt at home, too much so – perhaps that is what stopped me from reading on. Case closed there and then. [. . .] I am not trying to seem resistant to influences. I merely note that I have always been a poor reader, incurably inattentive, on the lookout for an elsewhere. And I think I can say, in no spirit of paradox, that the reading experiences which have affected me most are those that were best at sending me to that elsewhere. (*Letters* 2 464–5).

In a 1989 interview, Jacques Derrida adopted something of the same strategy towards 'This Strange Institution We Call Literature', of feeling 'too close' to the work of an author. Derrick Attridge asked: 'As far as I'm aware, you've never written on Beckett: is this a future project, or are there reasons why you have observed this silence?' 'This is an author to whom I feel very close, or to whom I would like to feel myself very close', Derrida replied,

but also too close. Precisely because of this proximity, it is too hard for me, too easy and too hard. I have perhaps avoided him a bit because of this identification. Too hard also because he writes – in my language, in a language which is his up to a point, mine up to a point (for both of us it is a 'differently' foreign language) – texts which are both too close to me and too distant for me even to be able to 'respond' to them. [. . .]

How could I write in French in the wake of or 'with' someone who does operations on this language which seem to me so strong and so necessary, but which must remain idiomatic? How could I write, sign, countersign performatively texts which 'respond' to Beckett? How could I avoid the platitude of a supposed academic metalanguage? (Derrida 1991: 60)

Derrida, too, sounds like something of a latecomer to a cultural flux already well in process, in transition, that he will reconstitute with a series of operations loosely termed deconstruction, and develop a way of speaking against a western tradition of metaphysics that he called the 'metaphysics of presence', introducing terms like trace, supplementarity, *différance* and repeatability into the critical and philosophical lexicon. Derrida seems to suggest that at best he might make manifest what is already latent in Beckett's operations on language and its fictive expression or representation as voice. He too seems to be resisting re-presentation, or simply restating, paralleling or performing Beckett's thought, linguistic operations or lines of flight in something of a metalanguage, and so the matter inevitably comes down to representation itself, to the issues with which Beckett himself struggled and contested and rejected, only to fall back, systemically, into representational inevitability – since consciousness, memory, signs and images are themselves in a sense repetitions, representations of a certain level of perception. Hence one is trapped in a representational bind, a rejection which reaffirms itself in its very rejection, but a re-presentation without originary presentation.

'No is all there is'

Much of Beckett's creative struggle was to find a new way – a third way, perhaps, his own way at least – to break free from or to rupture cultural expectations, linguistic presuppositions, cultural restrictions, the conventions of art in general, even of those most recently challenged and overcome, by performing what Derrida calls 'operations on this language which seem to me so strong and so necessary', by trying to recount the sentience, the feel, the affect of life, living through consciousness, with memory, in time, within a controlled flux of experience; a flux in which the 'I' is always fugitive, betrayed, the author performing riffs, variations on Rimbaud's 'Je est un autre' ('I is an other'), in a language, a failing medium, or rather in languages both idiomatic and foreign to speaker and listener, 'a "differently" foreign language', as Derrida put it, even as the author was disappearing into a textual aggregate both material and immaterial. Beckett would not so much replace language as a creative medium as go on to fold it into the image, the literariness of language devalued in favour of 'the ingenuous fibers / that suffer honestly'. The nature of the *image* as both material and ethereal, internal and external, is that defined by Henri Bergson in *Matter and Memory* and essentially adopted, subsequently, by Gilles Deleuze:

> I see plainly how external images influence the image I call my body; they transmit movement to it. And I also see how this body influences external images: it gives back movement to them. My body is then, in the aggregate of the material world, an image which acts like other images, receiving and giving back movement, with perhaps this difference only, that my body appears to choose, within certain limits, the manner in which it shall restore what it receives. (Bergson 1991: 19–20)

Beckett's version of what Bergson calls an image is stated with youthful explicitation in his 1929 essay on Joyce's *Work in Progress*, a sentence oft-quoted in the Beckettian discourse but seldom anchored or grounded, seldom glossed thoroughly, as perhaps being self-evident, the pugnacious Beckett addressing the decadent reader: 'You complain that this stuff is not written in English. It is not written at all. It is not to be read – or rather it is not only to be read. It is to be looked at and listened to. His writing is not about something; it is that something itself' (*Disjecta* 27). The sentence assumes and asserts a certain degree of materiality to thought, to memory, to language and to the image. By 1966 Beckett would disclose to the critic Colin Duckworth, who was editing a classroom edition of *En attendant Godot*, what amounted to a concise, even pithy, theory of theatre: 'I produce an object. What people make of it is not my concern' (Beckett 1966: xxiv). Language would remain, of course, but with story devalued, the drive of language towards representation at least exposed if not thwarted, language itself becomes opaque, substance, material. Writing to Georges Duthuit on 11 August 1948, amid a discussion of themes decidedly Bergsonian if not, anachronistically, Deleuzean, Beckett declares:

The mistake, the weakness at any rate, is perhaps to want to know what one is talking about. In defining literature, to one's satisfaction, even brief, where is the gain, even brief? [. . .] One must shout, murmur, exult, madly, until one can find the no doubt calm language of the no, unqualified, or as little qualified as possible. One must, no is all there is, apparently, for some of us, this mad little tally-ho sound, and then perhaps the shedding of at least a good part of what we thought we had that was best, or most real, at the cost of what effort. And perhaps the immense simplicity of part at least of the little feared that we are and have. But I am beginning to write. It has just struck midnight. Until tomorrow. (*Letters* 2 98)

Gilles Deleuze will call such 'operations on language', such shouts and murmurs, 'minor', and such writers, Kafka and Joyce among them, 'minoritarian'; and of Beckett's directly imagistic work in film Deleuze would call his single venture into that medium, 'The Greatest Irish Film (Beckett's 'Film')', because 'Becoming imperceptible is Life' (Deleuze 1997: 26). Much of Deleuze's analysis will detail and engage that struggle, Beckett's here and there, Beckett's now and then, Beckett's 'elsewhere', a way we now call Beckettian.

Herbert Blau describes his own engagements with Beckett thus: 'the shift from thinking *about* him to the sensation of thinking *through* him, by means of his thought, such as it was, in the extremity of meaning's absence' (Blau 2000: 2); that is, what Derrida has called the exhaustion of thematics. That 'exhaustion' keeps us within the text and breaks the 'indispensable' compact between artist and occasion, as Beckett put it in his oft-quoted 'dialogues' with Georges Duthuit published in 1949: 'The analysis between the artist and his occasion, a relation always regarded as indispensable, does not seem to have been productive either, the reason being perhaps that it lost its way in disquisitions on the nature of occasion' (*Disjecta* 144). The alternative is advanced by Duthuit early in his own disquisition on Tal Coat, as he announces 'The theory of the discreet overthrown. The world a flux of movement partaking of living time, that of effort, creation, liberation, the painting, the painter [all part of what Henri Bergson calls *durée*]. The fleeting instant of sensation given back, given forth [not, that is, merely simulated or represented] with context of the continuum it nourished' (*Disjecta* 101). Whose voice we hear in this disquisition attributed to Duthuit may be of more than scant interest as

Beckett was a puppeteer through much of these dialogues, Duthuit more often than not ventriloquised. Such a 'sensation' as Blau and, finally, Duthuit or Beckett suggests, then, informs Beckett's work. The issues of undermining both the metaphysics and physics of thereness, if there there is, or ever was, of presence, say, in favour of an elsewhere, and the dematerialisation of character in a literary transvaluation to voice, 'The theory of the discreet [as] overthrown', are especially slippery in the embodied art of theatre; but Beckett's theatrical art of dematerialising and de-theatricalising theatre, his shift from narratives to staged images, his dissolution of character, a devaluation of literariness, 'the loutishness of learning', become works that often trace traces.

Such an overview and critique of thereness and, or through, voice develop as not only central motifs in his *oeuvre* but as an heuristic that drives thought on, beyond impossibility, a way of moving that is neither linear nor forward, neither progressive nor regressive, neither originary nor teleological, not progress but process. The mysteries of voice as transcendent and so ethical, that is, categorical – or, on the other hand, internal, that is, personal, hermetic and monadic, and so hypothetical – remain as unresolved, as unresolvable tensions in Beckett's art that allow him to explore the infinite betweenness of such possibilities from at least Kant through, if not Husserl, then at least Derrida's critique of voice in Husserl's phenomenology, through, as well, Deleuze's redrafting of Henri Bergson, offering in Duthuit's phrase, 'The fleeting instant of sensation given back'. It is an art of the new, as Beckett describes it at the conclusion of his disquisition on Bram van Velde: 'For what is this coloured plane [the framed painting], that was not there before. I don't know what it is, having never seen anything like it before. It seems to have nothing to do with art [. . .]' (*Transition Forty-Nine*, December 1949: 126). The untethered, thereless voice, in all its conflicting mysteries, is the means, almost a method, of getting at thought's flow, thought's thinking itself into existence, beyond a thinker, that is, beyond anything but a trace of the Cartesian *cogito*, of consciousness as being and becoming, through, to borrow Derrida's neologism, *différance*, a process of movement, deferral and change, of differentiation, say, with neither genesis nor terminus. Among the last poems that Beckett wrote, 'Brief Dream', sent on a postcard to his British publisher, John Calder, he returns to these persistent preoccupations and paradoxes: a struggle towards the new only to find the familiar yet again, the new as always already familiar, the familiar always defamiliarised and so always again new, or rather re-newed:

> Go where never before
> No sooner there than there always
> No matter where never before
> No sooner there than there always.

From there, from or through voice, speech somehow disembodied, being dematerialised, the essays that follow go on – but go elsewhere, to the familiar 'never before'.

Notes

1. Heraclitus, *Diels*, Hermann, trans. John Burnet, at http://philoctetes. free.fr/heraclite.pdf (in Greek and English, last accessed June 2016). The fragment is translated on occasion as: 'The way forward and the way backward is one and the same.' For Beckett it is the 'way' that matters.
2. Derrida 1991: 60.
3. In a letter to Alec Reid of 17 January 1956, Beckett noted, 'Whoroscope and Proust belong to the ENS [*École normale supérieure*] years' (*Letters* 2 596).
4. See Greco Lobner 1997 and Quigley 2004.
5. Chronological details at http://jamesjoyce.ie/on-this-day-1-may (last accessed June 2016).
6. See also Ferrer and Aubert 1998.
7. See, for instance, Schork 1997: 38.
8. Succinctly outlined by Michael North at https://www.guernicamag. com/features/the-making-of-making-it-new (last accessed June 2016).
9. John Updike, *The New Yorker*, 19 December 1964, pp. 165–6.
10. The English translation by Richard Seaver would appear in *Merlin* II:3 (1954), pp. 144–59.

References

Bair, Deirdre (1978) *Samuel Beckett: A Biography*, New York: Vintage.
Beckett, Samuel (1966) *En attendant Godot*, ed. Colin Duckworth, London: George C. Harrap.

Beckett, Samuel (2012) *The Collected Poems of Samuel Beckett*, ed. Seán Lawlor and John Pilling, New York: Grove Press.

Bergson, Henri (1991) *Matter and Memory*, New York: Zone Books.

Blau, Herbert (2000) *Sails of the Herring Fleet: Essays on Beckett*, Ann Arbor: University of Michigan Press.

Connor, Steven (2009) 'Literature, Politics and the Loutishness of Learning', at http://www.stevenconnor.com/loutishness

Deleuze, Gilles (1997) *Essays Critical and Clinical*, trans. Daniel W. Smith and Michael A. Greco, Minneapolis: University of Minnesota Press.

Derrida, Jacques (1991) 'This Strange Institution We Call Literature', in *Acts of Literature*, ed. Derek Attridge, New York: Routledge.

Eliot, T. S. (1986) *The Use of Poetry and the Use of Criticism* (Charles Eliot Norton Lectures for 1932–33), Cambridge, MA: Harvard University Press.

Ferrer, Daniel and Jacques Aubert (1998) 'Anna Livia's French bifurcations', in *Transcultural Joyce*, ed. Karen Lawrence, Cambridge: Cambridge University Press, pp. 179–86.

Greco Lobner, Corinna del (1997) '*Anna Livia Plurabelle di James Joyce* by Samuel Beckett; James Joyce; Nino Frank; Rosa Maria Bollettieri Bosinelli', *James Joyce Quarterly* XXXV:1, pp. 180–3.

Monnier, Adrienne (1976), *The Very Rich Hours of Adrienne Monnier*, New York: Charles Scribners's Sons (reprinted Lincoln: Bison Books, 1996).

Putnam, Samuel et al., eds (1931) *The European Caravan: An Anthology of New Spirit in Literature, Part I: France, Spain, England and Ireland*, London: Brewer, Warren & Putnam.

Quigley, Megan M. (2004) 'Justice for the "Illstarred Punster": Samuel Beckett and Alfred Péron's Revisions of "Anna Lyvia Pluratself"', *James Joyce Quarterly* XLI:3, pp. 469–87.

Rabaté, Jean-Michel (2007) *1913: The Cradle of Modernism*, London: Wiley.

Schork, R. J. (1997) *Latin and Roman Culture in Joyce*, Gainesville: University Press of Florida.

Theory Matters

Beckett's Voice(s)

all sound his echo (*Watt*)

. . . not of one bird but of many . . . (Ezra Pound, *Canto 75*)

it's impossible that I should have a voice [. . .] this voice that is not mine, but can only be mine (*The Unnamable*)

All that Fall is a specifically radio play, or rather radio text, for voice, not bodies. I have already refused to have it 'staged' and I cannot think of it in such terms. A perfectly straight reading before an audience seems to me just barely legitimate, though even on this score I have my doubts. But I am absolutely opposed to any form of adaptation with a view to its conversion into 'theatre.' It is no more theatre than *End-game* [*sic*] is radio and to act it is to kill it. Even the reduced visual dimension it will receive from the simplest and most static of readings [. . .] will be destructive of whatever quality it may have and which depends on the whole thing's coming out of the dark. (Beckett to Barney Rosset, 27 August 1957, *Letters 3* 63)

Voice as disembodied entity, manifest sporadically, often of its own volition, in fragments, perceived piecemeal, echo of being, identity, self or others (even if falsely so), emanating from above or below, from within or without, is the heuristic that drives Samuel Beckett's supreme fictions, then manifests itself powerfully, if obliquely, slantingly, in the theatre that follows, beginning, perhaps, or at least overtly manifest, in 1957 with *All That Fall* for radio. Its sources are indeterminate, evasive, ghostly, receding, counterfeited, echoed, ventriloquised. It may be, finally – beyond the Belacquas, the Watts and Murphys, beyond the Didis

and Gogos, Hamms and Clovs, Winnies and Willies, even beyond
the Maddies and Dans – Beckett's most profound literary creation. He inherited a version of it from the early twentieth-century
Modernists – most directly from James Joyce, the surrealists,
and the Verticalists orbiting Eugene Jolas's *transition* magazine
in Paris – in the form of the interior monologue, which he then
stretched, extended and finally disbursed, scattered beyond cohesion, beyond recognition, beyond identity, even self-identity, as
the self in conversation with itself is often not self-presence but
counterfeit. Beckett's treatment of voice, or rather voices, of a
multivocal, indeterminate multiplicity, is thus a late, belated,
nomadic Modernism, post-Interior Monologue, less Joyce, James,
Bergson or Husserl, or others of the Modernist pantheon, than
Derrida (particularly on voice in Husserl) and Deleuze (*passim*),
and thus Beckett's art serves as an intervention into an ongoing
discourse among (mostly) twentieth-century European artists and
philosophers, even as it appears in the fictions or in performances
as little more than a murmur, ill heard, ill understood, ill recorded,
ill (re)presented, its sources unnamable: it 'is not a sound like other
sounds', Molloy tells us, 'that you listen to, when you choose, and
can sometimes silence, by going away or stopping your ears, no,
but is a sound which rustles in your head, without you knowing
how, or why. It's with your head you hear it, not your ears, you
can't stop it, but it stops itself, when it chooses' (*Three Novels* 40).

Writing for *The Guardian* on 19 August 2014, a perceptive
Marco Bernini comes close as he asks, 'to what extent are voices
in Beckett's fiction just metaphorical presences?': 'The qualities
of Beckett's voices (alien, autonomous, without a recognizable
source, and having aggressive or commanding contents) resonate
with and sometimes even match the phenomenology of auditory
verbal hallucinations (hearing voices in the absence of external
stimuli).' But for Bernini such a state, when it is not hallucinatory
or pathological, implies a presence, 'a recognizable source', a self
in conversation with itself in a language that re-presents presence,
and is thus the discourse, the monologue, even, of interiority,
what Bernini calls 'inner speech': 'Can Beckett's voices be interpreted as the fictional rendering of our inner monologues – of the
dialogues we constantly entertain within ourselves? Inner speech
is hard to stop or to escape from?' The rhetorical question is
evasive, of course; the implication is a self-presence, but Beckett's
voices with their own volition and detached from substance, from

materiality, from presence, often function as characters, as others, nameless, ghostly, hostile. It is Beckett's rupture of the Cartesian foundation of subjectivity, 'I am.' Beckett's own case is made most overtly, even ham-fistedly, early on, in the commissioned, pseudonymous, 1934 essay, 'Recent Irish Poetry', published in an Irish number of the London-based journal, *The Bookman*. This was Beckett's brash assertion of a Modernist sensibility even as he was already outgrowing it, his development of voice its pedigree. Beckett divides Irish poets between those aware of 'the breakdown of the object, whether current, historical, mythical or spook. [And] The thermolaters [. . .] never at a loss to know when they are in the Presence [. . . who would] like this amended to the breakdown of the subject. It comes to the same thing – rupture of the lines of communication' (*Disjecta* 70), even, or especially, self-communication. Witness as well an unpublished fragment of a prose text (Reading University Library MS 2910), dated 'Paris, Jan. 1977', 'The Voice', which exhibits affinities with *Company* with its references to the Ballyogan Road, Croker's Acres, his father's shade, and his green top-coat stiff with dirt and age, and which explores the vague relationship between Voice and Hearer, dramatised as if it were to be performed: '*Why die I not? My life is mud. I shall not be. O that I were. Perish the day. Let me be* (same flat tone)', then the voice breathless, faint and fading away.

Reduced to its fundamental sound, the mysteries of voice consists of a search for: 1) source, the location of the voice, within or beyond, always unnamable; 2) credibility or authenticity, that is, whether transcendent or delusional; and 3) significance, as marker of discrete, essential being or identity, selfness, say, and hence a self-presence, auto-affection; or external, as a cultural echo, itself often of a cultural echo, the voice, thus, not a spatial entity but a temporal movement, a flow across moments. These were issues that drove Beckett's art beyond the delineation of literary character, but even as character was fragmented and disbursed, voice separated from body, as in echo, say, its origin remained irresolute and grew increasingly so, part of the paradox of being and the enigma that drove the aporetics of Beckett's narratives of irresolution. The very insolubility of these difficulties, thus, guaranteed failure but provided as well the impetus for articulating the epistemological quandary beginning with, then moving beyond, *Watt*, through the crisis of epistemology into those of ontology and ethics.

Beckett's exploration of these questions admittedly took a variety of forms: an early fascination first with echo, then with schizophrenic voices; his need, expressed in the 'German Letter of 1937', to find amid the phonemics of voice some kind of Nominalist irony en route to the unword; his attempt in the fiction from *Watt* and *Three Novels* to *Worstward Ho* to determine the nature and location of that impossible imperative, that compelling need to express amid its acknowledged futility; and finally his (re) construction, his (re)representations in the theatre, of dramatic voices beyond the corporeal, beyond the constrictions and conventions of the interior monologue, beyond the coherence of ego and character, difficulties that dominated the mature fiction as well as the so-called late theatre.

Beyond such psychological, ontological and epistemological enigmas, Beckett's exploration of voice is consonant with one of the century's technological signatures, the projection, transmission and reception of not just coded data (with the telegraph, say), but of the human voice itself, wireless, voice separated from presence or source. The twentieth was the first century to confront such separation and then to store the results for retrieval and repetition in a form of electronic, disembodied memory. The invention of radio enabled the transmission of news across oceans and continents, but the invention of electronic, non-corporeal memory allowed its infinite repetition and redistribution. It is the shift from *All That Fall* to *Krapp's Last Tape*. Such developments spurred a popular entertainment industry based on individual desire and human absence. Music and the performing voice could be listened to at the time and place of an auditor's choosing, like a book; and the technical development of film allowed drama's separation from the presence of actors. The Parisian literary magazine with which Beckett was most closely associated, *transition*, was interested in the impact of the recorded voice and repeatable imagery on contemporary art. In response to Sergei Eisenstein's essay, 'The Cinematographic Principle and Japanese Culture' (*transition* 19/20, June 1930), editor Eugene Jolas offered a prescient *aperçu* of the future in his essay 'Towards New Forms': 'The development of the talking film and radio will doubtless have a revolutionary influence on the drama, among other things. And since sound seems to be the basis of the hear-play [Jolas's awkward neologism for the radio play] and the cinema-drama [do. film], it is safe to say that the problem of the new form will be the word' (1930: 104), or rather, 'the new form' will be voice. A voice and its image that 'comes to one in the dark' would profoundly effect drama, poetry and fiction in the new century and provide Beckett with the compelling metaphor for his aporetic art. And it would be Beckett who would exploit fully the possibilities of the disembodied voice in his fiction and drama.

Beckett was himself already exploring the intricacies of voice well before the appearance of Jolas's essay. A year earlier, for instance, he published 'Assumption' in *transition* 16/17 (June 1929), a story that opens with one form of the paradox: 'He could have shouted and could not' (*CSP* 30). 'Assumption' concerns the poet's need to 'whisper' the turmoil (i.e., alien or contrary voices) down, to dam the stream of cacophonous sounds before 'it' happens, the expulsion of a great storm of inchoate sound that threatens to overwhelm all. Through it Beckett would offer his reservations about the orphic authenticity of 'Verticalism' with its reconstituted Romanticism, the plunge into the depths of the artistic soul through which the artist ascends to divine heights and achieves near-perfect communion and communication, transcendence. His story, rather than affirming Jolas's 'New Romanticism' and the 'Revolution of the Word', asserts the failure of the poet to find his personal voice or to distinguish it from other myriad and ambient voices, the artist failing to ascend to divine heights, romantic clichés that were largely irrelevant to Beckett's enterprise. That search assumed classical echoes in *Echo's Bones and Other Precipitates* (1935) with the myth of Narcissus and Echo, or as in *Watt* where 'all sound his echo' (41) because 'all outside him will be he' (40); such is the definition of 'calm', 'premonitions of harmony' (40) for Watt. The poems are remnants or ghosts, afterimages, say, of what once was, arranged by a voice that is no more. *Dream of Fair to Middling Women* mocks the voice of 'the little poet' (26), but acknowledges Augustine's sense (*Confessions* 11:6) of that voice that 'passed by and passed away, began and ended; the syllables sounded and passed away, the second after the first, the third after the second, and so forth in order, until the last after the rest, and silence after the last' (cf. *Dream* 105, 137). This very Beckettian statement was recorded by Beckett in his *Dream Notebook* (1999a: 27) and deployed in 'Echo's Bones' (*CP* 15) and *First Love* (*CSP* 37); it is his first but lasting engagement with the disjunctions between transcendent and internal, between eternal and diurnal, between interior and exterior voices.

In *Murphy* casual ironies delineate key elements of this disjunction. Ticklepenny refers to 'the vocal stream issuing from the soul through the lips' (Beckett 1957: 85). This is Plato being mocked, but the source of the voice cannot be as easily dismissed. Rosie Dew uses the ouija board to access voices from the *au-delà* (98); the fakery is obvious, yet the phenomena persist. The patients in the M.M.M. offer written and verbatim reports of their inner voices (167–8); they may be paranoid, but their problems remain. Dr Killiecrankie has experience with the schizoid voice: 'It was not like a real voice, one minute it said one thing and the next minute something quite different' (185). In the French text Killiecrankie's Celtic background is particularised: conceived in the Shetlands, born in the Orkneys, and weaned in the Hebrides, he is a great admirer of Ossian, and 'croyait s'y connaître en voix schizoïdes. Elles ne ressemblaient guère aux voix hébridiennes, ni aux voix orcadiennes, ni aux voix shetlandiennes. Tantôt elles vous disent ceci et tantôt cela' (Beckett 1947: 135). Underlying such humbuggery is Beckett's visit with psychoanalyst Wilfred Bion (2 October 1935) to the Tavistock Clinic to hear Jung in the third of his Tavistock lectures describe how complexes may appear in visions and speak in voices, assuming identities of their own. Jung argued that unity of consciousness was an illusion, because complexes could emancipate themselves from conscious control and become visible and audible. For Beckett this was a critical insight, or confirmation of his determination that anything like an authentic, self-present voice would henceforth be attractive but decidedly problematic, unattainable, illusional.

Watt overtly explores variations of the schizoid voice. As Mr Spiro replies to his own questions, Watt hears nothing of this because of 'other voices, singing, crying, stating, murmuring, things unintelligible, in his ear' (*Watt* 29). This is followed by the first of many extended paradigms, one completely worked through, and although Watt understands little, or nothing, the coherence of the series testifies to some stability. Further on he hears a mixed choir, 'from without, yes really it seemed from without' (33); this time the paradigm approaches the irrationality of pi, as in the lyrics of Watt's threne which detail the ratio of days in the year over days in a week ('Fifty-two point two eight five seven one four' [33–4]). A second calculation for leap year ensues. At Mr Knott's house, Watt experiences many more such 'incidents of note', the force of which is to dislocate or untether his sense of reality and complicate the relationship between his inner and outer worlds. Most emblematic are his difficulties with the pot (81) and the process of 'reason' whereby he makes manifest the Lynch family to solve the problem of the famished dog. Abandoned by its inner rats (84), 'the last rats. For after these there would be no more rats, not a rat left', but then he 'was longing for a voice [. . .] with the old words' (84–5), as his world becomes increasingly 'unspeakable' (85). He begins to hear 'a little voice' (91) saying that Mr Knott is shy of dogs, but he does not know what to make of 'this particular little voice'. On leaving Knott's establishment (225), he has the curious experience of multiplicity, of seeing a figure that is and yet is not his self. At the station (234) he relives the experience of a woman named Price whose voice comes and goes; and, knocked to the ground (239), he distinguishes fragments from Hölderlin, the schizoid poet. The consequences of his illness are seen in Part 3, in his disintegrating discourse with Sam, the Cartesian *méthode* having succumbed under the weight of the trust placed in it. Derrida, in chapter six of *Voice and Phenomenon: Introduction to the Problem of the Sign in Husserl's Phenomenology*, calls the voice listening to itself 'the major instance of illusory self-transcendence'; the voice in *Watt* constitutes a warning of the fate awaiting those determined to eff the ineffable, the unnamable sources of voice.

Yet such warnings go unheeded, even by the author. The attempt to deconstruct, to decompose, to hear and to identify and name the voice is the incessant preoccupation of the *Three Novels*. That concern is anticipated in the 'German Letter of 1937', where Beckett overtly expressed his post-Mauthner distrust of language, and sought a means of boring holes in the silence, seeking not the 'apotheosis of the word' favoured by Joyce and Jolas, but rather something of the opposite, a 'literature of the unword' (*Disjecta* 171–3). What he thought desirable as a necessary stage was 'some form of Nominalist irony' as the basis for an irrational art. The word 'irony' is central. Wilhelm Windelband notes the consequences of assuming that universals cannot be substances (the Realist position), and asks what then they might be. Boethius had defined a word ('vox') as a 'motion of air produced by the tongue'; and with this the scope of an extreme Nominalism was given; universals are thus considered nothing but collective names and sounds that serve as signs for a multiplicity of substances or their accidents. Nominalism thus formulated (that is, lacking irony) was propounded and defended during this period with some of the intensity of the more recent poststructuralism, whose assumption of extreme Nominalism accounts for much in Beckett's writing, but not the ironic possibilities of 'something', a materiality, perhaps, seeping through. As Windelband notes, the *metaphysics of individualism* which corresponds to such a theory of knowledge' asserts that 'only individual things are to be regarded as substances, as truly real' (here he invokes *Roscellinus*), and this is a position that Beckett (more or less, at least for a time) found useful; 'universals are nothing but collective names, common designations for different things, sounds (*flatus vocis*), which serve as signs for a multiplicity of substances or their accidents' (Windelband 1938: 296). Such nominalist irony thus requires the level of detailed particularity one sees in *Murphy* and *Watt*, say, and such reconstituted scholasticism constitutes the background from which the experiments with voice emerge in the great writing of the middle period.

The poem 'bon bon il est un pays' of 1947 reminds us of Beckett's materialism as it dramatises the mind as place, a location to which the poet retreats to seek 'le calme, le calme' (*CP* 53); this is the realm sought by Malone (*Three Novels* 198), beyond the tumult, where he will never really be troubled by anything ever again. The advent of the voice disturbs that peaceful prospect, because it constitutes a different imperative. Molloy's quest for the self is equally a quest for the evasive voice. Anticipating the structure of the *Three Novels*, he cries out: 'this time, then another time perhaps, then perhaps a last time' (25). This is an outer not an inner voice, neither a presence nor its literary marker, the interior monologue, but it serves to focus the theme of voice's indeterminate and multiple sources. Molloy first intimates the inner voice when he hears the voice of a world collapsing endlessly (40). He chooses not to listen to that whisper, but it is not a sound like other sounds; 'it' stops when 'it' chooses, and he will hear it always, though it does not suit him to speak of it at this moment. But soon he hears 'the small voice' telling him to take his crutches and get out; and he obeys. So much for 'le calme' (59). He hears it again, telling him that that his region is vast (65), and he acknowledges that he is subject to its imperatives (86), more categorical than hypothetical, a commandment of reason and so a play on or with Kant's ethics of metaphysics. The voice that tells him to leave the forest manifests itself as a murmur, 'something gone wrong with the silence' (88), but at the critical moment he hears a voice telling him not to fret: 'Don't fret, Molloy, we're coming' (91), which may suggest Matthew 14:27 or Acts 23:11, the voice of the Lord saying, 'Be of good cheer'; it also anticipates the Pauline voice heard by the Unnamable.

Moran undergoes a similar but more emphatic imperative. His self-sufficiency and contentment are disturbed, and he is obliged to 'see about Molloy' (92) as his last moments of peace and happiness slip away. He recognises the silence 'beyond the fatuous clamour' (121), and early in his narrative he tells of the voice he listens to that needs no Gaber to make it heard, one that *seems* to be within but is ambiguous and not easy to follow, one he is just beginning to know, but one that he will follow 'from this day forth, no matter what it commands' (132). The voice doesn't get much more categorically imperative than that. When it ceases he will do nothing but wait (like the Unnamable) for its return. Tomorrow, he adds, he may be of a different mind; and, sure enough, he later recounts how he first heard that voice (a voice giving orders, a voice from *without*) on the way home, but paid little attention to it (169–70). In the final paragraph, however, he returns to that voice. He is getting to know it better now, beginning to understand what 'it' wants, to understand the ethics of it. It tells him to write 'this report' (ambiguous and not always easy to follow), which is simultaneously that which has just concluded and may include the next two volumes, which relentlessly go on.

Malone presents another variation of voice, that of an author who tells stories both to pass the time and to create avatars, puppets through which he may be heard; this compulsion towards identity will be stripped away in the endeavour to isolate the voice itself, the unaccommodated voice (just as Molloy has become an unaccommodated self). Malone will 'play' (180), but he recognises from the outset that (like St Paul, perhaps) he must put away playthings and find himself alone in the dark. The narrative is the account of movement towards that position, an *end* simultaneously the *beginning* of a third novel. Of stories, inventories, objects, he must divest himself, little by little, in order to try but fail to reach the great calm behind the tumult (198). He hears 'noises' (206), but has lost the faculty of 'decomposing' them (pun intended). The voice manifests itself in this text less directly than in the two flanking narratives, but Malone's sense that 'it's coming' (233) (death, identity, the voice, all?), like the images of St John that dominate the story, cries the way of one to come.

The search for the voice is finally the great theme of *The Unnamable*. The French and English texts vary in their beginnings, but the first paragraph of each concludes the same way: 'Je ne me tairai jamais. Jamais' ('I shall never be silent. Never', 294). The tone adopted is a composite biblical one. Like John (14:10) he must speak of things of which he cannot speak; like Paul (1 Corinthians 15:10) he invokes an authority that is not his own, 'yet not I, but the grace of God which was with me'; like Job (7:11) he is obliged to speak in the anguish of his spirit, in the bitterness of his soul; and, like Jeremiah (later said by Beckett to be the voice behind *Company*), he will utter his lamentations, but a distinction appears between a self which 'utters' and the 'not-I', which cannot so easily be identified. This is implicit in 'These things I say' (301), which echoes John 5:34: 'these things I say, that ye might be saved', the voice imagining 'a without' (305; the Calder text omits the crucial indefinite article); but above all is the paradox of 'this voice that is not mine, but can only be mine', one that must continue to utter, to invent voices 'woven into mine' (309), in order 'not to peter out' (307), or go silent (310). The paradox forms the dramatic conflict of Beckett's metonymic drama, *Not I*.

If the voice is not renewed, it will disappear one day (309). Mahood tells his tale, then is silent, 'that is to say his voice continues, but is no longer renewed' (325). The narrator is surrounded by such murmurs, vociferations, the 'burden' (refrain, pensum) of which is 'roughly' that he is sentient and so alive (335). But all this 'business about voices' requires to be 'revised' (336); he speaks of voices ('let them come'), but the problem remains that of 'Assumption': 'if I could only find a voice of my own, in all this babble' (438). Mahood and Murphy sometimes spoke, the Unnamable tells us, 'but it was clumsily done, you could see the ventriloquist' (348). Yet there is another sound which never stops (349), which forces the recognition that he is in a head, a skull, assailed with 'noises signifying nothing' (351), a voice which has 'denatured' him. He considers going deaf (354), invokes the conceit of a head growing out of the ear (356), a kind of transformer, the aural equivalent of the eye, of *percipi*, the paradox of no voice without a listener. If only the voice would stop (364), what could be worse (a soprano perhaps), he's in a dungeon (369), an oubliette, with a voice that never stops. He wishes it would stop, this blind voice, 'this meaningless voice which prevents you from being nothing' (372). He is the tympanum, vibrating (383), a between to inner and outer, and simultaneously part of, yet other to each.

These agonies culminate in a passage accentuating the contrast between 'my voice' and 'the voice' (393–4), the euphony in the French text (Beckett 1953: 177) between 'Ma' and 'La' rendering the difference more poignant. The Unnamable hears a voice failing, fears he is going silent, listens hard, intimates the real silence, then as he pauses for air, listens for his voice in the silence. It returns ('elle revient'), and with renewed breath he moves towards the end. The conclusion is itself inconclusive, the nature and location of the voice at the end as much a mystery as they were in the beginning. This may be implicit in the sub-atomic imagery which governs the novel, the old stable ego of self split, shattered to reveal a quantum world of non-Newtonian motion, in which the voice may be heard but not located, or located but not heard, and in which the very attempt to 'identify' it is of necessity doomed to frustration. Such uncertainty (in Heisenberg's sense of the word) suggests why the novel must end in impasse.

Yet since voice is in need of an auditor, a spectator, an audience, say, the paradox of *percipi* (no voice without a listener) is given a dramatic turn in the novel, and anticipates the structure of the dialogic within the monologic, an audience folded into the discourse, that informs much of Beckett's later drama. The Unnamable invokes an image of his audience, waiting for the show to begin, a free show, or perhaps performance is compulsory, 'it takes time, you hear a voice, perhaps it's a recitation, that's the show, someone reciting [. . .]' (*Three Novels* 381–2).

That final comment is, for all its innovative qualities, a retreat from the central problem of voice, an interlude (like others in *Malone meurt*) before Beckett resumed his quest for the voice, in *L'Innommable*. Curiously, at this creative junction, the drama lags behind the fiction with respect to Beckett's great theme, the voice in its plurality, in its multiplicity, returning to familiar motifs of Cartesian dualism, dialogue, pseudocharacters, in an exteriorised setting,

In the fiction that followed *Three Novels*, Beckett tried still to move (the paradox is implicit in this phrasing) beyond the impasse, to resolve the dilemma, to move beyond the interior monologue, the issue that of a voice within that is as often a voice without. *Texts for Nothing* explores this issue, but, unsurprisingly, with neither success nor resolution. These *Texts*, too, are failures, for at

best they rehearse yet again the 'old aporetics'. 'Text 2' acknowledges that 'it [voice] must be in the head' (*CSP* 106), 'Text 3' that
the voices are 'only lies' (109), that wherever they come from they
'have no life in them' (113). 'Text 4' raises the question, 'what
would I say, if I had a voice', only to conclude, 'this voice cannot
be mine'. 'Text 5' strains for a voice 'not from without', but fears
it might be 'the voice of reason' (118), hence an entertainment
of Kant's categorical imperative, different from 'all these voices,
like a rattling of chains in my head' (120). The awareness of 'that
other who is me' in 'Text 8' makes it difficult to accept 'this voice
as mine'; but 'Text 10' seeks 'a voice of silence, the voice of my
silence' (the disjunction still between 'la voix' and 'ma voix'). The
'vile words' of 'Text 11' make the narrator believe he's here, 'a
head with a voice belonging to it' (145); and that 'a voice speaks
that can be none but mine' (146). Yet in 'Text 12' it's 'not me'
('Not-I' in the accusative); and the final text begins by affirming,
'Weaker still the weak old voice that tried in vain to make me.'
The old paradox remains: 'No voice ever but in my life'; the imper-
sonal phrasing, 'it murmurs', and the partial resolution, 'nothing
but a voice murmuring a trace' (152). The image of 'trace' is by
definition ephemeral, a tiny flurry of dust disturbed by the breath,
evidence of the voice that was but cannot endure, leaving no trace
against the 'black nothing' (154), the voice that cannot speak yet
cannot cease. The 'impasse' has not been broken, but these *Texts*
testify to a continuing process, a voice that goes on.

While the issue remains unresolved in *How It Is*, it remains a
powerful heuristic. The novel begins by uttering three of Beckett's
certainties, birth, existence and death: 'before Pim with Pim after
Pim' (Beckett 1964: 7), then introduces the fourth, the voice that
was 'once without' and then 'in me', 'an ancient voice in me not
mine'. This restates the central thesis of *The Unnamable* and the
Texts for Nothing, the need to express as an obligation, a categorical imperative, or pensum. Before Pim the voice remains 'afar'
(13) but 'changeable' (15), 'once quaqua then in me' (20), 'barely
audible' (23) again, yet 'not mine' (40). With Pim the attention
moves to the voice of the other. Pim's voice is 'extorted' (21),
'there within an inch or two' (56), but his is not that ancient voice
the narrator seeks, and whether Pim has heard that voice or not
remains in doubt (74), heard any more than what the narrator
will utter when tormented by Bom (76). Again, Beckett invokes
the distinction between the voice that utters and the 'first voice'.

Whatever the status of the latter, 'above' or 'without' (79), it is 'only one voice my voice never any other' (87) that he hears and murmurs, though it be folly. It leaves, it returns (95), like that of the Unnamable. Part 2 ends with the restatement of the voice 'in me that was without quaqua', but introduces the notion of something transcendent or categorical, 'the voice of us all' (99), to be examined in Part 3. The notion is important, for it constitutes the difference between the narrator as sole elect played against the sense of universal experience, but by a rigorous process of categorical logic the voice comes 'back at last' (106), the universal (a choir, megaphones, 'the voice of us all'), and manifests itself as that of the self alone, just as the possibility of the many is ruthlessly reduced to the knowledge of the one (108, 114, 126 and 128), the categorical reduced to the hypothetical, the ethical reduced to the practical, pure reason reduced to practical reason. The given is the solitude (129), and the voice that recounts it is the sole means of living it; 'a past a present and a future' have been joined by the fourth inevitability, the voice, into a Bergsonian present. His life comprises 'bits and scraps strung together' (133) by 'an ancient voice ill-spoken ill-heard', the modality of both witness and scribe in doubt. The only conclusion (134) is that 'my life' is constituted by 'a voice without' (ill-spoken, ill-heard) which is now 'in me in the vault bone-white' (ill-heard, ill-murmured). But this is no advance on *The Unnamable*, nor even on the opening of *How It Is*, since no advance is possible beyond the logic that reduces 'this anonymous voice self-styled quaqua the voice of us all' to that of the 'single voice' within (139): 'this voice quaqua yes all balls yes only one voice here yes mine yes' (144–5). Any assertion of univocality is mocked by the dialogic, but when the panting stops what remains is finally 'only me yes alone yes with my voice' (146), for that is how it is, the identity between voice as coeval with self and voice as different, as other, as potentially universal remains unresolved, even unresolvable as the issues, voice(s) in phonic form, flow across time.

In *Company* the voice returns as memory, for the old themes are rehearsed once more, but even memory is often unrecognised or rendered unrecognisable by the sentient, perceiving, listening figure. Beckett considered calling the piece 'Verbatim' or simply 'Voice', but came to think of it as a text to 'keep going (company)' (Knowlson 1996: 574). Like other closed space tales, *Company* is neither memoir nor autobiography but an interplay, a multiplicity of voices, a fugue between one imagining himself into existence and an external voice addressing the hearer as 'you'. A voice (not 'the voice') comes from the dark (*Company* 3). It is company but not enough (5); it comes from first one quarter then another (9); and it ebbs and flows (11), comes and goes. The goal of the voice is 'To have the hearer have a past and acknowledge it' (24), or to create 'an addition to company' (41). But the images invoked are again ill-seen, and the voices are often false, fictions or figments whose role is that of aesthetic play, a devising for company, for one who at the end as in the beginning finds himself as he always was, alone.

Yet that voice, the enigmatic disembodied sound that swells out of the darkness like a radio transmission, for all its paradoxes and ambiguities, for all its irresolutions, remains Beckett's most profound, original and complex literary creation. Beckett returned to the structural idea of voice and echo that dominated his early poetry to provide the foundation for his pastiche in *Fin de partie*. In his 1967 staging of his 1957 play, he told the cast, 'The play is full of echoes, they all answer each other.' The echoes of *Endgame* are less bodiless voices than bodies with voices not their own; voices with indeterminate sources. Clov's opening monologue is already an echo, a repetition, the voice heard when one character echoes another. This becomes a central structural and thematic element of the play. The ontological, existential enigma in *Endgame* might be summed up thus: can a multiplicity and variety of voices make up an identity, a life?

That existential conception (not just figurative, nor metonymic, nor synechdochic, the part for the whole, say, but more radically and literally the part *as* the whole) informs much of Beckett's late metonymic theatre and became the rationale for a theatre of fragmentation. Shortly after writing *Fin de partie* Beckett responded to a request from the BBC to pursue the drama of pure voice. *All That Fall* began his infatuation with broadcast technology and allowed him to push the exploration of voice into hitherto unforeseen but perhaps inevitable realms. His first radio play was fairly conventional, relying on a bevy of semi-realistic sound effects and a plot that ends as the beginning of what may be a murder mystery. Hearing the BBC recording, Beckett incorporated the phenomenon of the recorded voice into his first English-language stage play, *Krapp's Last Tape*. As Krapp prepares for his annual birthday ritual, assessment of his rapidly failing life, he listens to tapes of past years, and the voice of memory is reified in the tapes stacked about his desk, weighing heavy on his desk as memories weigh heavy on his mind. The voices he hears are as strange and unrecognisable to him as if they were those of another or of others, which they are, in a sense. They must be *his* tapes, a record of *his* life, at least tapes made by him, but whether or not they capture, contain or represent his being, his identity, his self, his essence, is one expression of the paradox of voice. From here onward Beckett would explore on stage variations and extensions of the interior monologue, moving beyond its unity to multiplicities that defy the presence of theatre.

The success of *All That Fall* prompted Beckett in 1957 (before *Krapp's Last Tape*) to begin a second, more radical one-act radio piece, *Embers*, but he withheld it from the BBC until 1959. He spoke about its structure and problems to P. L. Mignon, and in so doing restated the paradox of voice. The play rests 'sur une ambi-guité: le personnage a-t-il une hallucination ou est-il en présence de la réalité?' (Zilliacus 1976: 83). Like *Endgame*, *Embers* is set on the margins of land and sea and so of interior and exterior. Henry alone, in all senses, speaks at first to the *au delà*, to his drowned father, whose death has haunted him since its occur-rence, then to his wife Ada about their daughter, Addie, the scenes replayed against the incessant sounds, the voice of the sea. Ada tells Henry that he will soon be quite alone with his voice, that there will be no other voice in the world but his. Whether the voices represent physical presences or are the product of Henry's mind, recurrent, unsettling echoes of his past, remains irresolute in both performance and reading, but such ambiguity substantially advances Beckett's manipulation of the medium and of the interi-ority of Modernism. Despite his initial reservations, *Embers* may be Beckett's most successful work for radio. It prompted a flurry of pieces for the medium, two of which were abandoned in the 1960s and resurrected in the 1970s (*Rough for Radio I & II*), and two that were mirror images of each other, one in French (*Cascando*), and one in English (*Words and Music*). The metaphor for *Rough I* is two knobs on a radio, but the work remains a weaker version of the theme treated masterfully in *Cascando* and *Words and Music*, the attempt to bring if not harmony between two forms of voice, words and music, at least peace.

With *Rough for Radio II* Beckett began to explore torture as a metaphor for creativity, and as such the radio play presages the last of his theatre works, *What Where*. The radio 'rough' or sketch includes characters whose names invite allegory: 'Animator', with a cylindrical ruler, accompanied by 'Stenographer' and a mute named 'Dick', who wields a bull's pizzle (a dried penis). The victim, bound, gagged, blindfolded, ears plugged, and hooded, is called 'Fox', a fricative, the voiceless form of 'Vox', or voice. The session begins, like *Endgame*, with an unveiling of the 'ravishing' F/Vox, whom the 'same old team' prods to speech or confession. The difficulty is access to the voice as well as its veracity once tapped, but the overt or too-obvious links between voice and repressed memory may account for Beckett's decision to jettison the work, at least for a decade.

In 1964 the voice in Beckett's theatre took a dramatic turn towards the ethereal, the ghostly, where all that remained of the characters was their voices, figures who were only echoes of their lives. *Play* too has a decided musicality about it as three apparently post-mortem figures or voices function as instruments played by a light. Side by side, the figures or icons never speak to one another but respond only to a mechanical stimulus, the inquisitorial light functioning as a conductor as a fourth character in what becomes, at Beckett's designated speed, an orchestration of sounds rather than a comprehensible narrative.

Beckett's first teleplay, *Eh Joe*, features a voice grown aggressive, antagonistic, an assailant, as it insinuates itself into Joe's consciousness to torment him over a suicidal lover. This voice is anticipated in the Unnamable's 'I can't stop it, I can't prevent it, from tearing me, racking me, assailing me' (*Three Novels* 307). Joe struggles to suppress it (although its emergence seems not to surprise him) as he has suppressed the voices of his family. The assailant voice calls Joe a 'mental thuggee', and the smile at the end, added to Beckett's production of the play but available in no published text, suggests that Joe is at least temporarily successful at suppressing the voices. This voice, the voice of a former lover, appears to emanate from 'that penny farthing hell you call your mind', but it is not just memory of a dead past. The antagonistic voice rehearses details of a former lover's suicide that neither she nor Joe could know first-hand and that the dead lover could not report. Yet Beckett insisted on the concrete reality of the assailing voice, insisting to Siegfried Melchinger, 'It is a concrete person for Joe ... he invents himself what he thinks he hears ... She really whispers in him. He hears her. Only if she lives can he have the wish to kill her. She is dead, but in him she lives. That is his passion: to kill the voices, which he cannot kill' (Kalb 1991: 103). She is both material and ethereal, person and figment, both internal and external; the broader problem of where the voice is ultimately located remains, of necessity, unresolved.

Beckett's *tour de force* of the staged voice is a pair of plays written in English just before his seventieth birthday, and which were performed in that honour. *That Time* and *Footfalls* opened at London's Royal Court Theatre in May 1976, the latter directed by Beckett and starring Billie Whitelaw. In *That Time*, Listener, a floating head some ten feet above stage level, listens to three voices, A, B and C, recite what are apparently memories of his past. The voices come from afar, from both sides of the theatre and above. Each tells a story whose details, like those in *Company*, correspond, if loosely, to those of Beckett's own life. Only the face of Listener is seen, with the hair spread out so that the audience seems to be looking down on a figure in bed, perhaps. The rest of the stage is dark, which focuses attention on the face, but the face is off centre, suggesting that although it is the only physical representation on stage it is not the sole focus of attention. The three voices that speak continuously (with the exception of two pauses and the last 23 seconds of the play) are thus 'central'. Like Krapp's tapes, they seem to represent the same person at different stages in his life, but those stages are fictions. Voice A in middle age tries to remember his childhood, voice B in young adulthood likewise, and voice C in old age likewise as well. Yet the stories are alien, voices of another, Listener barely responding to them until the end where a smile like that which ends *Eh Joe* in Beckett's staging appears, not to suggest success in stilling the voices necessarily but in having arranged their succession in a serial and so artful pattern.

Written to accompany *That Time*, *Footfalls*, featuring an aged, pacing woman in tattered nightwear, is divided into four parts, each separated by chimes, which grow fainter in each of the four soundings. In Part I the pacing May addresses the voice of her dying mother, whom May is apparently attending at her last, the mother in her nineties, May in her forties. In Part II Woman's Voice (the Mother's, apparently) observes and narrates her daughter's obsessive pacing through which the daughter affirms her existence; her perception of the material sounds of her footsteps and the dragging of her tattered nightwear thus offer some confirmation of her material corporeality. The 'Sequel' begins Part III of the play,

May's story. May, who herself may simply be narrated, a product of voice, narrates herself (in both senses), a semblance of what the audience thinks it sees on stage. Her anagrammatic other, Amy, is represented in dialogue with her mother, Mrs Winter, concerning the former's attendance at Evensong: 'I saw nothing, heard nothing, of any kind. I was not there' (*CDW* 402–3). Part IV has proven consistently difficult in production, so brief the fourth chime and so empty the stage. Beckett took great pains with this coda to suggest its thematic significance, emphasising that the thought-tormented body pacing before the audience is and is not there, or rather exists only within the embedded narratives of the play, constructed by the interplay of bodiless voices. The final ten seconds with 'No trace of May' is a crucial reminder that May was always 'not there', or there only as a 'trace', a whisper, a voice. Such dramatic absence, such bodiless presence anticipates the ghostly works for television, where being is twice removed (because of the medium), and the late plays, *Ohio Impromptu*, *Rockaby*, and *What Where*.

In *What Where*, a dimly lit megaphone (in the original, unrevised and only officially published text) speaks first, announcing images of the last five beings, 'In the present as were we still' (*CDW* 470). The apparently authoritative voice of Bam, as bodiless megaphone or (later) shimmery light or hologram, is already a voice from beyond the grave, according to Beckett. Four characters, Bam, Bom, Bim and Bem (a fifth unseen, incorporeal player [Bum?] is being 'worked over' as the play opens), nearly identical in appearance, their names differentiated by a single vowel (see Rimbaud's poem 'Voyelles'), are represented as if they existed. Bam's voice (V) controls the action, switching light (of memory and imagination) on and off the playing area, or the space of memory, to initiate action. In recasting the play for television, Beckett drastically altered the visual imagery of his first version and simplified dialogue and action, trimming the false starts, revising away much of the metatheatrical, internal revisions of the original. In Stuttgart the speaking voice became a huge, distorted face of Bam, refracted, diffuse, and dominating half the television screen. In his Stuttgart notebook Beckett wrote that 'S (Stimme [Voice]) = mirror reflection of Bam's face' (Beckett 1992: 7–8, 11). This death mask replaced the suspended 'small megaphone at head level' of the original publication; as Beckett noted, 'Loudspeaker out'.

The image that now intrigued him was the hooded statue of John Donne, the shrouded Dean of St Paul's spectral in his sculptured rendering. The two staged Bams, however, two stage or video representations and their corresponding voices, are not the same entity, not two versions of the same body, character, or even voice. In the Stuttgart TV production the difference between the two was achieved mechanically. 'There was a slightly higher frequency in [the voice] of the younger Bam, and a lower, deeper effect in the older Bam', according to cameraman, Jim Lewis (cited in Beckett 1999b: 451). In both French and English stage productions that followed Beckett's revised text for television, the vocal difference was achieved by recording and altering V to create, as Walter Asmus suggests, 'the ghost Bam, dead Bam, distorted image of a face in a grave, somewhere not in this world any longer, imagining that he comes back to life in the world, dreaming and seeing himself as a little face on the screen' (Fehsenfeld 1986: 238). In the Stuttgart notebook Beckett wrote, 'S's voice prerecorded. Bam's, but changed.' Shortly thereafter he added, 'Bam's voice in dialogue with some colour. S [Stimme] colourless' (Beckett 1992: 11). Instead of players in long grey gowns, their corporeality suspect, the four figures of the revised *What Where* appeared as floating faces dissolving in and out of the TV screen, which became the field of memory to replace the lighted rectangle of the stage, in a dialectic ballet of 'disappearance and manifestation'. Neither representation of Bam is material or corporeal, finally, Beckett representing instead a spectral or dreamed image and its mirror reflection. The rest of the figures of *What Where* are also ghosts, all the more so as they are re-presented by the patterns of dots on the TV screen. Whatever characters or bodies finally exist in *What Where* are created by voice, less absent presences than present absences. Such a treatment of dramatic figures simultaneously effaces and re-inscribes the body in the body of Beckett's drama.

What Where was the last of Beckett's completed stage and television works, and being is finally voice. To Charles Juliet Beckett said that he could spend hours sitting quietly, doing nothing but listen to his inner voice and observe his inner life. That comment could gloss much of Beckett's creative output, coupled as it inevitably is with the disappearance of the body, both its literary representation as character and the self. To Juliet he noted that he had eliminated self increasingly from his work: 'In the end you don't know who is speaking any more. The subject disappears completely. That's the end result of the identity crisis' (Juliet 1995: 7). As the subject disappears so does its literary emblem, the body. What remains is its echo, its recording, its trace, its footfalls, its voice.

References

Beckett, Samuel (1947) *Murphy*, Paris: Bordas, Collection Les Imaginaires, #5.

Beckett, Samuel (1953) *L'Innommable*, Paris: Editions de Minuit.

Beckett, Samuel (1957) *Murphy*, New York: Grove Press.

Beckett, Samuel (1964) *How It Is*, New York: Grove Press.

Beckett, Samuel (1992) '*What Where*: The Revised Text', ed. with Textual Notes by S. E. Gontarski, *Journal of Beckett Studies* (New Series) 2:1 (autumn), pp. 1–25.

Beckett, Samuel (1999a) *Beckett's Dream Notebook*, edited, annotated and introduced by John Pilling, Reading: Beckett International Foundation.

Beckett, Samuel (1999b) *The Theatrical Notebooks of Samuel Beckett, Vol. 4: The Shorter Plays*, London: Faber & Faber; New York: Grove Press.

Derrida, Jacques (2011) *Voice and Phenomenon: Introduction to the Problem of the Sign in Husserl's Phenomenology* (Studies in Phenomenology and Existential Philosophy), trans. Leonard Lawlor, Evanston: Northwestern University Press. (This retranslation supersedes the David Allison translation of 1973 from the same publisher.)

Eisenstein, Sergei (1930) 'The Cinematographic Principle and Japanese Culture', *transition: An International Quarterly for Creative Experiment*, 19/20, pp. 90–103.

Fehsenfeld, Martha (1986) 'Everything Out But The Faces': Beckett's Shaping of 'What Where' for Television', *Modern Drama* 24:2, 229–40.

Jolas, Eugene (1930) 'Towards New Forms', *transition: An International Quarterly for Creative Experiment*, 19/20, pp. 104–6.

Juliet, Charles (1995) *Conversations with Samuel Beckett and Bram van Velde*, New York: Dalkey Archive Press.

Kalb, Jonathan (1991) *Beckett in Performance*, Cambridge: Cambridge University Press.

Knowlson, James (1996) *Damned to Fame: The Life of Samuel Beckett*, London: Bloomsbury.

Windelband, Wilhelm (1938) *A History of Philosophy, with Special Reference to the Formation and Development of its Problems and Conceptions*, trans. James H. Tufts, 2nd edn, New York: Macmillan.

Zilliacus, Clas (1976) *Beckett and Broadcasting: A Study of the Works of Samuel Beckett for and in Radio and Television*, Turku, Finland: Abo Akademi.

2

From Unabandoned Works:
Beckett's Short Prose

... what would I say *if* I had a voice, who says this saying it's me? (Text IV, *Texts for Nothing*)

And dream of a way in a space with neither here nor there where all the footsteps ever fell can never fare nearer to anywhere nor from anywhere further away. (Fizzle 8, 'For to end yet again')

While short fiction was a major creative outlet for Samuel Beckett, it has attracted only a modest readership. Such neglect is difficult to account for given that Beckett wrote short fiction for the entirety of his creative life, and his literary achievement and innovation are as apparent in the shorter works as in his more famous novels and plays, if succinctly so. Christopher Ricks, for one, has suggested that the 1946 short story 'The End' is, 'the best possible introduction to Beckett's fiction' (1967: 148–9). Yet few anthologists of short fiction, and in particular of the Irish short story, include Beckett's work. Beckett's stories have instead often been treated as anomalous or aberrant, a species so alien to the tradition of short fiction that critics are still struggling to assess not only what they mean – if indeed they 'mean' at all – but what they are: stories or novels, prose or poetry, rejected fragments or completed tales. William Trevor has justified Beckett's exclusion from *The Oxford Book of Irish Short Stories* by asserting that, like his countrymen Shaw and O'Casey, Beckett 'conveyed [his] ideas more skilfully in another medium' (Trevor 1989: xvi). But to see Beckett as fundamentally a dramatist who wrote some narratives is seriously to distort his literary achievement. Beckett himself considered his prose fictions 'the important writing' (Lake 1984: 133). Such omissions are all the more curious given that

Beckett's short prose approaches Trevor's characterisation of the genre as 'the distillation of an essence'. Beckett's prose pieces are the product of some sixty years of expulsion and distillation, of excising excess and extraneity, and through that process novels were often reduced to stories, stories pared to fragments, first abandoned then unabandoned and 'completed', if that is the word, through the act of publication. When that master of the Irish short story, Frank O'Connor, noted that 'there is something in the short story at its most characteristic [–] something we do not often find in the novel – an intense awareness of human loneliness' (1985: 19), he could have been writing directly about Beckett's short prose. As Beckett periodically confronted first the difficulties then the impossibility of sustaining and shaping longer works, as his aesthetic preoccupations grew more contractive than expansive, short prose became his principal narrative form – the distillate of longer fiction as well as the testing ground for occasional longer works – and the theme of 'human loneliness' pervades it.

Beckett's own creative roots, furthermore, were set deeply, unavoidably, in the tradition of Irish story-telling that Trevor valorises, 'the immediacy of the spoken word', particularly that of the Irish *seanchaí*. Although self-consciously experimental, self-referential, and often mannered, Beckett's short fiction never wholly abandons the culturally pervasive traditions of Irish story-telling and its focus on orality, an oral tradition with its emphasis on voice. Even when his subject is the absence of subject, the story the impossibility of stories, its form the disintegration of form, Beckett's short prose can span the gulf between the more fabulist strains of Irish story-telling and the aestheticised experimental narratives of European modernism, of which Beckett was a late if formative part. Self-conscious and aesthetic as they often are, Beckett's stories gain immeasurably from oral presentation, performance, and so they have attracted theatre artists who, like Joseph Chaikin, among others, have adapted the stories to the stage, or who like Billy Whitelaw and Barry McGovern have simply read them in public performance, the modes of performance and reading often coeval.

Much of Beckett's short prose inhabits the margins between prose and poetry, between narrative and drama, and finally between completion and incompletion. The short work 'neither' has routinely been published with line breaks suggestive of poetry, but when British publisher John Calder was about to gather 'neither' into the *Collected Poems*, Beckett balked because he considered it a prose work, a short story. Calder relates the incident in a letter to the *Times Literary Supplement* (24–30 August 1990): he had 'originally intended to put it in the *Collected Poems*. We did not do so, because Beckett at the last moment said that it was not a poem and should not be there' (895).

'From an Abandoned Work', furthermore, was initially published as a theatre piece by the British publisher Faber & Faber after it was performed on the BBC Third Programme on 14 December 1957 by Patrick Magee. Although 'From an Abandoned Work' is now generally grouped with Beckett's short fiction, Faber collected it among four theatre works in *Breath and Other Shorts* (1971). That grouping, of course, punctuated its debut as a piece *for* performance.[1] It might be argued, then, that 'From an Abandoned Work' as a hybrid text could as well be anthologised with Beckett's theatre. It is no less 'dramatic', after all, than *A Piece of Monologue*, with which it shares a titular admission of fragmentation. Even as Beckett expanded the boundaries of short fiction, often by contracting the form, his stories retained that oral, performative quality of their Irish roots. What many an actor has discovered is that even Beckett's most intractable fictions, like the *Texts for Nothing*, 'Enough', or 'Stirrings Still', share ground with theatre and so maintain an immediacy in performance that makes them accessible to a broad audience.

With the exception of *More Pricks than Kicks*, which, with its single, unifying character, Belacqua Shuah, is as much a novel as a collection of stories,[2] and the 1933 coda to that collection, 'Echo's Bones' – which Beckett wrote as the collection's tailpiece but which was first rejected by the publisher, Chatto and Windus, then by Beckett himself for subsequent editions, then by the Beckett Estate for *Samuel Beckett: The Complete Short Prose*, and published only, and finally, independently, edited and annotated by Mark Nixon, in 2014 – the entire output of Beckett's short fiction from his first published story, 'Assumption', which appeared in *transition* magazine in 1929 when he was twenty-three years old, to his last, which were produced nearly sixty years later, shortly before his death, attain a greater recognition and weight in the sequential gathering of *Samuel Beckett: The Complete Short Prose*. In failing health and stirring little from his Paris flat, Beckett managed creative stirrings still in 1986, the title he gave three related short tales dedicated to his friend and long-time American publisher, Barney Rosset. In between, Beckett used short fiction to rescue what was in 1932 a failed and abandoned novel, *Dream of Fair to Middling Women*, salvaging two discrete segments of that unfinished (and published only in 1992) work as a short fiction sequence, adding eight fresh, if fairly conventional, tales (or chapters) to fill out *More Pricks than Kicks* (1934), a work whose title alone, although biblical in origin, ensured its scandalous reception and eventual banning in Ireland. In 1945–6, Beckett turned to short fiction to launch 'the French venture' producing four *nouvelles*: 'Premier amour' ('First Love'), 'L'Expulsé' ('The Expelled'), 'Le Calmant' ('The Calmative'), and 'La Fin' or 'Suite' ('The End'), which he considered long enough to be published as a stand-alone book. These stories, 'the very first writing in French',[3] tapped a creative reservoir, for a burst of writing followed: an attempt at a novel in French, *Mercier et Camier*, scheduled to be published by Bordas in 1946, two full-length plays, *Eleuthéria*, 1947, scheduled for publication by Les Edition Minuit in 1951, and *En attendant Godot (Waiting for Godot)* in 1948, and the much, and justly, celebrated novel sequence *Molloy, Malone meurt (Malone Dies), L'Innommable (The Unnamable)* (1946–50). When the frenetic creativity of that period began to flag, Beckett turned afresh to fragments, short fiction, heeding his imperative to 'go on', producing thirteen brief tales grouped under a title adapted from the phrase conductors use for that ghost measure which sets the orchestra's tempo. The conductor calls his silent prelude a 'measure for nothing'; Beckett called his prose stumblings and stutterings *Texts for Nothing*. For Beckett these tales 'express the failure to implement the last words of *L'Innommable*: "il faut continuer, je vais continuer"' ('I can't go on, I'll go on').[4]

By the 1940s Beckett had thus abandoned the literary use of his native tongue. Writing to George Reavey about 'a book of short stories', Beckett noted on 15 December 1946, 'I do not think I shall write very much in English in the future' (Lake 1984: 81). But early in 1954 Beckett's American publisher, Barney Rosset, suggested that he return to English: 'I have been wondering if you would not get almost the freshness of turning to doing something in English which you must have gotten when you first seriously took to writing in French.'[5] Shortly thereafter, Beckett began a new English novel, which he first abandoned then published in 1958 as 'From an Abandoned Work'. In a transcription of the story, a fair copy made as a gift for a friend, Beckett appended a note on its provenance: 'This text was written 1954 or 1955. It was the first text written directly in English since *Watt* (1945)' (Lake 1984: 90). Almost a decade intervened between *Fancy Dying*, portions of which, in French and English (with German translations of both), were published as *Faux Départs* to launch a new, German, literary journal, *Karsbuch* No. 1 in June of 1965.[6] That abandoned novel developed into at least *All Strange Away* (where although 'Fancy is her only hope', 'Fancy dead') and its sibling, *Imagination Dead Imagine*, but was the impetus for several other *Residua* as well. Although these works were apparently distillations of a longer work, Beckett's British publisher treated the 1,500-word *Imagination Dead Imagine* as a completed novel, issuing it separately in 1965 with the following gloss: 'The present work was conceived as a novel, and in spite of its brevity, remains a novel, a work of fiction from which the author has removed all but the essentials, having first imagined them and created them. It is possibly the shortest novel ever published.'

In between Beckett completed an impressive array of theatre work, from *Fin de partie* (*Endgame*) (1957) to *Play* (1964), including *Krapp's Last Tape* (1958) and *Happy Days* (1961), both in English, and another extended prose work, *Comment c'est* (*How It Is*), itself first abandoned, then 'unabandoned' in 1960. A fragment was published separately as 'L'Image' in the journal X in December of 1959. The English version, 'The Image', was published posthumously in a translation by Edith Fournier in *Samuel Beckett: The Complete Short Prose, 1929–1989* (1995). Another segment of *How It Is* was published as 'From an Unabandoned Work' in *Evergreen Review* in 1960.[7] For the next three decades, the post-*How It Is* period, Beckett would write in French and English denuded, distilled tales in the manner of *All Strange Away*, stories that focused on a single, often static image 'ill seen' and consequently 'ill said', residua which resulted from the continued impossibility of long fiction. As the titles of two of Beckett's late stories suggest, these are tales 'Heard in the Dark', stories, that is, that featured voice, stories which were themselves early versions of the novel *Company*. And in a note accompanying the French manuscript of 'Bing', translated into English first as 'Pfft' but quickly revised to the equally onomatopoetic 'Ping', Beckett noted: 'Though very different formally these two MSS ["Bing" and *Le Dépeupleur*] belong together. "Bing" may be regarded as the result or miniaturisation of "Le Dépeupleur" abandoned because of its intractable complexities' (Reading University Library MS

1536/1). Abandoned in 1966, *Le Dépeupleur* was subsequently unabandoned, 'completed' in 1970, and translated as *The Lost Ones* in 1971. Throughout this period Beckett managed to turn apparent limitations, impasses, rejections into aesthetic triumphs. Adapting the aesthetics of two architects, Mies van der Rohe's 'less is more' and Adolf Loos's 'ornament is a crime', Beckett set out to expunge 'ornament', to write 'less', to remove 'all but the essentials' from his art, to distill his narratives and so develop his own astringent, desiccated, monochromatic minimalism, miniaturisations, the 'minima' he alluded to in the 'Fizzle' called 'He is barehead'. As Beckett's fiction developed from the pronominal unity of the four *nouvelles* through the 'pseudocouple' of *Mercier et Camier,* to the disembodied voices of the *Texts for Nothing* towards the voiceless bodies of *All Strange Away* and its evolutionary descendant *Imagination Dead Imagine*, he continued his ontological exploration of being as becoming in narrative and finally of being as narrative, producing in the body of the text the text as body. If the *Texts for Nothing* suggest the dispersal of character and the subsequent writing beyond the body, *All Strange Away* signalled a refiguration, the body's return, its textualisation, the body as voiceless, static object, or the object of text, unnamed except for a series of overdetermined geometric signifiers, being as mathematical formulae.

In the life of the mind, 'seat of all', as the narrator of *Worstward Ho* reminds us, any rendering is mutable, ephemeral, spectral, immaterial, its material existence thus doubtful. Its forces are memory and imagination, each infused with the other, but its products, its images, diffuse as they appear, are vital and can comprise a unity created by the power of imagination. Beckett was well aware that the Romantic poet Samuel Taylor Coleridge divided the activity of mind into two categories, fancy and imagination, the latter superior to the former. Of the imagination, then, Coleridge would tell us in his *Biographia Literaria* of 1817, 'It dissolves, diffuses, dissipates, in order to recreate; or where this process is rendered impossible, yet still at all events it struggles to idealise and unify. It is essentially vital, even as all objects (as objects) are essentially fixed and dead.' To such flux of the mind Coleridge added a shaping force, 'the esemplastic [or shaping] power of the poetic imagination'. Beckett had been exploring the vitality of imagination, in one form or another, for most of his writing career, nowhere more directly than in *Imagination Dead*

Imagine,[8] a development not only of preliminary versions, 'Fancy Dying', and rendered in a set of four 'Faux Départs' (*CSP* 271–4), but a re-rendering of a longer work, *All Strange Away* (*CSP* 169–81), published finally in 1976 by the Gotham Book Mart in New York with fifteen illustrations by Edward Gorey. Of the cluster of experimental and related fragments and tales, *Imagination Dead Imagine* is the more controlled, concentrated, coherent, abstracted, accessible and moving as readers are asked to entertain the implications of a mental paradox, the death of imagination; its demise, however, is itself a creative act, an act of imagination, and thus in its death or dying a new beginning emerges and, in a continuing process, its product is, in Coleridge's term, esemplastic. Beckett's poetic narrative thus explores possibilities of imagination at points of extinction and renewal, images vanishing and absences materialised. That is, the theme of the imagination's dying yet conscious of its own decline, its own demise, is itself regenerative. The fourth section of a preliminary *Faux Départs* of the 1960s ends thus: 'When it [the light] goes out no matter, start again, another place, someone in it, keep glaring, never see, never find, no end, no matter' (*CSP* 273). That 'no end' signalled a new beginning as Beckett did 'start again'.

Set, if that is the word, in a vault, sepulchre, or rotunda of sorts, amid the familiar closed space of much of Beckett's later fiction, the spatial climate arbitrary, both with regards to temperature and illumination, 'two white bodies', alive, since the mirror mists, male and female are presented in positions mathematically defined, but their two gazes (the devouring 'eye of prey', so called) rarely meet, and the identity of each, identified in the *Faux Départs* and *All Strange Away* with 'women's faces on the walls' or as 'Jolly and Draeger Praeger Draeger', are finally barely perceptible, a 'white speck lost in whiteness'. In *All Strange Away*, the narrator is imagining or re-imagining images of a former lover, Emma. In *Imagination Dead Imagine* the lineaments, the details, the specifics have blurred or vanished, references to a world outside the enclosure disappear. What remains are hermetic images without external reference, images in and of themselves. There is movement, if ever so slight, but where movement is perceptible there is life, a life force, vitality, even at its 'meremost minimum', as Beckett reminds us in his late masterwork, *Worstward Ho*. The subject of these late tales is less the secret recesses of the repressed subconscious or the imagination valorised by Romantic poets and painters than the dispersed, post-Freudian ego, voice as alien other. As the narrator of Fizzle 2, 'Horn came always' (i.e., at night), suggests, 'It is in the outer space, not to be confused with the other [either inner space or the Other], that such images develop' (*CSP* 230).

Despite such dehumanised immobility, these figures (one hesitates to call them characters) and their chronologically earlier disembodied voices retain a direct and fundamental dramatic quality of which Beckett was fully aware. Despite occasional protestations to the contrary, Beckett encouraged directors eager to stage his prose. Actors then have intuited what literary critics have too often failed to articulate, that even Beckett's most philosophical and experimental short fictions have an immediacy and emotional affect, 'the immediacy of the spoken voice', which makes them accessible to a broad audience and places them firmly within a tradition of Irish story-telling.

Beckett's first short stories, 'Assumption', 'A Case in A Thousand', 'Text' and 'Sedendo et Quiescendo',[9] may retain the rhetorical ornament and psychological probing characteristic of much high Modernism. These stories, the latter two fragments of a then-abandoned novel, are finally uncharacteristic of the narrative diaspora Beckett would eventually develop, but they are central to understanding its creative genesis. Beckett's first two stories, for instance, were written as if he were still preoccupied with literary models. In the first case Beckett seems to have been reading too many of Baudelaire's translations of Poe; in the second too much Sigmund Freud. But it was with such derivative short fiction that he launched a literary career in 1929, less than a year after having arrived in Paris, in Eugene Jolas's journal of experimental writing, *transition*. Jolas was in the midst of championing James Joyce's *Finnegans Wake* by publishing not only excerpts from the *Work in Progress* but essays about it as well. Beckett had impressed Joyce enough that he was offered the opportunity to write an essay comparing Joyce to three of the latter's favourite Italian writers, Dante, Bruno and Vico, for a volume of essays defining and defending the *Work in Progress*. Along with the essay, Jolas accepted a short story from Beckett, 'Assumption', which opens with an antinomy that would eventually become a Beckettian signature, 'He could have shouted and could not' (*CSP* 3).

The story details the fate of a young, anguished 'artist' who struggles to retain and restrain 'that wild rebellious surge that aspired violently towards realization in sound' (4). The silent, unnamed protagonist, however, commands a 'remarkable faculty of whispering the turmoil down' (3). He can silence 'the most fiercely oblivious combatant' with a gesture, with 'all but imperceptible twitches of impatience' (3). He develops as well an aesthetics which separates Beauty from Prettiness. The latter merely proceeds 'comfortably up the staircase of sensation, and sit[s] down mildly on the topmost stair to digest our gratification' (4). More powerful are sensations generated when 'We are taken up bodily and pitched breathless on the peak of a sheer crag: which is the pain of Beauty' (4). The Romantics might call such emotional impact sublime; in the twenty-first century we would deem it affect, a function of art, which, in 1929, Beckett was already developing. The remainder of 'Assumption' develops just such an aesthetics of affect, the pain of beauty or the beauty of pain, which emotions echo the German Romanticism Beckett never quite purged from his art. As the artist struggles to restrain the animal voice which 'tore at his throat as he chocked it back in dread and sorrow', an unnamed Woman enters. She flatters and finally seduces the *artiste manqué*, and 'SO [sic] each evening in contemplation and absorption of this woman, he lost part of his essential animality' (6). After he is seduced, 'spent with extasy [sic]', the dammed 'stream of whispers' explodes in 'a great storm of sound' (6–7). The story ends with the sort of epiphany that Beckett would recycle in the final line of 'Dante and the Lobster': 'They found her caressing his wild dead hair' (7). 'Assumption' works through (and finally against) the image of a Promethean artist: 'Thus each night he died and was God [the Assumption of the title?], each night revived and was torn, torn and battered with increasing grievousness ...' (6). But whether or not the artist transcends the worldly through this experience to unite with something like the Idea, or pure essence, transcends Schopenhauer's world of representation to achieve the pure will, or whether the title refers simply to the arrogance of such desire, may be the crux of the story. The protagonist's romantic agony (in both senses of that phrase) may simply describe post-coital depression, and so travesty the belaboured agonies of a would-be artist.

When Beckett came to publish another story in *transition* in March 1932, he selected an excerpt from the stalled novel *Dream of Fair to Middling Women*, which he called 'Sedendo et Quiescendo' (but which appeared as 'Sedendo et Quiesciendo'). The story includes a sonnet from the protagonist, Belacqua Shuah, to his lover, the Smeraldina, which developed the same sort of yearning for transcendence and union with the 'Eternally, irrevocably one' evident in 'Assumption'. The means to this end was to 'be consumed and fused in the white heat / Of her sad finite essence . . .' (*CSP* 13). In the sonnet the speaker claims that '[I] cannot be whole . . . unless I be consumed', which consumption provides the climax to 'Assumption.' The parallels between story and sonnet extend to the recycling of imagery and phrasing: 'One with the birdless, cloudless, colourless skies' (untitled sonnet to the Smeraldina, 13); 'he hungered to be irretrievably engulfed in the light of eternity, one with the birdless cloudless colourless skies' ('Assumption', 7). Even the image of the 'blue flower' reappears: 'Belacqua inscribed to his darling blue flower some of the finest Night of May hiccupsobs that ever left a fox's paw sneering and rotting in a snaptrap' ('Sedendo et Quiescendo', 13); 'He was released, acheived [*sic*], the blue flower, Vega, GOD . . .' ('Assumption', 6).

Beckett's fourth published story, 'A Case in a Thousand', appeared in *Bookman* in August of 1934 along with his critical article, 'Recent Irish Poetry', the latter, however, signed with the pseudonym, Andrew Belis. 'A Case in a Thousand' features one Dr Nye who 'belonged to the sad men' (*CSP* 18). Physician though he is, Dr Nye 'cannot save' himself. He is called in on a case of surgeon Bor who had operated on the tubercular glands of a boy named Bray, who had then taken a turn for the worse. 'Dr Nye found a rightsided empyema' (19) and then another on the left. He discovered as well that the boy's mother, who has been barred from the hospital excepting an hour's visit in the morning and another in the evening but who maintains a day-long vigil on the hospital grounds until her appointed visiting hour, is actually Nye's 'old nurse' who on their meeting reminds him that he was '"always in a great hurry so you could grow up and marry me"' (20). Mrs Bray, however, 'did not disclose the trauma at the root of this attachment' (20). There are then at least two patients in this story, the Bray boy and Dr Nye. As the boy's condition worsens and a decision about another operation must be made, the doctor regresses, 'took hold of the boy's wrist, stretched himself all along the edge of the bed and entered the kind of therapeutic trance that he reserved for such happily rare dilemmas' (21). At that moment Mrs Bray 'saw him as she could remember him' (21), that is, as the boy she nursed. The young Bray does not survive the operation, but after the funeral the mother resumes her vigil outside the hospital as if her child were still alive – as in a sense he is. When Nye appears, 'she related a matter connected with his earliest years, so trivial and intimate that it need not be enlarged on here, but from the elucidation of which Dr Nye, that sad man, expected great things' (24). The undisclosed incident, at once a 'trauma at the root of this attachment' and an incident so 'trivial and intimate that it need not be enlarged on here' (24), is at the root of the story as well. The matter is certainly sexual, particularly Oedipal, and at least one critic, J. D. O'Hara, has surmised that the 'trivial and intimate' incident involves the young Nye's curiosity about female anatomy, in particular whether or not women have penises. Dr Nye's nurse may have answered the question by anatomical demonstration, and the unexpected disclosure may have left the young Nye impotent, which condition would help explain why as an adult Nye was 'one of the sad men'. The 'Case in a Thousand', then, is not (or not only) the young boy's empyema but Nye's disorder, impotence perhaps, as well.

Thereafter, Beckett returned to his stalled and incomplete novel, *Dream of Fair to Middling Women*; having published two excerpts as separate stories, 'Text' and 'Sedendo et Quiescendo', he now cannibalised two of its more detachable pieces, 'A Wet Night' and 'The Smeraldina's Billet-Doux', retaining the protagonist, Belacqua Shuah, to develop an episodic novel, *More Pricks than Kicks*, whose lead story, 'Dante and the Lobster', was published separately in *This Quarter* in December of 1932. (The story 'Yellow' was also published separately in *New World Writing* but not until November of 1956, twenty-two years after the publication of the novel.)

Beckett's subsequent venture into short fiction began just after the Second World War, after the writing of *Watt*, when he produced four stories in his adopted language. Originally, all four of the French stories were scheduled for publication by Beckett's first French publisher, Bordas, which had published his translation of *Murphy* in 1947, for which, as Beckett notes, 'they have paid me handsomely enough (for one used to British generosity) both for my translation and an advance on royalties. [. . .] It is a great relief for me to have my literary affairs centralised in this way, by a firm prepared to act in a sense as my agents [the firm was negotiating the rights to *Watt* as well] as well as my publishers' (*Letters* 2 48). But as Beckett approached the success he had worked assiduously to achieve, Bordas dropped plans to issue *Mercier et Camier* and *Quatre Nouvelles* when sales of the French *Murphy* proved disastrous, the volume selling fewer than 100 copies. Pierre Bordas noted that the firm sent out over 200 copies of *Murphy* for review and not a single piece about it appeared (*Letters 2* 73n4). Beckett's comment: 'The French *Murphy* fell still born from the press, as I think Dr J. said' (actually, Alexander Pope) (*Letters 2* 71, 73n4). Subsequently, Beckett suppressed for a time the French novel and one of the stories, 'First Love'. The remaining three *nouvelles* of 1946 were finally published in France by Les Editions de Minuit (1955) and in the US by Grove Press (1967) in combination with thirteen *Texts for Nothing* ('First Love' being published separately only in 1970). Although conjoined in publication, the two sets of stories remained very separate in Beckett's mind, as he explained to Joseph Chaikin as he resisted Chaikin's theatrical mixing of the *Stories* and *Texts*, noting that, '*Stories* and *Texts for Nothing* are two very different matters, the former the beginning of the French venture, the latter in the doldrums that followed the "trilogy".' When Chaikin persisted, arguing that *Stories* and *Texts for Nothing* could all be read as tales for 'nothing', Beckett corrected him by return post, 'Have only now realized ambiguity of title. What I meant to say was *Stories. Followed by Texts for Nothing*.'[10]

The four stories, 'First Love', 'The Expelled', 'The Calmative' and 'The End', written before, almost in anticipation of, the *Three Novels* and the thirteen *Texts for Nothing*, form the bookends to Beckett's great creative period, which Hugh Kenner memorably dubbed 'the siege in the room that was to last until 1950' (1968: 24), and which in some regards was anticipated by the final two paragraphs of 'Assumption'. *Stories* and *Texts for Nothing* seem as embedded within *Three Novels* as Beckett's first two full-length plays, *Eleuthéria* and *En attendant Godot* (*Waiting for Godot*), are embedded within the novels, the plays written, as Beckett confessed, 'in search of respite from the wasteland of prose' he had been writing in 1948–9 (cited in Brater 1994: 8). In fact, the unnamed narrator of this four-story sequence, almost always suddenly and inexplicably expelled from the security of a shelter, an ejection that mimics the birth trauma, anachronistically anticipates the eponymous Molloy, as in the post-mortem story 'The Calmative', and remains a theme through *Fizzles* where in 'For to end yet again', 'the expelled falls headlong down' (*CSP* 245).

In these four stories what has been and continued to be one of Beckett's central preoccupations developed in its full complexity: the psychological, ontological, epistemological, narratological bewilderment at the inconsistency, the duality or multiplicity of the human predicament, the experience of existence. On the one side is the post-Medieval tradition of humanism that develops through the Renaissance into the rationality of the Enlightenment. Its ideology buttresses the capacity of humanity to know and adapt to the mechanism of the universe and to understand humanity's place in the scheme. This is the world of the school-room and laboratory, the world of mathematics and proportion, the world of Classical symmetry, of the pensum. For Beckett's narrators the punctum, the lived, sentient experience of existence, the being in the world, punctures and deflates that humanistic tradition, the empiricism of the classroom, although the latter never loses its appeal and is potentially a source of comfort (although it apparently destroys Watt). The opening of 'The Expelled', for instance, focuses not on the trauma of rejection and forcible ejection but on the difficulty of counting the stairs down which the narrator has, presumably, already been dispatched. There is little resentment here at the injustice of having been ejected from someplace like a home. The focus of injustice in Beckett is almost never local, civil, or social, but cosmic, the injustice of having been born, after which one finds one's consolations where one may – in mathematics, say. As the protagonist of 'Heard in the Dark 2' (the 'summerhouse' episode of *Company*) suggests, 'Simple sums you find a help in times of trouble. A haven . . . Even still in the timeless dark you find figures a comfort' (*CSP* 250–1). The experience of living is dark, mysterious, inexplicable, cthonic, in many respects Medieval but without the absolution of a benign deity. Such dissociation had preoccupied Beckett in his earlier work, chiefly in *Dream of Fair to Middling Women*, *Murphy*, *Watt*, and the long poem, *Whoroscope*, through the philosophical meditations of the seventeenth-century philosopher and mathematician, René Descartes, that is, in terms of the conflict between mind (pensum) and body (punctum), although Schopenhauer's division of the world in terms of the will and its representations is never very far from the foreground, nor is Kant's distinction between categorical and hypothetical imperatives, the former ethical the latter merely good (individually). Here the hormonal surges in even a spastic body like Murphy's conspire against the idealism and serenity of mind (or soul, or spirit). But in the four *Stories* Beckett went beyond Descartes and descended further into the inchoate subconscious of existence, rationality and civilisation, beyond even the Freudian Eros and the Schopenhauerian Will into the more Jungian Collective Unconscious of the race, and the four separate narrators (or the single collective narrator called 'I') of these *Stories* confront those primeval depths with little sense of horror, shame or judgement. The stories retain an unabashedly Swiftian misanthropy: 'The living wash in vain, in vain perfume themselves, they stink' (*CSP* 26). In 'The Expelled' grotesqueries acquire comic effect even as they disclose psychoanalytic enigmas: 'They never lynch children, babies, no matter what they do they are whitewashed in advance. I personally would lynch them with the utmost pleasure' (*CSP* 52). The theme will re-surface in the 1957 radio play *All That Fall* when Dan Rooney asks wife Maddy, 'Did you ever wish to kill a child . . . Nip some young doom in the bud' (*CDW* 191). This is depersonalised humanity sunk in on itself: 'It is not my wish to labour these antinomies, for we are, needless to say, in a skull, but I have no choice but to add the following few remarks. All the mortals I saw were alone and as if sunk in themselves' (*CSP* 70). It is a descent, most often into an emblematic skull, from which Beckett's fiction, long or short, will never emerge. The image anticipates not only the skullscapes of the *Three Novels*, but the dehumanised, dystopic tale, *The Lost Ones*, and what is generally called the post-*How It Is* prose. Such a creative descent into 'inner space', into a monadic world of liminal consciousness, had been contemplated by Beckett at least since the earliest stages of *Watt*. In the notebook and subsequent typescript versions of the novel Beckett noted, 'the unconscious mind! What a subject for a short story' (cited by Ackerley 1993: 179). 'The Expelled' seems a fulfilment of such a wish, to plumb 'perhaps deep down in those palaeozoic profounds, midst mammoth Old Red Sandstone phalli and Carboniferous pudenda . . . into the pre-uterine . . . the agar-agar . . . impossible to describe' (cited by Ackerley 1993: 179).

But while character names may shift in the four stories (Lulu, for instance, becomes Anna in *First Love*), the narrating consciousness, the 'I' of these stories, remains more or less cogent, intact, coherent, psychologically and narratologically whole and at least pronominally namable. And something like representable external reality still exists, even as it is folded in on itself and so inseparable from the consciousness perceiving it. Writing subsequently three interrelated and sequential novels dubbed incorrectly the Trilogy, Beckett continued to probe the 'pre-uterine'. It is a period during which Beckett pushed beyond recognisable external reality and discrete, recognisable literary characters, replacing them with something like naked consciousness or pure being (living or dead is not always clear) and a concatenation of voices.

The *Texts for Nothing* are then, as Beckett tried to explain to Chaikin, a major leap beyond the four *Stories*. To use the current historical markers, they represent a leap from Modernism to at least late or second-generation Modernism, from interior voices to multiple exterior voices, from discrete internality to blended externality. Beckett's fragments are in fact no longer 'completed' stories but shards, *aperçus* of a continuous unfolding narrative, glimpses at a never to be complete being or story. The *Texts for Nothing* would redefine at least Beckett's short fiction, if not the possibilities of the short story itself, as narrative or story per se was finally discarded (as it was for the most part in the *Three Novels*), replaced by attempts of consciousness to perceive, comprehend, or create first a life, then a more or less stable, static image, an essence, failing at the latter no less often than at the former. 'No need of a story', says one of the voices, 'once there is speech no need for a story, a story is not compulsory, just a life, that's the mistake I made, one of the mistakes, to have wanted a story for myself, whereas life alone is enough' (*CSP* 116). The struggle of the protean narrators of the four *Stories* and the *Three Novels* was to create a narrative to capture or reflect, to present at least a segment of a life in a work of art – that struggle has been abandoned with and mocked in the *Texts for Nothing*. If 'life' and so story assume character, the voice has made yet another mistake, for the coherent entity which in literature we call 'character' is itself disbursed amid a plurality of disembodied voices and echoes whose distinctions are unclear and whose sources are unknowable. The disembodied voice captivated Beckett from his earliest creative years when he took the image of Echo as the literary emblem for his first collection of poems, *Echo's Bones*. Echo, an Oread or mountain nymph, pined away for the love of Narcissus until all that remained of her was her voice. *Texts for Nothing* could as easily have been called *Echo's Bones* as well, and from then on Beckett would never again create anything like literary characters save for an unnamed (even unnamable) narrator straining to see images and hear sounds, almost always echoes – bodiless voices or later voiceless bodies, origins unknown. In Beckett's tribute to painter and friend, Bram van Velde, the *témoignage* 'La Falaise', the window through which the observing 'you' views the cliff both separates him from and joins him to the cliff in a process which blends perception and imagination. In these late works the artist figure inhabits a no man's land, 'an unspeakable [because unnamable?] home' in 'neither', neither wholly self nor wholly other. In theatrical adaptations of his prose, Beckett retained such paradoxes of self by insisting on the separation of character and narrative, and such separation was evident in almost every stage adaptation of his prose works that he himself had a hand in. These then are the limitations, the necessary incoherence and fragmentation within which the writer is obliged to work in the post-Auschwitz era in order to convey the punctum, the affect, the experience of living in the world: 'I'm here, that's all I know, and that it's still not me, it's of that the best has to be made' (*CSP* 113). Because of such an impasse, narrative (at least as we've known and expect it, even among the more experimental Modernists) 'can't go on', and yet somehow is obliged to 'go on'. How it goes on is in fits, sputters, stutters and not so much starts as re-starts, in imaginative ventures doomed to fail. As it had in *The Unnamable*, all pretence to artistic completion was abandoned, even in the titles of these later works, not only to suggest that the individual works are themselves incomplete, unfinished, but that completion is beyond human experience. The thirteen *Texts for Nothing* are merely numbered, for instance, and Beckett went on to write stories with titles like 'Lessness', 'From an Abandoned Work', *Fizzles* (*foirades* in French), and *Residua*. But these tales are no more unfinished works of art than those paintings by Matisse or Picasso, among others, that retain raw, unpainted, exposed canvas.

What one is left with after the *Texts for Nothing* is 'nothing', incorporeal consciousness perhaps, into which Beckett plunged afresh in English in the early 1950s to produce a tale rich in imagery but short on external coherence. 'From an Abandoned Work' deals with three days in the life of the unnamed narrator, an old man recalling his childhood, which was as uneventful as it was loveless, except, perhaps, for words, which 'have been my only loves, not many' (*CSP* 162). The father died when the narrator was young, and he lived with his mother until she died. The narrator's life is ordered by motion, movement, the daily journey and return:

'in the morning out from home and in the evening back home again' (159). He had taken long walks with his father, and those have continued even after the father's death. His motion, however, is directionless, 'I have never in my life been on my way anywhere, but simply on my way' (156). In contrast to his own patterned motion, he retains 'Great love in [his] heart for all things still and rooted' (155). A great deal of hostility remains in the parental relationship, however: 'ah my father and mother, to think they are probably in paradise, they were so good. Let me go to hell, that's all I ask, and go on cursing them there, and them looking down and hear me, that might take some shine off their bliss' (159). In fact, his admission that he may have killed his father, 'as well as [his] mother' (159), suggests a consciousness permeated with guilt. The events of the days grow more bizarre. There is 'the white horse and white mother in the window' (160–1). Another day, 'I was set on and pursued by a family or tribe of stoats' (161). The narrator, moreover, experiences inexplicable periods of rage: 'The next thing I was up in the bracken lashing out with my stick making the drops fly and cursing, filthy language, the same over and over, I hope nobody heard me' (163). The most comprehensive reading of this enigmatic text is the one offered by J. D. O'Hara in which he sees the word 'work' of the title as referring not to a work of art, the story itself, but to a session of psychotherapy. Freud often spoke of his therapy sessions, for instance, as working through psychological problems. What is abandoned for O'Hara, then, is not a narrative or story, which is in this reading complete, but the therapy, which is never completed and so abandoned. The emotional tensions, then, are never resolved, the anxiety never relieved, the personality never integrated. For O'Hara:

> the protagonist has divided his feelings for his parents into love and hatred, has expressed that hatred to us while concealing it from the world, and has repressed his love and displaced it into a love of words, of animals, of this earth, etc. In all this he has expressed his love of self while expressing his hatred of that self by youthful punishment in the walks, by future punishment in hell, and by present punishment among the rocks, isolated from all humans. (O'Hara 1997: 96)

It took almost a decade for Beckett to put such psychological strangeness away. When he returned to short fiction in the early 1960s it was to reshape the remains of aborted longer fiction yet again, a work tentatively entitled *Fancy Dying*, a short excerpt of which, in French and English, was published in 1965 as *Faux Départs*. The work suggests, however, less a false start than a major aesthetic shift, a rejection of the journey motif and structure (incipient in *Murphy* and *Watt* and fully developed in *First Love* and the fiction through 'From an Abandoned Work'), a return to which might have signalled the death of creative imagination: 'Out of the door and down the road in the old hat and coat like after the war, no, not that again' to Beckett's (or the narrator's) new imaginative preoccupation, 'A closed space five foot square by six high, try for him there', a space in which he would conduct exercises in human origami, all with a rechristened pronoun through which to tell his story, 'last person' (*CSP* 169). For the opening of *All Strange Away* Beckett would delete the first three words of the sentence above, but 'A closed space' ('Closed place' opens Fizzle 5) would come close to describing the creative terrain which Beckett's short fiction would hereafter inhabit. And if an impasse were reached in such imaginative spelunking, the light (of imagination?) go out, 'no matter, start again, another place, someone in it . . .' (169).

The British novelist David Lodge's analysis of one of Beckett's 'closed space' tales, 'Ping' ('Bing' in French), originally a segment of *Le Dépeupleur* (*The Lost Ones*), is a cogent reading of this cryptic tale, and so of much of Beckett's late prose: 'I suggest that "Ping" is the rendering of the consciousness of a person confined in a small, bare, white room, a person who is evidently under extreme duress, and probably at the last gasp of life.' Such is what passes for plot in Beckett's late prose, and Lodge goes on to suggest that:

> 'Ping' seems to record the struggles of an expiring consciousness to find some meaning in a situation which offers no purchase to the mind or to sensation. The consciousness makes repeated, feeble efforts to assert the possibility of colour, movement, sound, memory, another person's presence, only to fall back hopelessly into the recognition of colourlessness, paralysis, silence, oblivion, solitude. (Lodge 1968: 86)[11]

Lodge struggles to re-situate 'Ping' within a more or less traditional, realistic frame, an exercise that Gilles Deleuze would call reterritorialisation: an expiring consciousness in search of meaning. The questions which Lodge defers, however, are the narratological ones: who is the figure to whom all is 'known'? By whom is the image described 'never seen'; to whom is it repeatedly 'invisible'? Certainly not the reader to whom even these white on white images are strikingly visible, for the reader, like the narrator, sees them clearly if fleetingly in his mind's eye through the imaginative construct we call literature, fiction. The figure described, the narrator hints, is 'perhaps not alone', and so the possibility exists of others in other worlds, whose perceptions likewise fail. Although the story-line of the late tales is fairly simple, as Lodge suggests, or rather as he constructs it, narratologically they are more complex. The reader's focus is not only on a figure in a closed space, but on another figure and a narrator imagining them and others, who likewise imagine. We have then not just the psychologically complex but narratologically transparent image of a self imagining itself, but a self imagining itself imagining itself and potential others, often suspecting that it is being imagined itself.

In these late tales the mysterious narrator is often recorded in the midst of the fiction making process. Beckett's subject here is then less the objects perceived and recorded, a process, of necessity 'ill seen' and so 'ill said', but the human imagination. In his seminal study, *The Sense of an Ending: Studies in the Theory of Fiction*, the critic Frank Kermode quotes Hans Vaihinger on the human impulse of fiction-making: fictions are 'mental structures. The psyche weaves this or that thought out of itself; for the mind is invention; under the compulsion of necessity [in Beckett, the "obligation to express"], stimulated by the outer world, it discovers the store of contrivances hidden within itself' (Kermode 1979: 40, citing Vaihinger's *The Philosophy of As If*). Beckett's late short fiction, the post-*How It Is* prose, constitutes a record, a catalogue of those discoveries, even as it opens new lands for discovery, and so the late work may have more in common with that of American poet Wallace Stevens, say, in his celebration of the imagination, than with many other writers of short fiction.

Such then is the rarefied world of Beckett's late short fiction, from *All Strange Away* to 'Stirrings Still', short tales that in fundamental ways are almost indistinguishable from the late novels, as the late prose is almost indistinguishable from the late theatre. Despite his early insistence on keeping 'our genres more or less distinct',[12] Beckett seemed in this later phase of his work to have stretched beyond such limitations, beyond generic boundaries to examine the diaphanous membrane separating inside from outside, perception from imagination, self from others, past from present, narrative from experience, 'neither' wholly the one nor wholly the other. Despite such psychological and philosophical flux, an almost frustrating thematic irresolution, this controlled flux, this literary oscillation between waves and particles, these stories retain a direct dramatic and poetic simplicity as if they had been spoken into a tape recorder. Taken together Beckett's short prose pieces not only outline his development as an artist, but suggest as well Beckett's own view of his art, that it is all part of a continuous process, a series. Writing to George Reavey on 8 July 1948, for instance, Beckett noted, 'I am now retyping, for rejection by the publishers, *Malone Meurt* [*Malone Dies*], the last I hope of the series Murphy, Watt, Mercier & Camier, Molloy, not to mention the 4 Nouvelles & Eleuthéria' (Lake 1984: 53). That series did not, of course, end with *Malone Meurt*. It continued for another forty years to 'Stirrings Still'. The post-*How It Is* stories were then just the latest in a series whose end was only Beckett's own. In these generically androgynous stories, tales, pieces, Beckett produced a series of literary hermaphrodites that echo each other (and the earlier work as well) like reverberations in a skull, where all sound is echo. Taken together the stories suggest the intertextual weave of or a collaboration between Rorschach and Escher.

Notes

1. The work finally seems to have wound up anthologised with Beckett's prose via an exchange between publishers. The dramaticule *Come and Go* was originally published by John Calder in the UK, to whom the work is dedicated. Faber has subsequently published *Come and Go* in anthologies of Beckett's drama, and Calder published 'From an Abandoned Work' in anthologies of Beckett's prose. Beckett's short story 'Lessness' was also performed on the BBC, on 25 February 1971, with Donal Donnelly, Leonard Fenton, Denys Hawthorne, Patrick Magee and Harold Pinter.

2. Even Beckett's earliest critics like Dylan Thomas referred to *More Pricks than Kicks* as a novel; see *New English Weekly*, 17 March 1938, pp. 454–5.

3. Letter to American publisher, Barney Rosset, dated 11 February 1954. The Beckett/Rosset letters are cited from the S.E. Gontarski Grove Press Research Materials at Florida State University,

http://fsuarchon.fcla.edu/?p=collections/controlcard&id=4024 (last accessed June 2016).

4. Ibid.

5. Rosset letter to Samuel Beckett, 5 February 1954.

6. A reference to this abandoned work appears in 'Why Actors Are Fascinated by Beckett's Theatre', *The Times*, 27 January 1965, p. 14: 'Mr. Beckett is at present finishing a novel called *Fancy Dying*, and also writing a play' – the latter presumably *Play*. The source of the information is apparently Jack MacGowran, who was not only playing in *Endgame* at the time but also preparing a one-man performance of Beckett's prose writings which became *Beginning to End*.

7. 'From an Unabandoned Work', *Evergreen Review* 4:14 (September-October 1960), pp. 58–65.

8. *Imagination Dead Imagine / Imagination mort imaginez* was written in French in 1965 and published in *Les Lettres nouvelles* 13 (October–November 1965), pp. 13–16, thence translated for *The Sunday Times*, 7 November 1965, p. 48. It was published independently (Minuit, 1965) in a special edition of 612 numbered copies, and then included in the collection *Têtes-mortes* (1967), pp. 49–57. An English text appeared *hors commerce* from Calder & Boyars (1965), 100 copies on handmade paper, numbered and signed, before the trade edition (1966); thence in *No's Knife: Collected Shorter Prose, 1945–1966*, Calder Publications, April 1967, with two numbered, limited editions of 100 cased copies in 8vo., series A and B, A bound in quarter white calf over grey Buckram boards and B bound in full Buckram, both signed by the author and printed *hors commerce*. The first American printing was in *Evergreen Review* 10:39 (February 1966), pp. 48–9. It has since appeared in the *Samuel Beckett Reader* (Calder & Boyars, 1967); *Modern Short Stories*, ed. Robert Taubman (Penguin, 1969), pp. 329–31; *First Love and Other Shorts* (Grove, 1974); *I can't go on, I'll go on*, ed. Richard Seaver (Grove, 1976); and the *Complete Short Prose* (Grove, 1995), from which the *Fancy Dying* quotations are taken (*CSP* 272–3).

9. The title alludes to Dante's *Purgatorio*, 'Sedendo et quiescendo anima efficitur prudens' (roughly: sitting quietly the soul acquires wisdom).

10. Copies of the Joseph Chaikin/Samuel Beckett correspondence are on deposit at the Stanley E. Gontarski Samuel Beckett Collection at Trinity College, Dublin.

11. Lodge's essay was reprinted in Lawrence and Federman 1979: 291–301. The original publication of the essay, however, contains line

numberings to the original publication of 'Ping' in *Encounter* 28:2 (February 1967): 25–6.

12. This oft-quoted letter to Barney Rosset of 27 August 1957 objects to a staging of *All That Fall* and a film of *Act without Words*. Beckett's full wording is: 'If we can't keep our genres more or less distinct, or extricate them from the confusion that has them where they are, we might as well go home and lie down' (*Letters* 3 64).

References

Ackerley, Chris (1993) 'Fatigue and Disgust: The Addenda to *Watt*', *Samuel Beckett Today/Aujourd'hui: Beckett in the 1990s*, Vol. 2 (January).

Asmus, Walter D. (1986) 'Rehearsal Notes for the German Premiere of Samuel Beckett's *That Time* and *Footfalls*', in S. E. Gontarski, ed., *On Beckett: Essays and Criticism*, New York: Grove Press (second edition, London: Anthem Press 2012).

Brater, Enoch (1994) *The Drama in the Text: Beckett's Late Fiction*, Oxford: Oxford University Press.

Graver, Lawrence and Raymond Federman, eds (1979) *Samuel Beckett: The Critical Heritage*, London: Routledge & Kegan Paul.

Kenner, Hugh (1968) *Samuel Beckett: A Critical Study*, Los Angeles: University of California Press.

Kermode, Frank (1979) *The Sense of an Ending: Studies in the Theory of Fiction*, New York: Oxford University Press.

Lake, Carlton (1984) *No Symbols Where None Intended: A Catalogue of Books, Manuscripts, and Other Material Relating to Samuel Beckett in the Collection of the Humanities Research Center*, selected and described by Carlton Lake, Austin, TX: Humanities Research Center.

Lodge, David (1968) 'Some Ping Understood', *Encounter* (February), pp. 85–9.

O'Connor, Frank (1985) *The Lonely Voice: A Study of the Short Story*, New York: Harper & Row.

O'Hara, J. D. (1997) *Samuel Beckett's Hidden Drives: Structural Uses of Depth Psychology*, Gainesville: University Press of Florida.

Ricks, Christopher (1967) 'Mr Artesian', *The Listener* (3 August). Reprinted in Graver and Federman 1979: 286–91.

Trevor, William, ed. (1989) *The Oxford Book of Irish Short Stories*, Oxford: Oxford University Press.

3

The Conjuring of Something Out of Nothing: Beckett's 'Closed Space' Novels

... this seemed rather to belong to some story heard long
before, an instant in the life of another, ill told, ill heard, and
more than half forgotten. (*Watt*)

... and only half seen so far a pallet and a ghostly chair. Ill half
seen. (*Ill Seen Ill Said*)

In the mid-1960s, Samuel Beckett's fiction took a dramatic turn,
away from stories featuring the compulsion to (and so solace in)
motion, towards stories of stillness or some barely perceptible
movement, at times just the breathing of a body or the trembling of
a hand. These 'closed space' stories often entailed little more than
the perception of a figure in various postures. The journey theme
had been a feature of Beckett's fiction from *Murphy* and *Watt*, and
it culminated in the body of French fiction: the four French *Stories*
of 1946, the three collected novels, *Molloy*, *Malone Dies* and *The
Unnamable*, the fictive fragments, written to reach beyond the
impasse of *The Unnamable*, collected as *Texts for Nothing*, and
the great post-*Unnamable* novel, *How It Is*. Motion had offered
Beckett's 'Omnidolent' creatures a degree of solace, something of
a respite from assailing voices: 'As long as I kept walking I didn't
hear [the cries] because of the footsteps' (*CSP* 45), the narrator
of *First Love* reminds us. But it was the fact of movement rather
than any particular destination that consoled, as the narrator of
'From an Abandoned Work' makes clear: 'I have never in my life
been on my way anywhere, but simply on my way' (*CSP* 156). The
shift from journeys, a movement from and return to some shelter
or haven, often 'home', to the 'closed space' tales is announced in
the fragments and *Faux Départs* that eventually develop into *All
Strange Away* (1963–4) and its sibling *Imagination Dead Imagine*

(1965): 'Out the door and down the road in the old hat and coat like after the war, no not that again.' The more *imaginative* alternative was now: 'A closed space five foot square by six high, try for him there' (*CDW* 272). The change necessitated a new character as well, the nameless 'him' who became Beckett's second major fictional innovation. The first was 'voice', that progressive disintegration of literary character that dominated the journey fictions from *Watt* through 'From an Abandoned Work' and included most of Beckett's major novels – and made occasional appearances in 'closed space' tales like *Company* and *Ill Seen Ill Said*, for instance. The second is 'him', or on occasion 'her', 'one', or 'it', pronominal objects of narrator's creation, the narrator himself often a creation, 'devised', a 'him' to someone else's imaginings.

These 'closed space' tales not infrequently resulted in intractable creative difficulties, literary cul-de-sacs into which Beckett had written himself, and so were abandoned.[1] As often they were unabandoned, resuscitated, revived and revised as Beckett periodically returned to his 'trunk manuscripts', and that stuttering creative process of experiment and impasse, breakthrough and breakdown, was folded into the narratives themselves. These are tales designed to fail, which were continued until they did fail, and then continued a bit further. As these stories were begun, abandoned, recommenced, and ended yet again, they often existed in multiple versions most of which were, at one time or another, published, like the abandoned *Faux Départs* called *Fancy Dying* at one point, which developed into two published versions in the mid-1960s, *All Strange Away* and *Imagination Dead Imagine* – and similarly, the triplet of mid-'70s 'Still' stories: 'Still', 'Sounds', and 'Still 3'. These stories featured a narrative consciousness straining to see and hear images that may come from within or without, and sometimes both simultaneously, resulting in what the narrator of *Ill Seen Ill Said* calls the confusion of 'That old tandem': 'the confusion now between real and – how say its contrary? No matter. That old tandem. Such now the confusion between them once so twain' (*Nohow* 72).

One of the abandoned (but unpublished) tales from the 1970s is called 'Long Observation of the Ray' (1976), written apparently on the way to *Ill Seen Ill Said* and of which critic Steven Connor has said: 'It forms a link between two important preoccupations in Beckett's [late] work, the preoccupation with cylinders and enclosed spaces to be found in *The Lost Ones*, 'Ping', *All Strange*

Away and *Closed Space* [*sic*, i.e., the *Fizzle*, 'Closed Place'], and the preoccupation with the dynamics of looking which runs from *Play* and *Film* through to *Ill Seen Ill Said*' (Connor 1992: 79), and, one might add, *Worstward Ho*. These 'closed space' tales feature a narrator as a seeing, creating eye and so, perhaps, an 'I', as site of seeing, and saying the seeing. The difficulties of perception and conception, memory and imagination, and the presentation or representation of both in language, became the focus of much of this late and most experimental fiction, as a devouring eye, 'the eye of prey' as it is called at the end of *Imagination Dead Imagine*, that witnesses and devours, consumes.

The masterwork of this period of narratological experiment, the seeing in a closed space where the homophones 'seen' and 'scene' are coeval, is the sequence of novels written in the early 1980s and collected under Beckett's title, *Nohow On*: *Company* (1980), *Mal vu mal dit* (*Ill Seen Ill Said*) (1981), and the work Beckett deemed 'untranslatable', *Worstward Ho* (1983).[2]

Although they were written in sequence and bear a close kinship to one another, Beckett himself resisted using the word *trilogy* to describe them, as he had with his first collection of novels.[3] Although 'trilogy' has since become their sobriquet, Beckett consistently rejected it. When British publisher John Calder, for instance, asked him on 29 December 1957, 'May we use a general title "Trilogy" on the jacket with the three books listed underneath?' Beckett replied on 6 January, 'Not "Trilogy", I beseech you, just the three titles and nothing else.' By the end of the year, Calder still lacked a comprehensive title, and he queried Beckett again, proposing to substitute the word *trinity* for *trilogy*. 'I can think of no general title', Beckett replied on 19 December 1958: 'TRINITY would not do. It seems to me the three separate titles should be enough' (*Letters* 3 187).

With his American publisher, Barney Rosset of Grove Press, Beckett took the identical position, writing on 5 May 1959: 'Delighted to hear you are doing the 3 in 1 soon. Simply can't think, as I told Calder, of a general title and can't bear the thought of [the] word trilogy appearing anywhere. [. . .] If it's possible to present the thing without either I'd be grateful. If not I'll cudgel my fused synopses [*sic*] for a word or two to cover it all' (*Letters* 3 230).

Both American and British editions finally appeared as *Three Novels* followed by the titles of the individual works as Beckett

requested, but critics have triumphed where publishers failed. The *Three Novels* are consistently referred to as 'The Trilogy' in the critical discourse, a phrase occasionally italicised as if it were the official title of the work, although the 1979 Calder licensed reprint from Picador is blatantly called *The Beckett Trilogy: Molloy, Malone Dies, The Unnamable*. Although pleased with the Grove and Calder collections, Beckett himself consistently referred to the anthology as the 'so-called trilogy'.

For subsequent collections Beckett was more forthcoming, offering *No's Knife* for Calder's expanded edition of what at Grove was simply *Stories and Texts for Nothing, Residua* for the early 'closed space' tales, and for his second collection of novels, his second '3 in 1', Beckett 'cudgelled his fused synopses' yet again to supply a title. As Calder notes on the jacket to the British edition, 'the overall title, *Nohow On*, the last words of *Worstward Ho*, have [*sic*] been given to the trilogy by the author'. Calder's use of the word 'trilogy' is surprising given the correspondence above, and at least one critic, novelist and former book review editor of the *Irish Times*, John Banville, has taken him to task for such cavalier terminology. In fact, Banville, objects to the collection in general because it fails to achieve – to his eye at least – the integration (or disintegration) of the first 'trilogy', in which 'Each successive volume in the series consumes its predecessor, swallowing and negating it, in a way entirely consistent with Beckett's stated artistic aims. No such unity is apparent in *Nohow On*' (Banville 1992:

20).[4] Admittedly, the aporia, disintegration and lacerating comedy (the 'mirthless laugh' of *Watt*, say, played over three volumes) of the first 'so-called trilogy' are missing from the second, but certainly Beckett's aims, stated or otherwise, had decidedly changed in the intervening thirty-five years, and to measure the themes and form of the earlier against those of the latter is to ignore that fact.

Trilogy or not, the three novels of *Nohow On* form a cohesion of their own, unified, as much of the 'late' fiction, by an extended exploration of the imaginative consciousness, narratives that seem to have more in common with the spatiality of painting than the chronicity of traditional story-telling, the themes of 'decreation' of the earlier trilogy replaced by 're-creation', the virtual tableaux of the latter perpetually forming and re-forming so that the spatiality of the images is more dynamic than static. But such imaginative play is not just play, not, that is, frivolous or gratuitous. As Frank Kermode recognised, after Coleridge, 'The imagination . . . is a form-giving power, an esemplastic power, it may require . . . to be preceded by a "decreative" act, but it is certainly a maker of orders and concords' (1979: 144). For the critic Nicholas Zurbrugg: 'Beckett seems to have abandoned his early images of partially resigned, partially grotesque, and partially impassioned anguish for carefully crafted images of affection, grace and harmony' (1991: 45). In Kermode's terms the *Nohow On* 'trilogy' is a fiction of order and concord.

While the title Beckett chose for his second '3 in 1' may suggest the inevitable impasse in the ineluctable aesthetic march 'ill-ward' or 'worstward', the final accent of the title falls on continuation, even if regressive, as the novels offer at least the possibility of respite and even occasional pleasure in the play of mind – admittedly cunning, duplicitous, inconsistent, and dissembling, but also company. The title forms finally the classically shaped Beckettian paradox, the aporia of 'how' framed by 'no' and its mirror image 'on'. As John Banville put it, 'to have *said* nohow on is already to have found a way forward' (1992: 18). The theme echoes Edgar in *King Lear*, 'the worst is not / So long as we can say "This is the worst"' (IV.1, 29–30). 'Nohow on', then, is less a statement of impasse than a soupçon to a discourse on method, the accent on the final 'on' producing 'Beckett's antithetical power to becalm and console' (Zurbrugg 1991: 45). 'From where she lies she sees Venus rise' (*Nohow* 49), the narratological voice of *Ill Seen Ill Said* tells us opening that narrative, and immediately thereafter offers the brief sentence that becomes the novel's refrain, 'On', a word which in *Worstward Ho* is folded into the pun 'so on'.

The three novels of Beckett's second '3 in 1' appeared hard upon each other in a creative burst reminiscent of Beckett's 'siege in the room' of 1945–50. On 20 November 1958 Beckett wrote nostalgically about that period to Barney Rosset while lamenting the growing professional demands on his time, particularly from the theatre:

> When I get back from London [where he was 'overseeing' the world premiere of *Krapp's Last Tape* and helping with the revival of *Endgame* at the Royal Court Theatre] if I can't get on with any new work I'll start on the translation of *Textes pour Rien*. I made a balls of the new act in French I was telling you about. I'll try it again, but I'm not even sure it's viable in the present setup. I feel I'm getting more and more entangled in professionalism and self-exploitation and that it would be really better to stop altogether [i.e., theatre] than to go on with that. What I need is to get back into the state of mind in 1945 when it was write or perish. But I suppose no chance of that. (*Letters 3* 177)

By the late 1970s, Beckett would hardly have perished had he stopped writing, but he seemed soon after to return to his creative sources to produce the three novels of *Nohow On* in rapid succession, three longer works that stood almost in defiance of the contemporary critical cant which saw his work lapsing (or collapsing) into inevitable and imminent silence. Some early critics had confused Beckett's pursuit of a 'literature of the unword' (a phrase he used in a 1937 letter to acquaintance Axel Kaun) with the cessation of creation – an active 'unwording of the world', as critic Carla Locatelli (1990) phrases it – with a passive silence, a retreat into quiescence. In the 'closed space' tales, however, Beckett seems to take some consolation and even pleasure in 'unwording the world', even as the enterprise was doomed to failure given the imagination's persistence even in the face of the death of imagination. Rather than rejecting language, he seems to have continued to explore its tenacious power to represent even as it was being reduced, denuded, stripped bare. The images of the 'closed space' novels (and stories) disappear, vanish, or are discarded from the virtual space of consciousness, only to reappear through the imagination's ineluctable visualisation and the tenacity of language to represent. Even when the imagination is dead, a perverse consciousness struggles to imagine its death, which paradox seems to have launched Beckett on the enterprise of the late, 'closed space' fiction. Beckett's sudden creative expansiveness with the *Nohow On* novels confounded those critical predictions of a lapse into silence. With the turn of a new decade Beckett seems to have disentangled his complicated life as a leading man of letters and returned to his creative sources, the wellhead he celebrated in the radio play *Words and Music*, returned to the conditions of the late 1940s and the 'siege in the room' that produced the first '3 in 1'.

These three late novels, then, form something of a family triptych (or trilogy, or trinity, if we must) with *Company* featuring a man/son in old age (as will *Worstward Ho*), *Ill Seen Ill Said*, a ghostly woman/mother in old age (as will *Worstward Ho*, as well), and finally in *Worstward Ho* itself, a nearly mystical union (anticipated in *Company* and even earlier in 'From an Abandoned Work') of father and son moving motionlessly. *Company*, the first in the series, is dominated by scenes long associated with Beckett's early life and which not only appeared periodically in his work but may have assailed him psychologically as well until the very end. The story of learning to swim at the Victorian sea-water baths in Sandymount called 'The Forty Foot'[5] is rendered as childhood terror in *Company*: 'You stand at the tip of a high board. High above the sea' (*Nohow* 12). The scene appeared in *Watt* as well where the image troubled a weary Watt's dreams: 'into an uneasy sleep lacerated by dreams, by dives from dreadful heights into rocky waters, before a numerous public' (*Watt* 222). The image or memory haunted Beckett's poem of 1930 which featured this incident, 'For Future Reference':

> And then the bright waters
> beneath the broad board
> the trembling blade of the streamlined divers
> and down to our waiting
> to my enforced buoyancy.[6]

And according to Herbert Blau, Beckett was wrestling with just this image in the nursing home shortly before his death when he asked Blau directly, 'What do you think of recurring dreams? I have one, I still have it, always had it, anyway a long time. I am up on a high board, over a water full of large rocks [. . .] I have to dive through a hole in the rocks' (Blau 1991: 218).

Likewise, the scene of an inquisitive child returning with his mother from Connolly's store and testing her patience by raising the question about the distance of moon from earth is another of those recurring scenes, if not recurring dreams: 'A small boy you come out of Connolly's store holding your mother by the hand' (*Nohow* 6). The question engenders a sharp reply in *Company*: 'she shook off your little hand and made you a cutting retort you have never forgotten' (*Nohow* 6). The mother's retort was even sharper in 'The End' (1947): 'A small boy, stretching out his hands and looking up at the blue sky, asked his mother how such a thing was possible. Fuck off, she said' (*CSP* 81); and in *Malone Dies*: 'The sky is further away than you think, is it not, mama? . . . She replied, to me her son, It is precisely as far away as it appears to be' (*Three Novels* 98). But such scenes even if rooted in Beckett's childhood are no more frequent than the persistent literary allusions to Dante and Belacqua, the Florentine lute-maker stuck in Limbo: 'the old lutist cause of Dante's first quarter-smile and now perhaps singing praises with some section of the blessed at last' (*CSP* 60). And Belacqua himself may have been the model for Beckett's closed space figures: 'huddled with his legs drawn up within the semi-circle of his arms and his head on his knees' (*CSP* 27), like Botticelli's illustration of him for the *Divine Comedy*.

These scenes from childhood have tempted his early biographer (among others) to suggest that *Company* (and so much of Beckett's work) was coded autobiography: 'You were born on an Easter Friday after long labour' (*Nohow* 24–5), as Beckett himself was, for example. For some critics the mother-haunted *Ill Seen Ill Said* reflects the author's struggling through images of his own mother, May Beckett, whose namesake appears in the play *Footfalls* as well. And the mystical union of father and son in *Worstward Ho* may owe much to memories of a son's walks with his father through the Irish countryside (an image of which the film documentary called *Silence to Silence*, produced by Radio Telefís Éireann, makes much). The image appears even more direct and autobiographical in *Company*: 'Halted too at your elbow during these computations [of his daily steps or footfalls] your father's shade. In his old tramping rags. Finally on side by side from nought anew' (*Nohow* 9). But such autobiographical emphases ignore the undercutting of empiricism that runs through these works, the rejection of the 'verifiability' of immediate knowledge and sensory data, since in Beckett's fictive world all is re-presentation, always already a repetition. The search for an originary model for the fictive images ignores or subverts the very nature of these late fictions where the narrator himself is a 'Devised devisor devising it all for company' (33). The narrator is, after all, in *Company*'s most persistent pun, 'lying' from the first. Even if we identify certain of the images in Beckett's fiction as having parallels in his personal life, this information tells us little about their function in the narrative. Childhood memories, like literary allusions, are themselves 'figments', 'traces', 'fables' or 'shades', a mix of memory, experience, desire and imagination.

Company then, like the other 'closed space' tales, is neither memoir nor autobiography, but a set of devised images of one devising images. To Beckett's mind at any rate, *Company* was an interplay of voices, a fugue between a hearer, 'H. Aspirate. Haitch' (*Nohow* 22), and on occasion 'M', while 'Himself some other character. W. Devising it all himself included for company' (31), imagining himself into existence, the external voice addressing the hearer as 'you' on occasion (42), voice trying to provide hearer with a history and so a life. The hearer is puzzled by the voice because it is not only sourceless but appears false, not his, and so the 'life' not 'his' either, the tale not autobiographical: 'Only a small part of what is said can be verified' (3), the narrator of *Company* reminds us. Stories of what may or may not be images from the narrator's past have tended to sound to him like incidents in the life of another, a situation *Company*'s unnamed narrator shares with Watt: 'this seemed rather to belong to some story heard long before, an instant in the life of another, ill told, ill heard, and more than half forgotten' (*Watt* 74). What passes for memories are images often ill seen and, of necessity, ill said. In fact, both voices of *Company* are false; that is, they are fictions, figments of imagination whose function, like much of art, is aesthetic play, company for a narrator who is finally and fundamentally, 'as you always were. Alone' (46). Of representations, then, 'Even M must go. So W reminds himself of his creature so far created. W? But W too is creature. Figment' (33). The company of *Company*, then, is not the nostalgia of memory regained, the past recaptured, a stable past, but the solace of the 'conjuring of something out of nothing' (39), that is, nothing but memory.

That memories are indistinguishable from imaginings in the process of mind, both ill seen and ill said, is as much the subject of the *Nohow On* novels as any autobiographical strain. In *Ill Seen*

Ill Said, the only one of the three novels written directly in French (*Company* having been written in English, translated/transformed into French, and then retranslated into English), a desiring eye, 'having no need of light to see' (*Nohow* 50), is in relentless pursuit of a ghostly old woman whose 'left hand lacks its third finger' (67) and who is 'drawn to a certain spot. At times. There stands a stone. It it is draws her' (52). The closed space here is a cabin in the midst of 'Chalkstones'. Not only are these ghostly, imagined images ill seen, but they are ill said because the right word is always the 'wrong word': 'And from [the cabin] as from an evil core the what is the wrong word the evil spreads' (50). There are, in fact, two eyes in this narrative: 'No longer anywhere to be seen. Not by the eye of flesh nor by the other' (56). An 'imaginary stranger' (53) also appears, as well as a group of witnesses. And as she walks from cabin to stone, she is observed, perceived, witnessed, 'On the snow her long shadow keeps her company. The others are there. All about. The twelve. Afar. Still or receding' (55). The movement of these 'guardians' is such that they always 'keep her in the center' (60).

But to see this tale, and so all the 'closed space' tales, as purely fictive, imaginative play with no reference beyond itself, to an external world or a narrator's memory, say, is to oversimplify as much as to see them as veiled autobiography, and the narrator cautions against such in what amounts to a summary of the narrative. This mingling of voice and images, memory and imagination, internal and external, fiction and its opposite causes 'confusion' through which the narrative sifts:

> Already all confusion. Things and imaginings. As of always. Confusion amounting to nothing. Despite precautions. If only she could be pure figment. Unalloyed. This old so dying woman. So dead. In the madhouse of the skull and nowhere else. [. . .] Cooped up there with the rest. Hovel and stones. The lot. And the eye. How simple all then. If only all could be pure figment. Neither be nor been nor by any shift to be. Gently gently. On. Careful. (58)

In *Worstward Ho* the images are iller seen still and so iller said as we move worstward, but we are still in 'the madhouse of the skull', where mind is necessary if only to feel pain (90). As Beckett outlined the themes of *Worstward Ho* in the early drafts, it was clear that in addition to the 'pained body' and 'combined image of man and child', we have 'The perceiving head or skull, "Germ of all"'.[7] But the term 'all' already contains a paradox that threatens to block the narrative. Can the skull be 'Germ of all' (91), that is, even of itself: 'If of all of it too?' (91). Can it then perceive itself if there is, to adapt Jacques Derrida's dictum, no outside the skull. From what perspective or grounding could it then be perceived? If 'all' happens inside the skull, is skull, somehow, simultaneously inside skull as well: 'In the skull the skull alone to be seen' (102)? That is, by extension, the starer is also seen, presumably, by the starer, or, read as a single sentence, the following sequence or image so suggests: 'The staring eyes. Dimly seen. By the staring eyes' (102); or again, skull as 'Scene and seer of all' (101). Such epistemological and perceptual enigmas, 'That head in that head' (100), shift the narrative focus from image to language and back, and so to the complicity of language in the act of representation and the creation of images, where the void is 'Rife with shades. Well so mis-said. Shade-ridden void' (101). If the pivotal word, what in *A Piece of Monologue* is called 'the rip word' (*CSP* 269), in *Ill Seen Ill Said* is 'less', in *Worstward Ho*, like *Company*, it is 'gone': 'Gnawing to be gone. Less no good. Worse no good. Only one good. Gone. Gone for good. Till then gnaw on. All gnaw on. To be gone' (*Nohow* 113). But denial re-invokes, reconstitutes the image or the world, the gone always a going. That is, writing about absence reifies absence, makes of it a presence, as writing about the impossibility of writing about absence is not the creation of silences but its performance and so representation. (Beckett's silences have always been wordy.) As the image shifts in *Worstward Ho* from skull, 'Germ of all' (91) or 'The so-said seat and germ of all' (100, 104), to the language (re)presenting it, the narrator tries to break free of words, or the ooze, 'only words gone, ooze gone. Till somehow ooze again and on. Somehow ooze again' (110), that is, words, 'As somehow from some soft of mind they ooze' (107) and so persist. To evade representation yet again, the gaper, the longing, preying perceiver, substitutes the word 'blanks', 'Blanks for nohow on' (105) or 'Blanks for when words gone' (112) – still, however, a word – and then simply a dash, ' – '. But the dash, too, is sign or signification, which recalls the conventions of referring to proper names and places in nineteenth-century Russian fiction. The closer we come to emptying the void, of man, boy, woman, skull, the closer void itself comes to being an entity imagined in language, its own image and so no different from man or boy, woman or skull, even as it dims. The desire to worsen language and its images generates an expansion of imaginative possibility in the attempt to shape experience. The drive worstward is, thus, doomed to fail, and so all that an artist can do, Beckett has been saying for some half-century, is 'Try again. Fail again. Fail better' (89) or 'Fail better worse now' (91), even as such persistent and inevitable failure produced the exquisite *Worstward Ho*.

With the 'closed space' novels, in which change and so time persists, Beckett did something innovative not only with his own fiction but with fiction in general – a reduction of narrative time to points of space, which, like all points, occupy, paradoxically, no space and so are a no thing, a nothing. With the development of the 'closed space' images in the mid-1960s, Beckett turned from his own earlier work, by then his own narrative tradition, and thereby provided himself with enough creative thrust, movement, flow to sustain him for the rest of his creative life. It is an aesthetics of impoverishment, of apparent diminution, of subtraction that finally added up to some of the most carefully crafted and emotionally poignant tales of the late modernist period. 'It was his genius', notes John Banville, 'to produce out of such an enterprise these moving, disconsolate, and scrupulously crafted works which rank among the greatest of world literature' (1992: 20).

Notes

1. For a fuller account of the stories abandoned and subsequently rescued, see Chapter 2.
2. The work has since been translated into French by Edith Fournier as *Cap au pire* (Paris: Editions de Minuit, 1991).
3. *Molloy*, 1951 (Grove Press, 1955), *Malone meurt*, 1951 (*Malone Dies*, Grove Press, 1956), and *L'Innommable*, 1953 (*The Unnamable*, Grove Press, 1958).
4. 'Now the term "trilogy" is not sacrosanct, but this offhand use of it is startling, to say the least' (Banville 1992: 20).
5. For additional details and pictures of the location see Eoin O'Brien's extraordinary pictorial survey of Beckett's Ireland, *The Beckett Country* (O'Brien 1986: 85–7).
6. *transition* 19/20 (June 1930), pp. 342–3. The poem is reprinted in full in Harvey 1970: 299. Harvey traces the image through the poem commenting in the first footnote on the poem's opening quatrain: 'A clear analogy to diving from a height and penetrating beneath a surface.'

7. For a full account of the early drafts of *Worstward Ho*, see Renton
   1992: 99–135.

References

Banville, John (1992) 'The Last Word', *The New York Review of Books*,
13 August.

Blau, Herbert (1991) 'The Less Said', in Joseph H. Smith, ed., *The World
of Samuel Beckett* (Psychiatry and the Humanities, Vol. 12), Baltimore:
Johns Hopkins University Press.

Connor, Steven (1992) 'Between Theatre and Theory: "Long Observation
of the Ray"', in John Pilling and Mary Bryden, eds, *The Ideal Core of
the Onion: Reading Beckett Archives*, Reading: Beckett International
Foundation.

Harvey, Lawrence E. (1970) *Samuel Beckett: Poet and Critic*, Princeton:
Princeton University Press.

Kermode, Frank (1979) *The Sense of an Ending: Studies in the Theory of
Fiction*, New York: Oxford University Press.

Locatelli, Carla (1990) *Unwording the World: Samuel Beckett's Prose
Work After the Nobel Prize*, Philadelphia: University of Pennsylvania
Press.

O'Brien, Eoin (1986) *The Beckett Country*, Dublin: The Black Cat Press.

Renton, Andrew (1992) '*Worstward Ho* and the Ends of Representation',
in John Pilling and Mary Bryden, eds, *The Ideal Core of the Onion:
Reading Beckett Archives*, Reading: Beckett International Foundation.

Zurbrugg, Nicholas (1991) 'Seven Types of Postmodernism: Several
Types of Samuel Beckett', in Joseph H. Smith, ed., *The World of
Samuel Beckett* (Psychiatry and the Humanities, Vol. 12), Baltimore:
Johns Hopkins University Press.

4

Beckett's 'Imbedded' Poetry and the Critique of Genre

In the *Oxford Book of Modern Verse 1892–1935*, 378 numbered poems idiosyncratically 'Chosen by' William Butler Yeats and published in 1936, Yeats not only affirmed the modernism of 'aestheticist' Walter Pater by including him in this volume but also declared him a poet by lineating a single sentence from Pater's essay on the *Mona Lisa*. That generic border between prose and poetry had, of course, been breached on the continent at least half a century earlier by Baudelaire, perhaps the inventor of the modern as an 'ism', who had shown the way in his posthumously published *Petits Poemes en prose*, the collection much more commonly known *as Le Spleen de Paris* (1869). Baudelaire's heir, Arthur Rimbaud, followed with the visionary surrealities of *Une Saison en enfer* (1873, translated as *A Season in Hell*) and *Iluminations* (1874), where language breaks its tether to our mundane world. James Joyce, of course, offered a like decoupling in *Finnegans Wake*, where the rubric is bound to example: 'Hear we here her first poseproem. [. . .]' (*FW* 528). For Joyce the 'poseproem' had the requisite musicality of poetry but its language took on a materiality as well, a linguistic opacity whereby words function more like things than referential transparencies or signposts to a stable, knowable world. Rimbaud and Joyce put the lie to any suggestion that the prose poem (or 'poseproem') was other than a discrete genre, merely something potentially akin to vignette. Theirs were decidedly unlineated poems. Yeats found in Pater the British equivalent of Baudelaire's final poetic project: 'Who among us on his more ambitious days has not dreamed of the miracle of a poetic prose, musical but with neither meter nor rhyme, supple enough and rugged enough to lend itself to the lyrical movements of the soul, to the undulations of reverie, to the jolts and spasms of conscience?' (Baudelaire 2000).[1] Yeats heard that music in Pater, whose prose seemed metrical to the poet's ear, and he noted in his 'Introduction': 'Only by printing it in *vers libre* can one show its revolutionary importance. Pater was accustomed to give each sentence a separate page of manuscript, isolating and analyzing its rhythm' (Yeats 1936: viii). Yeats's assertion in a high-profile publication that, at very least, certain of Pater's sentences had the crafted and rhythmic qualities of poetry also implies that, more broadly, something had slipped along generic borders late in the nineteenth century. For the modern the barrier separating poetry from prose was made of sand, and such slippage as Yeats describes was the way of Beckett as well, as he notes in the self-translated, untitled French poem, '*my way* is in the sand flowing / between the shingle and the dune' (*CP* 57, emphasis added). Much of Beckett's work results from or resides in that slippage 'between the shingle and the dune', contributing to the genealogy of what Marjorie Perloff has called 'this odd verse-prose ambiguity' (1986: 192).

The young (and brash) Beckett may have castigated Yeats and the Irish poetical revival as wallowing in so much Irish dung – in his critique of the revival, 'Recent Irish Poetry', he excoriated Yeats's easy associations with the Celtic Twilight and its celebration of song. Yet Beckett remained a musical poet all of his life, beginning and ending his career with verse. As with many a Modern, the border between Beckett's poetry and his prose is often amorphous or ambiguous, since his prose shares the rhythms of his verse and not all of his poetry is stanzaic. His prose, moreover, often incorporated poems imbedded in the narrative in various ways. The fact that his prose features characters themselves poets further complicates the issues, since Beckett's fictive poets are seldom spared the lash. In the novel *Dream of Fair to Middling Women* (about which Beckett admitted [on 12 July 1931 to Charles Prentice]: 'You're right about my top heavy Sedano et Quiescendo, though the title's meant to embrace the following section also: They Go Out for the Evening. And of course it stinks of Joyce in spite of most earnest endeavors to endow it with my own odours. Unfortunately for myself that's the only way I'm interested in writing' [*Letters 1* 81]) and the derivative short story, 'A Wet Night', the poseur Chas rehearses a potential performance of a poem as something of a party trick; his hope is 'to put across this strong composition and cause something of a flutter' (*Dream* 119). This 'strong composition' is the eighteen-line poem 'Calvary by Night', which is both part of the narrator's travesty of Chas and also a poem the author published under his own name in *The European Caravan* in 1931. The poem, apparently composed simultaneously with and published before the novel was completed in 1932, was deemed at once worthy of publication and worthy of ridicule. For the novel and short story versions, for example, Beckett undercut its (perhaps now embarrassingly) overt Romanticism, altering that Romantic symbol of longing, the 'blue flower' of Novalis, to the 'blue bloom' of self-abuse, the altered line picking up the onanism of Leopold Bloom (but echoing the surname of Novalis as well) with its imagery of rockets and the floating bloom (of sperm, presumably). Within the fictions then, the poem becomes an image of masturbatory self-indulgence. Beckett travestied another of his early poems again in *Dream* (70–1) and in an excerpt from the novel published separately as 'Sedendo and Quiescendo' (1932).[2] The single-sentence sonnet was presumably written to his cousin Peggy Sinclair as a tribute: 'At last I find in my confusèd soul', with its emphasis on 'merged stars' (revised to 'syzygetic stars' for the novel) and the 'birdless, cloudless, colorless skies'. Beckett's early Romanticism may be deflected in the prose but remains unrepressed, as the 'syzygetic stars', presumably the couple in full rut, need be 'Conjoined in the One and the Infinite!'; lust is conjoined to divinity at the, well, hip. But this poem is travestied in the novel and subsequent story as so much sentimentalism: 'inscribed to his darling blue flower', this 'finest Night of May hiccupsob that ever left a fox's paw sneering and rotting in a snaptrap' (*CSP* 28). Beckett withheld subsequent requests to reprint both poems (among others he considered juvenilia), even as his British publisher, John Calder, claimed that in *Collected Poems in English and French* he had collected '*all the work* [i.e., poetry] previously published in English with the addition of previously uncollected pre-war poems and *some* recent ones' (*CP* ix, emphasis added). But perhaps Calder simply meant all the poems in English published separately as poems and not those imbedded in the prose.

By the writing of *Watt* something had overtly slipped, as Arsene informs us, and that slippage dominates the 254-page prose masterwork: 'Something slipped. There I was, warm and bright, smoking my tobacco-pipe, watching the warm bright wall, when suddenly some little thing slipped, some little tiny thing. Gliss – iss – iss – STOP!' (*Watt* 42–3). Arsene depicts life along 'the long shifting thresholds' that he, Watt, his narrator, Sam, and the narrator of the 1948 poem, 'my way is in the sand flowing',[3] tread. The slippage effected Arsene's 'personal system' that 'was so distended [. . .] that the distinction between what was inside it and what was outside it was not at all easy to draw. Everything that happened happened inside it, and at the same time everything that happened happened outside of it' (43). That is, something had slipped along the border separating subject and object, inside and outside, as it will have in *The Unnamable* and at the opening of *Endgame* as well. Such slippage dramatised the 'breakdown of the object' that Beckett described in 'Recent Irish Poetry' (1934), a breakdown that might be amended to include a 'breakdown of the subject [as well]. It comes to the same thing' (*Disjecta* 70). Beckett's most direct poetic expression of Arsene's slippage is in, after Goethe's *Harzreise im Winter*, 'The Vulture', where sky, skull and earth are one as someone is 'dragging his hunger through the sky / of my skull shell of sky and earth'.

But *Watt* contains what appears to be self-plagiary as well. Arsene's speech, where 'all sound his [or *is*] echo' (41), also contains a more direct echo of Beckett's poetry, the 1937 poem 'Dieppe', here more fully realised in its context: 'your dead walk beside you, on the dark shingle the turning for the last time again to the lights of the little town' (40). This passage, also in the German Romantic tradition of early Beckett, is after Friedrich Hölderlin's elegiac *Der Spaziergang* (a walk or stroll, usually edifying, like that of a *flâneur*[4]). Beckett published 'Dieppe' separately after the war in *Les Temps Modernes* 2.14 (November 1946) and in *The Irish Times* (9 June 1945) and later allowed its collection and translation in the tri-lingual *Gedichte* (*Poetry*) (Limes Verlag, 1959). Beckett's English rendering follows the French poem as the shingle is now 'dead' and 'lights of the town' become 'the lights of old':

> Again the last ebb
> The dead shingle
> The turning then the steps
> Towards the lights of old

Translating *Watt* into French in 1967 (ostensibly with 'Ludovic et Agnès Janvier en collaboration avec l'auteur', an attribution that has mysteriously vanished from current reprints), Beckett (or Ludovic and Agnès Janvier) translated from the English 'pose-proem' and not from either of its 1938–9 verse versions thus: 'les routes loin de tout où vos morts marchent à vos côtés, sur les galets nocturnes chaque fois pour la dernière le demi-tour vers les feux du bourg' (40).

By 1961 Beckett took the musicality of creativity as the subject of two dominantly aural works, the twin radio plays: *Words and Music* first, followed almost immediately by *Cascando*, the latter itself after a thirty-seven-line poem of lost love published in the *Dublin Magazine* 11:3 (October–December 1936) and later also collected in *Gedichte* (1959). The poem imbedded in the former, Words's (Joe's) final lyric, was extracted from the play and published separately, at Beckett's suggestion, as 'Song' in *Collected Poems 1930–1978* (1984), but without the second part, 'Then down a little way.' The poem that emerges from the dialogic competition between words and music is finally offered discrete from context and as a coda to the 1984 collection of poems (which volume includes 'Tailpiece' from the 'Addenda' to *Watt* as well).

The sand border, moreover, allows passage in either direction. The short work 'neither' was originally published in the *Journal of Beckett Studies* No. 4 (1979) with lineation suggestive of poetry. When John Calder was about to include the 'poem' in the *Collected Poems 1930–1978*, Beckett resisted because he considered it a piece of prose, that is, a short story. Subsequently, it was scheduled for but inadvertently omitted from *The Collected Shorter Prose 1945–1980* (John Calder, 1984). It was finally printed but in a corrupt version in the posthumous collection, *As the Story Was Told: Uncollected and Later Prose* (John Calder/Riverrun Press, 1990). The printing was further corrupted not only by the introduction of erroneous information (the story, identified in the *Journal of Beckett Studies* as 'written by Samuel Beckett in September 1976 to be set to music by Morton Feldman', is described in *As the Story Was Told* as having been 'Written for composer Morton Feldman, 1962'). When 'neither' was finally collected the title was capitalised and instead of printing the word omitted from the *Journal of Beckett Studies* version included instead the copy editor's query marking the place of the lost word. That is, the question mark was taken by the printer as an addition to the text and was retained in publication; line six (in the collected edition) then reads, 'doors once? gently close, once turned [. . .]' instead of 'doors once neared gently close, once turned [. . .]'. Moreover, since the piece is a work of prose, there is no question of retaining the stanzaic lineation of the *Journal of Beckett Studies* version, but the *As the Story Was Told* version retains that poetic lineation.

While much study of Beckett's work has explored the issues of what Ruby Cohn has called 'jumping genres', almost all of that has focused on the adaptation of prose works (or television works) to the stage. Moreover, studies of Beckett's poetry, few as they are, too often fail to address the critical implications of the sort of generic slippage between prose and poetry detailed above, even as such slippage is central to our understanding of Beckett's critique of genre itself, his interrogation of formalist distinctions and literariness, of Romanticism and Modernism, an interrogation at the heart of his creative enterprise. The singular exception to such neglect is Marjorie Perloff's work on Beckett's late prose which she sees as part of 'the gradual and inevitable evolution of the free verse lyric [. . .] into a literary mode that can accommodate verse and prose [. . .]' (1986: 204). But Beckett's lifelong preoccupation with poetry, manifest even in the early fiction, in the dazzling poetry of the plays of the 1980s like *Rockaby* and *Ohio Impromptu*, and in the teleplays, the most obvious of which features Beckett's return to Yeats in '...but the clouds ...', remains unexplored. Most telling is perhaps Beckett's rewriting of Baudelaire near the end of *Endgame*. Hamm quotes from 'Recueillement', 'Tu réclamais le soir; il descend; le voici', imbedding the transliteration into his own narrative; in Beckett's English: 'You cried for night; it falls; now cry in darkness' (*Endgame* 83). But Hamm as poet (or the poetics of the rest of Hamm's evolving chronicle) remains under-explored critically even as the play itself, perched on the border of land and sea, invites a critique of the slipping borders of theatre, prose narrative and poetry, a play in which, like *A Piece of Monologue*, 'Everything that happened happened inside it, and at the same time everything that happened happened outside of it' (*Watt* 43). Arsene, another of Beckett's fictive poets, is also a genre theorist, whose simple mantra, 'all slips', itself a critique of genre, we, like Watt himself, have too often failed critically to acknowledge or heed.

Notes

1. From Baudelaire's 'Preface' to *Le Spleen de Paris*, the quotation is used as an epigraph to *The Prose Poem: An International Journal*.
2. 'Sedendo et Quiesc[i]endo', *transition* 21 (March 1932), pp. 13–20; reprinted in *CSP*.
3. First published in *Transition Forty-Eight*, No. 2 (June 1948), p. 96.

4. See also Stefan Wolpe's 1924 *lied* of the Hölderlin poem and Caspar David Friedrich's sublime painting, *The Wanderer Above the Sea Fog*.

References

Baudelaire, Charles (2000) 'Preface', *Le Spleen de Paris*, Paris: Gallimard.

Beckett, Samuel (1984) *Collected Poems 1930–1978*, London: John Calder.

Perloff, Marjorie (1986) 'Between Verse and Prose: Beckett and the New Poetry', in S. E. Gontarski, ed., *On Beckett: Essays and Criticism*, New York: Grove Press, pp. 191–206.

Yeats, William Butler, ed. (1936) *The Oxford Book of Modern Verse 1892–1935*, New York: Oxford University Press

5

Art and Commodity:
Beckett's Commerce with Grove Press

In one sentence, how would you epitomize those goals you
have sought to achieve in your lifetime, and the contribution
you have sought to make? (Request to SB from *Who's Who in
America*)

Amid the intense theorising of 'Three Dialogues: Samuel Beckett
and Georges Duthuit', one discovers what appears to be a reluctant admission, an acknowledgment, a summary of a materialist
theory of art, even as it is dismissed: 'The realization that art has
always been bourgeois, though it may dull our pain before the
achievements of the social progressive, is finally of scant interest' (Beckett 1949: 123–4). Despite Beckett's casual dismissal, the
statement seemed significant enough for him to revise and reprint it
in two subsequent publications, one in French and one in English,
tributes to the struggling painter Bram van Velde.[1] In fact, Beckett
leads his tribute essay with this simultaneous admission and dismissal, only the crucial subordinate clause, the quasi-Freudian
acknowledgment of art's potential palliative effect, 'to dull our
pain', omitted; that is, the admission of an aesthetic function to art
is expunged in reference to van Velde. The relation of art to bourgeois culture may have been declared 'of scant interest' to Beckett
as he focused on other features of the art work, particularly the
paradoxical relation between artist and occasion, but Beckett's
denial reinserts the denied into the equation and so constitutes
something of a reaffirmation, the denial of occasion seeming to
double back on itself to become something of a fresh occasion,
a danger that Beckett acknowledged. Evading the material and
bourgeois, Beckett recognised, may be futile, his evasion leading
back to the terrestrial, the quotidian, the diurnal, the mundane.

The issue that Beckett skirts in his commentary, what amounts to a politics of art, its uneasy, often occluded association with commodity and commerce, is, of course, most evident in theatre, where property is rented from its owners, presumably an author (or designate), packaged, and resold to the public, but it remains a defining feature of all art. Like painting, writing in all its genres is inextricably tied to the *quid pro quo* world of commerce. Most literary publications and theatrical performances, especially in late capitalist societies, require investors, those bourgeois replacements for patrons who exhibit something less than altruism in their economic support for the arts. They expect something tangible in return for their outlay. As uninterested as he appeared to be in the *quid pro quo* world he so castigated in *Murphy*, Samuel Beckett himself, like the unfortunate Murphy, was tied ('ti-ed') to it, and the arc of his literary reputation was inextricably linked to the world of commerce. Murphy avoided that world as best he could, succeeding only in the eradication of his material self from the material world. Beckett, on the other hand and for a time, flogged his wares almost door to door. That this link between art and commerce has been under-examined by cultural critics in general and analysts of Beckett's work in particular is surprising given the trend in contemporary culture to rate creative achievement in terms of cash value, sales and attendance figures: platinum CDs, weekly box-office take, Christie's sale prices, and bestseller lists. Barney Rosset, Beckett's first and only American publisher, took on Beckett, son of a successful Dublin entrepreneur, as an author in June 1953 for his aesthetic and political qualities, but Rosset, son of a wealthy, successful Chicago banker, was always a commercial publisher who expected to, indeed, who needed to, earn a return on his investment, even from avant-garde authors. Admittedly, his publishing enterprise was funded by a personal fortune, but it would soon vanish, as it did in the 1970s, without substantial capital return.

Beckett's alliance with Grove Press was literary and aesthetic, certainly, but the association was also commercial, a relationship Beckett acknowledged, accepted, and supported. The dearth of analysis of that relationship suggests something of a critical blind spot, a refusal to confront the material circumstances of art. In *Institutions of Modernism: Literary Elites and Public Culture* (1998), for instance, Lawrence Rainey traces the assimilation of art and commodity, or art by commodity, to the social provocations of the Futurists between 1912 and 1914, as artists had 'to come to terms with the new institutions of mass culture and assess their bearings on the place of art in the cultural marketplace'. Such reassessment precipitated 'a permanent collapse of all distinctions between art and commodity, [and effected] the perceptible and irreversible levelling of both within the single and amorphous category of commodity' (Rainey 1998: 38–9). This is the world in which Beckett worked, and his recognition 'that art has always been bourgeois' reaches further than Rainey's assessment, to suggest that to be an artist was not only to fail on the highest of aesthetic planes, but to be something of a huckster as well.

A neophyte publisher, Rosset saw the economy of publishing, and so of literature, clearly and early on. He built his enterprise, which would feature Beckett and other writers of the European avant-garde, as something of a second phase of Modernist publishing with emphases on a little literary review, the *Evergreen Review* (later just *Evergreen* in its glossier, more commercial format), and limited editions, author-signed artefacts that were not designed as books to be read but as cultural and commercial investments, the reading of which would devalue them. Grove's marketing strategy for *Waiting for Godot* was in 1954 decidedly populist, Rosset offering the paperback *Godot* (E-33) for $1.00, a strategy to broaden sales, particularly among the young and particularly at performances.[2] Shortly thereafter Rosset followed with a $1.00 *Proust* (E-50), writing to Beckett on 25 January 1956:

> I would love to do the *Proust* book and your letter goaded me into action. I snatched it off the shelf in East Hampton and handed it to the printer today for a printing estimate. My idea is that we will bring it out, at $1.00 if possible, in February or thereabouts of next year. This time ALL of the royalties can go directly to you [since the work was written in English, not French]. If this meets with your approval, let me know and I will send you a letter of confirmation and even dredge up some sort of a modest advance.[3]

Beckett was enthusiastic about such market expansion that accompanied low-cost books.

But Rosset also targeted another market, this one more upscale. In 1956 Grove followed the format for *Molloy* (E-18, $1.75) with *Malone Dies*, publishing it in an Evergreen paperback format (E-39, $1.25), but unlike *Molloy*, the hard-bound edition of *Malone Dies* was a limited edition of 500 copies (selling for $3.75). Rosset was tentative about the publication of Beckett's novels, especially *Molloy*, which he would use finally to test the limits of censorship in America. Cautioned by Beckett and on advice of his legal staff, Rosset published *Molloy* exclusively in hard cover, its distribution restricted to New York bookshops that had requested it, as he told Beckett on 24 September 1955: 'Copies of *Molloy* are in all the New York City bookstores that wanted them, but distribution across the rest of the country has not yet gone out. The post office is now examining the book and I am sure their decision will be very amusing if not pleasing.' In this instance the United States Post Office, as official censor of a United States still subject to the Comstock laws, raised no objection to the book,[4] and Rosset proceeded with a paperback publication of *Molloy* the following year, concurrent with the release of *Malone Dies*. Although actually released in 1956, the paperback *Molloy* retained the 1955 publication date as if it were published simultaneously with the hard cover.

The following year, March 1957, Rosset began printing signed editions of Beckett's work, first with *Murphy*, publishing it in a hard-bound edition ($3.50) but also offering a specially bound, limited edition of 100 numbered copies signed by the author. *Endgame* appeared in four editions the following year: an Evergreen Book (E-96), a hard-bound edition, a specially bound limited edition of 100 copies, and a special edition of twenty-six copies signed by the author. At the same time, the $1.00 *Proust* was also issued in a hard-bound edition, and a limited edition of 250 copies signed by the author. By 1958 the economic stakes increased yet again and, once translated, *The Unnamable* was published in *five* editions, that is, as both a cultural and an overtly commercial artefact: an Evergreen Book (E-117, $1.45), a cloth-bound edition like *Molloy* and *Malone Dies*, a specially bound limited edition of 100 numbered copies, a specially bound and signed edition of twenty-six copies, numbered A through Z, and a specially bound and signed edition, *hors commerce*, numbered 1–4. The publishing pattern of *The Unnamable* was repeated the following year for *Watt*: a trade paperback (E-152, $1.75), a cloth-bound book ($3.50), a specially bound limited edition of 100 numbered copies, a specially bound and signed edition of twenty-six copies, lettered A–Z, and four copies *hors commerce*, numbered 1–4. Rosset thus set about encouraging investment in the avant-garde in general and in Beckett's work in particular, and for that he needed Beckett's participation, and so Beckett went into what Rosset's assistant Judith Schmidt would call the 'autograph business'. In a letter of 1 December 1956, Beckett accepted Rosset's strategy: 'I shall be delighted to sign as many sheets as you please of *Proust* and *Murphy*' (*Letters* 2 681; the annotation to this sentence in the *Letters* [682n8] incorrectly declares these works published by Grove only in 1958, although both were published in 1957). And Beckett continued to support Rosset's books-as-investment strategy, Beckett signing and promoting books, numbered and limited editions, for the collector's market, and personalised autographs of general editions for special clients. And Rosset (or the British publisher John Calder) prevailed upon Beckett to write, even if not directly, the occasional book blurb, in this case for Beckett's friend, Robert Pinget, whose novel *The Inquisitory* (1966) is called in a blurb attributed to Beckett, 'One of the most important novels of the last ten years'. Admittedly, the prose sounds little like Beckett, but his name is attached to it on the book's cover. As part of the Grove Press marketing strategy, Beckett was very much in the American book business.

What Rosset seems to have understood, instinctively perhaps, was that an anti-bourgeois art needed substantial and broad bourgeois support, and that Beckett's name and image already had considerable commercial cachet by the 1950s. That cachet would only increase with the award of the International Publisher's Prize in 1961, which he shared with Jorge Louis Borges and which Grove Press engineered for its author and promoted heavily, and the Nobel Prize in 1969. In an advert run in the *New York Times* following the first award, Grove announced its author (and his image) directly to the American intellectual middle class, emphasising the monetary value of the award and ignoring its co-winner. Grove's ability to promote its authors, who were predominantly counter-cultural, not mainstream, increased dramatically with the conversion of what was at first a small, literary, house journal, the *Evergreen Review*, issued quarterly, into the monthly glossy called *Evergreen* (starting with issue No. 32 [April–May 1964]), which Rosset would use not only to promote Grove's authors and publications but to make news as well.

The change was pugnacious in a number of ways, not the least of which was its social provocations. With No. 32, advertising increased but much of it was politically driven, advertising as editorial, a form of capitalism in the service of a revolution that Rosset seems to have invented. *Evergreen* continued its commitment to experimental writing, like William Burroughs's neo-Dadaist 'Cut-Ups Self-Explained', but the No. 32 issue also tested the censorship standard for visual art with a portfolio of double-exposed nudes by American photographer Emil J. Cadoo. The photos also exposed *Evergreen* to criminal prosecution. On 12 June 1964, detectives of the Nassau County, New York, Vice Squad raided the printing plant on Long Island and carried off 21,000 unbound copies of *Evergreen* No. 32. Rosset retaliated by publishing yet another Cadoo nude in No. 33, and explained the police seizure of No. 32 in a short note called simply 'About *Evergreen Review* no. 32'. But No. 33 was also seized; this time the offending item was a poem by Judith Malina, co-director, with Julian Beck, of the Living Theatre, 'last performance at the living theatre invective'. The poem concluded, 'I suggest an overthrow of all governments by love. / I suggest direct action: / Ergo: Fuck the USA'. No. 34 contained yet another Cadoo photograph as well as the sort of works that were becoming *Evergreen*'s signature: Susan Sontag's now-famous 'Against Interpretation', Hubert Selby's 'The Queen is Dead', anticipating Grove's publication of Selby's controversial stories, *Last Exit to Brooklyn*, and Samuel Beckett's *Play*, seized as part of the police action.

For the new *Evergreen*, subscribers were asked to 'Join the Underground', of which Beckett was very much a part. *Evergreen Review* No.1 (1957) contained Beckett's 'Dante and the Lobster' (24–36), which revived interest in *More Pricks than Kicks*. This first issue also contained ten poems by Beckett reprinted photographically from *Echo's Bones*, omitting only 'Alba', 'Dortmunder' and 'Malacoda'. Thereafter, Beckett appeared regularly in *Evergreen Review*, with ten texts published between its first and final issues, and he remained integral to the new *Evergreen* as well with five further texts appearing.[5] The *Evergreen Review Reader, 1957–1967* (Grove Press, 1968) reprinted 'Dante and the Lobster' (3–8) and 'The Expelled' (448–54). When Grove fell on hard financial times in 1970–71, Rosset nonetheless tried to revive its now infamous magazine, publishing a Dell paperback (No. 95, 1972), and another the following spring (No. 96), the latter with the 'Complete Text of Samuel Beckett's *The Lost Ones*'. Grove tried a tabloid edition devoted to *Last Tango in Paris* (No. 97; rpt. [Dell] as an '*Evergreen Review* Special'), but by 1973 the magazine had lost its audience. Rosset attempted again to revive *Evergreen* with

No. 98 (1984), and this revival, too, featured Beckett (the plays *Ohio Impromptu*, *Catastrophe*, and *What Where*), but the publication could neither attract nor sustain an adequate readership. The underground had either surfaced or was dispersed. In all, Beckett appeared in eighteen issues over a twenty-seven-year period. Some of the most important (and most accurate) printings of his work appeared in *Evergreen Review*, notably *Play* (No. 34) and *The Lost Ones* (No. 96). In addition to a substantial advertising campaign in the *New York Times*, Rosset could splash Beckett's image across the pages of *Evergreen*, even for such slight works as the collection called *Cascando* in the advert but *Cascando and Other Short Dramatic Pieces* (1968) in its published version. As the advert suggests, the particular work seems less important than its giving Grove the opportunity to splash Beckett's powerful, iconic visage across a full page of the journal.

Rosset was thus keen to publicise his new author in all available venues, and Beckett was only too willing to participate in the preparations and publicity. On 25 July 1956, Rosset asked for Beckett's help in preparing a programme of public readings:

> First, read the enclosed letters [from the YM-YWHA Poetry Center in New York]. They give the idea – a program of readings of the writings of one SAMUEL BECKETT. I am absolutely terrified at the idea of being in charge of it and being expected to say something, so you <u>must</u> help me.
> We need – A program
> Readings from poetry – *Echo's Bones*
> 'Whoroscope'
> Other things which I may not know about. Perhaps a French poem or two if either Marshall or Epstein can read in French.
> Prose – *Proust*
> Anything else which I may not know about.
> Stories – *More Pricks Than Kicks*
> Other stories unbeknownst to me
> Novels – *Murphy*
> *Watt*
> *Molloy*
> *Malone Dies*
> *L'Inno* [*L'Innommable*]
> and other things such as *Fin de Partie*, *Textes de Rien* [*sic*] and so forth.

So out of all this richness we must put together something to take up about 1hr and 45 minutes, including whatever little words I may have to contribute – which means some kind of biographical background on you and some sort of setting for each piece.

Naturally it would be wonderful if any section of something not yet published could be read because that would help to draw attention to the whole affair – and if if IF <u>IF</u> I could persuade you to stop in at a recording studio, either for tape or disque, and read a section of something yourself, then I think we would have something of truly great interest to the people here. [. . .] If you do not want to go into a studio then all you need is a friend with a tape recorder. I have one, many of my friends do also, so the same thing must exist in quantity in Paris – as a matter of fact I had one there in '48. Had the silly idea I could write by speaking to the damn machine and then type it off.[6]

That's all for the program for the moment – but I am counting on you like a man waits for that last drink two minutes before the pub closes.[7]

Replying to Rosset on 1 August 1956, Beckett agreed: 'Of course I shall give you all help I can with the readings programme. With regard to choice of texts, do you want me to make suggestions? I am quite happy to leave it to you. But go canny on the early stuff. [. . .] Tell the Poetry Center how pleased I feel and how honoured' (*Letters* 2 642–3). Beckett then immediately began making arrangements for recordings of material in French, and agreeing to record his own reading:

With regard to some readings in French, I have approached Martin and Blin with the suggestion that the former should record Lucky's speech and the latter a passage from *L'Inno* or a *Textes pour Rien*. They would both be very glad to do this, and no doubt would do it without payment if necessary, but I feel they should be paid something. I play with the idea of doing a short text in English and another in French myself. I think I'll have at least a shot at it, and then withhold it if too awful. It was all very well for Joyce with his fine trained voice, but when you have a gasp-croak like mine you hesitate. (*Letters* 2 642)

And Beckett seemed to allow Rosset a free hand for his introduction of biographical material: 'With regard to your presentation [i.e., introduction] I am not worrying, you are as well able as any and better than most to say what little there is to say about me. But needless to say any help or information I can give you are unreservedly at your disposal' (*Letters 2* 642). Rosset followed up quickly on 20 August 1956; after dispensing with some early business, he notes:

> Second – for what is important – The Reading.
> All constantly on my mind since I got your MOST welcome letter. I was very happy to get your concurrence and your views. Perhaps I could go back over your letter in the same order you mention things.
> I certainly do want you to make suggestions on the readings. Please give me as many as you can dredge up.
> In *Murphy* the 'Amor Intellectualis etc'. would be fine, even though I think that perhaps more of the quality of the writing comes out in other parts.
> What about 'Dante and the Lobster' from *More Pricks than Kicks*.
> And for the recordings – both Poetry Center and I extremely happy and pleased that you will do something yourself – a text in English and one in French sounds perfect – CROAK ON. [. . .]
> Alvin Epstein told me that he would like to read something in French – perhaps some poetry. What would you suggest?
> A passage from *L'Inno* (translation in progress) would be very good idea—and also newsworthy.
> Am looking forward to seeing the English text 'From an Abandoned Work'. What is a TCD [Trinity College Dublin] magazine. We certainly might get some USA periodical to use it.
> *Proust* is in the works – will publish it in first half of '57. Other publishers notified.

Beckett replied on 30 August 1956 with his own programme outline (*Letters 2* 646).

With strong interest in non-print media, Rosset was also keen to develop a line of commercial recordings, and a Columbia two-LP version of *Godot* (produced by Michael Myerberg, liner notes by Goddard Lieberson; Caedmon TRS 352 CSM 914–1–2) had already been recorded by the time of the proposed Poetry Center readings. In his liner notes Lieberson says of the audio recording that music, or rather electronic sound, 'was occasionally called for to sustain moods or atmosphere which had been created on stage through visual means, either by actors or through scenery'.

To these dramatic enhancements Beckett made no objection. He noted to Rosset on 30 August 1956:

> I saw Lieberson of Columbia Rdgs who gave me the Godot record. I find it quite good, as a record, especially Act 1 where Pozzo is remarkable. The sound element (finger on chords of grand piano blown up through micro) is hardly disturbing, except perhaps at end of 1st act. Some changes and interpolations annoyed me mildly especially at the beginning of Act II. I thought Vladimir very wooden and did not agree at all with Epstein's remarkable technical performance in the tirade. The boy I thought very good. (*Letters 2* 646–7)

Rosset himself took the initiative in 1957 to record Alan Schneider's Obie Award-winning production of *Endgame* at the Cherry Lane Theatre for Grove Press. The performance was published in two versions, as a two-disc, high-fidelity recording in Grove's short lived Evergreen Records series (as EV 003) and a second version with the full Evergreen text fitted into the album, the package then containing both text and recording. Taking his cue from Lieberson, Rosset also added some original music by David Amram, or low-level sounds, to the performance. To these Beckett objected, and Rosset tried to have them removed. Most of the music was deleted, but not all of it. Vague sounds still underlie the opening of each act. But Beckett was finally pleased with the results, writing to Rosset on 5 May 1959: 'I played the *Endgame* record and liked it. Clov's feet, trailing ladder, ticking at end, excellent. Of the four I preferred Nell. Hamm was inclined to declaim. Clove a bit wooden though he improved as it went. Music all right. On the whole a fine job. Thanks to you all' (*Letters 3* 229). In December of 1984, however, Beckett and Rosset took a more strident position on the issue of music in *Endgame*. In the *New York Times* coverage of the JoAnne Akalaitis-directed *Endgame* at the American Repertory Theatre, which included an 'overture' by Philip Glass, Samuel G. Freedman cited Rosset as follows, 'As for the music, Mr. Rosset said that Mr. Beckett opposes the addition of music to any of his plays and ordered a score by David Amram excised from the original production of "Endgame" in 1959.'[8]

The final recording that Rosset helped oversee was the historic production of *Krapp's Last Tape*, by Theater 1960 at Provincetown Playhouse, with Donald Davis, directed by Alan Schneider. *Krapp*, along with Edward Albee's *Zoo Story*, with which *Krapp* was paired, was cited as a 'Distinguished Play', Donald Davie as 'Distinguished Actor', at the 1960 Obie Awards. The awards prompted the release of the production as an LP version (New York: Spoken Arts #788) in 1960, distributed in Britain by Argo [RG 220], and by HEAR, Home Educational Records, London (1964). But, alas, no recording of the poetry programme that Beckett outlined, and certainly no recordings of Beckett's performances, have been discovered.

Judith Schmidt joined Grove as Rosset's personal assistant in April of 1956 and went on to become head of Grove's subsidiary rights division. She was Beckett's principal liaison with Grove during the growth years of both the Press and the Beckett business, and she fully understood the economic requirements of publishing and what was required of Grove authors. Moreover, as Grove Press grew in size and stature, Rosset was distracted by other, often ancillary projects, most involving the battle against censorship in the US, in print and increasingly in film. Subsequently, more and more of the correspondence with Beckett was taken over by various members of the staff, most conspicuously by Judith Schmidt and by editor and Beckett translator Richard Seaver, among others. On occasion Beckett seems frustrated by the plurality of his Grove correspondents. On 3 July 1958 he asked Rosset to drop him a note 'in your own wild old fist' (letter in Rosset archive but not included in *Letters 3*). But overall he established strong working and personal relations with those at Grove involved with his work. On 31 May 1962 Schmidt wrote to Beckett regarding the Obie Award for Alan Schneider's Cherry Lane production of *Happy Days*:

> I guess Alan gave you the details of the Obie awards. The certificate will be sent.[9]
>
> I saw Ruth White there and she very hesitantly asked about your possibly signing a copy of HAPPY DAYS for her. She said she had been trying to work up the courage to ask you yourself. This really should have occurred to me months ago, and I should have written to ask you, but my mind is not functioning terribly well. Would you sign a copy for her and another for John C. Becher? I took the liberty of telling her that I thought you would be very happy to do it.

On 15 September 1962 Beckett wrote to Schmidt that he would sign books for John Becher and Ruth White, as requested, and pass them on in Paris to Richard Seaver, who in turn would relay them to the actors. Becher's copy, however, went missing since, on 6 December 1962, Schmidt wrote Beckett:

> John C. Becher called this week to say that he never received the signed copy of HAPPY DAYS. Unfortunately, I had mailed the book to him about three months ago, so it was too late to check with the Post Office. Would you mind inscribing another copy and mailing it whenever it is convenient? Mr. Becher sounded so disappointed when he heard that the book had been mailed, and was presumably lost.

On 12 December, Beckett replied to Schmidt and agreed to sign another copy for Becher. On 27 January 1964 Schmidt wrote to Beckett:

> Please sign as many copies of POEMS as you can spare. I think we sent you about 20, but if you have given some away, or would like to keep some, it doesn't matter. Ten or fifteen will do for us. Barney would like to give them to a few people – mainly people at Grove, I think. He would also like you to sign about 10 copies of HOW IT IS. I'll send them on to you. Hope it's OK.

Away in London rehearsing *Endgame* with Jack MacGowran and Patrick Magee, a production he deemed 'very exciting. They are both marvelous', Beckett got back to the publishing business in Paris and replied to a series of Schmidt's letters on 7 February, referencing her letter of 27 January 1964: 'Very sorry to have forgotten to sign *Poems*. Shall do so tomorrow and send them Mon. at latest. Also very gladly 10 copies of *HII* when they arrive' (letter in Grove archive not included in *Letters 3*).

By 7 March Beckett wrote to say he had completed his tasks: 'Thanks for letter of March 5 [. . .]. Glad the *Poems* arrived safely. The 10 signed copies of *How It Is* left a few days ago' (letter not included in *Letters 3*). By 1967 the signings had become a business, big business, and Schmidt wrote to Beckett on 23 August:

> It looks as though the autographing business is picking up. I have a letter from a man and enclosures of the last page of *Godot* and the same for *Happy Days*, plus a typed copy of a poem by you, for which he wants three signatures. I frankly hesitate to send these on to you, and I fear that we may be getting many of these in the future. I can tell

people that you do not give out autographs – shall I do that? Please let me know your decision.

I'm afraid that you may soon be swamped with these requests.

And swamped he was, but such was the business of authorship, particularly with Beckett's American publishing house, the activity of which exploded after the Nobel Prize was awarded.

Since Grove commissioned most of the English translations, Schmidt would handle considerable international translation rights as well as performance rights, and she was ever faithful to her task, mindful and respectful of Beckett's desire to maintain the integrity to his work in an age of increasing commercialisation. On occasion, however, Beckett would override her diligence. Writing to the director of a theatre programme in Milwaukee, Wisconsin on 15 November 1965, Schmidt noted sternly:

I have your letter of the 12th. I am sorry, but we cannot authorize you to produce the Beckett mime with the changes you mentioned. I really would prefer that Mr. Beckett made this decision himself, and I am sending him a copy of your letter, but I doubt that we will receive an answer before the 22nd.

I do know that Mr. Beckett expects that his directions be followed exactly, and when he says 'a little pile of clothes' he means 'a little pile of clothes' [. . .] [A]s far as the elimination of clothes is concerned, you definitely do <u>not</u> have authorization to proceed, and we prefer that you cancel the production rather than change the stage directions given by Mr. Beckett. Please let us know your decision immediately.

I think you misunderstood my letter about the performance of *Act Without Words I*. [. . .] I told you that 'We generally do not give permission for one of the Beckett plays to be produced in any way other than the exact way in which Mr. Beckett wrote it, but if your reading of stage directions was clear to the audience, no harm was done.' I certainly did not mean this to be an authorization to you to change the stage directions in other works by Samuel Beckett.

Such is the position that Grove took and enforced as guardian of Beckett's work. On this occasion, however, Beckett relented and wrote across the bottom of Schmidt's letter, almost whimsically, 'Dear Judith, Let him do it. Love Sam'.

The number of such requests in the Grove files is staggering and suggests what Beckett saw as the burden of authorship. As his reputation grew requests to Grove Press for information about him, honours offered him, or permissions to produce one sort of production or another became legion, so that Beckett was grateful to have his American publisher, as was the case with his French publisher, filter most of such quotidian correspondence. It was left to Grove then to sort through the correspondence, to separate requests from students working on theses of various sorts, composers desiring to develop operas around one or another of the dramatic works, directors wanting to adapt prose works to the stage or to alter one or a group of texts for performance, and the like.

On 15 January 1965, Schmidt wrote to Beckett about correcting and updating his entry for *Who's Who in America*, which Grove was quite willing to do for its author: 'Enclosed is a copy of proof sent to us by WHO'S WHO IN AMERICA. They're correcting for their new edition. If all of the information is accurate, don't bother to answer (I'm referring to the personal information. I'll check publication dates here, and also add dates for PLAY and POEMS in ENGLISH.' Two years later, 7 March 1967, the reference book wanted more detailed information for its 35th edition:

Dear Mr. Beckett:
    Because your accomplishments and influence have been so extensive, we would be honored if you would consider the following question for us:
'In one sentence, how would you epitomize those goals you have sought to achieve in your lifetime, and the contribution you have sought to make?' [. . .] Such a summation would provide precious insight and clarity in a world of confused reportage and interpretation. It would serve not only our living hundreds and thousands of readers the world over, but generations hence ... because *Who's Who in America*, from its first appearance in 1899, has become established as a reliable, objective, and singular form of historical record.

Such requests continued to grow, so little wonder Beckett (and Suzanne) considered the Nobel Prize a catastrophe, and as a result Beckett withdrew further from the commercial world of publishing. Unlike the publicity that Grove generated for Beckett's International Publisher's Prize, the Nobel Prize was underplayed, the only tribute being a sixteen-volume celebratory edition, *The Collected Works of Samuel Beckett* (1970), the first uniform edition of Beckett's work. In it only scant reference was made to the Prize, and that only on the inside back flap of the dust jacket, where Dr Karl Glerow of the Swedish Academy is quoted: 'In the realms of annihilation, the writing of Samuel Beckett rises like a miserere from all mankind, its muffled minor key sounding liberation to the oppressed and comfort to those in need.' Whether or not Dr Glerow's poignant tribute actually describes Beckett's work, the one-sentence summary that *Who's Who in America* sought two years earlier is less an issue than Grove's validating the summary in all sixteen of its tribute volumes. As important, the Nobel Prize finally allowed Samuel Beckett to become 'Samuel Beckett', an image of an author Beckett created and one who succeeded, finally, where Murphy failed. That image is perhaps best summarised by Rosset himself, who finally, on 16 December 1982, wrote a long apology to Beckett for the distribution of his work to a broad American public and pleading for a cessation of that distribution, a plea which was apparently ignored. The letter, moreover, details a rift between Beckett's American and French publishers, the latter, according to Rosset, undermining the work of the former, a rift that would only grow over the years as Rosset began losing control of the rights to Beckett's work in America.

> Dear Sam,
>   Enclosed is a piece which I thought might be of some interest or even amusement, regarding the use of *Ill Seen Ill Said* in *The New* Yorker.[10] Quite good, I thought.
>   Sam – Please! – understand, I had <u>nothing</u> to do with offering, aiding and abetting, or anything else, in sending your work to that magazine. Not only do I consider it wrong to give to them, but I also find the people there to be personally insufferable. Neither *Rockaby* nor *Ohio Impromptu* were offered to *The New Yorker*. The same holds for *Company* and *Worstward Ho*. The problem lies with the pieces written first in French. They apparently go straight to [Georges] Borchardt who acts as the 'owner' of the rights for this country. When we contract for the book rights, we at least control those, but in the first instance we are powerless. The submissions to *The New Yorker* were done without ANY consultation with us. I feel certain that if Jerome [Lindon] understood your feelings about this he would tell Borchardt to cease and desist immediately. Borchardt is acting as if

perhaps another American publisher might pop up to do *Catastrophe*. [. . .] Why not tell them to withdraw *Catastrophe* from *The New Yorker*? This very moment I called Borchardt to tell him what I am telling you, but he is on vacation. [. . .]

When Jerome contracts with you for a text written in French, he gets English translation rights. This gives him some sort of vague right to have Borchardt hustle off and sell something to *The New Yorker* without consulting us. The fact that Borchardt magnanimously sent us 10% of the fee received from *The New Yorker* changes nothing.

I was absolutely stunned when he informed us of the sale of *Catastrophe* to *The New Yorker*. Sam, I can only believe that Jerome has not been aware of your objection to this procedure. Please, for <u>my</u> sake, do tell him, and clarify this extremely upsetting problem. Remember, Borchardt is trying to fulfill his job as an agent. *The New Yorker* fees are unusually large and therefore enticing. Who knows, perhaps Jerome thinks that Borchardt is consulting with me. First of all, he is not, but perhaps in some way or other Jerome got the feeling that he was doing so. This time I sent you a copy of Borchardt's letter, giving me the 'fait accompli.'

Rosset's phrase, 'What has happened here is absolutely wrong', is at least ambiguous. Certainly, he is objecting to the interference by Beckett's French publisher in the American market, but the sort of exposure that publication in *The New Yorker* represented is exactly the sort that Rosset struggled so hard and long to generate for his author. At this point, Rosset's position was very different from his initial appeal to Beckett in June 1953: 'Believe me, we will do what we can to make your work known in this country.' Whether or not Rosset was being disingenuous in this appeal to Beckett is less important here than how the letter outlines the nature of fundamental changes in both author and publisher in the thirty years between 1953 and 1982, as Beckett withdrew from, could afford to withdraw from, the *quid pro quo* world of publishing commerce, and Rosset increasingly took on the role not of promoter but of protector, if not of his author then at least of the image of his author.

Notes

1. First in *Bram van Velde* (1958) and then in English by Grove Press in 1960 as an Evergreen Gallery Book, Book 5 (E-174).

2. Substantial expense was saved on the $3.00 cloth edition by eliminating the production photos from the hardcover edition and reducing the size of the 1951 publicity photograph of Beckett, the latter originally published internally (eliminated) and on the back cover (reduced in size).

3. All letters to and from Barney Rosset and the Grove Press staff are in the Barney Rosset/Grove Press archives now at the George Arents Research Library at Syracuse University, the John J. Burns Library, Boston College and the Stanley E. Gontarski Grove Press Research Materials at Florida State University, Special Collections . All letters to and from Alan Schneider are published in Harmon 1998. All material is used with the permission of the principals.

4. It was immediately banned in Beckett's homeland, however, as Beckett noted in his letter to Rosset of 2 February 1956.

5. These texts are: 'From an Abandoned Work', 3 (March 1957), pp. 83–91; *Krapp's Last Tape*, 5 (1958), pp. 13–24; 'Text for Nothing I', 9 (1959), pp. 21–4; 'Embers', 10 (Nov.–Dec. 1959), pp. 28–41; 'From an Unabandoned Work', 14 (Sept.–Oct. 1960), pp. 58–65; 'The End', 15 (Nov.–Dec. 1960), pp. 22–41; 'The Old Tune', 17 (March–April 1961), pp. 47–60; 'The Expelled', 22 (Jan.–Feb. 1962), pp. 8–20; 'Words and Music', 27 (Nov.–Dec. 1962), pp. 34–43; 'Cascando', 30 (May–June 1963), pp. 47–57. In the new *Evergreen*: 'Play', 34 (Dec. 1964), pp. 42–7; 'Imagination Dead Imagine', 39 (Feb. 1966), pp. 48–9; 'The Calmative', 47 (June 1967), pp. 47–9, 93–5; 'Eh Joe', 62 (Jan. 1969), pp. 43–6; and *Lessness*, 80 (July 1970), pp. 35–6.

6. This production, which did not produce a tape for the Poetry Center reading, may have nudged Beckett towards what became *Krapp's Last Tape*. It also suggests Rosset's profound interest in media evident throughout the letters. This preoccupation has deep roots. After his discharge from the US Army on the last day of 1945, Rosset returned to Chicago to develop some direction to his life. He moved to New York City in January of 1947 to capitalise on his military training as a photographer and began making documentary films. The one product of his company, Target Films, was the documentary (or docudrama) *Strange Victory*, which was released in June 1948. Although praised by, principally, the press of the American left for its anti-segregation theme, the film failed financially. It had more success abroad, however. Despite attempts to suppress it, the film was shown at the Venice Film Festival in September 1948, and won prizes at the Karlovy-Vary film festival and at the Venice

Film Festival. By 5 September 1948, Rosset and his live-in partner, the painter Joan Mitchell, had settled into Paris at 73 rue Galande in the 5eme district. On 15 December 1948 Rosset and Mitchell took *Strange Victory* to Prague and by 26 December he had sold it to Ceskoslovensky Statni Film for $3,000. By 21 January 1949 the couple moved to the south of France where Rosset thought that Mitchell might recover more quickly from her winter-induced illness. By 9 March they had settled into the Villa Le Pin in Le Lavandou, where, Rosset wrote to his office at Target Films, 'Joan is painting and I am writing'. Rosset and Mitchell were married in Le Lavandou and returned to the United States shortly thereafter, where Rosset eventually found his *métier*, not as a filmmaker or a writer, but as a publisher. In many regards much of the activist and anti-racist political agenda that coalesced with the making of *Strange Victory* became the political core of Grove Press as well, positions with which Samuel Beckett was wholly sympathetic.

7. The editors to the Beckett *Letters* 2 claim that this letter 'has not been found' (644n1).

8. See http://www.nytimes.com/1984/12/08/theater/associates-of-beck ett-seek-to-halt-production.html (last accessed June 2016).

9. Although Beckett's *Happy Days* won the Obie for 1961–2 for Best Foreign Play, Walter Kerr (1/3 of the committee with Edward Albee and Jerry Tallmer) registered his displeasure by abstaining. Ruth White was cited for Distinguished Performance (Actress), a category just short of Best Actress. No directing award was given that year, a snub, perhaps, of Alan Schneider. This would be Beckett's second Obie for Best Foreign Play, the first for *Endgame* in 1958, with Nydia Westman also winning Distinguished Performance (Actress) for her portrayal as Nell.

10. The text of *Ill Seen Ill Said* was interspersed with ten cartoons (*The New Yorker*, 5 October 1981, pp. 42–58). See Perloff's full article and a sample page from *The New Yorker* in Gontarski 1986: 195. Despite Rosset's plea, *Catastrophe* appeared in *The New Yorker* on 10 January 1983 (p. 27). 'The Cliff' appeared after Beckett's death on 13 May 1996 (p. 84). Two Beckett letters appeared in *The New Yorker* under the title 'Who Is Godot?: The playwright explains (or doesn't) his craft' in the double summer issue dated 24 June and 1 July 1996 (pp. 136–7). The first is to Michel Polac dated January 1952, trans. Edith Fournier. Polac was presenting excerpts from *En attendant Godot* on his Paris radio show. Declining to be interviewed, Beckett nonetheless sent this letter by way of 'introduction';

it was read on air by Roger Blin. For details of this first 'performance' of *En attendant Godot*, Beckett's letter in French, and in another translation, see Moorjani 1998. The French text (with a variation from Beckett's original) appeared in *Le Nouvel observateur* (24 October 1996). The second letter was written under similar circumstances to Desmond Smith, who was producing *Waiting for Godot* in Canada. Both assert Beckett's standard position on interpretation, as to Smith: 'I am quite incapable of sitting down and writing out an "explanation" of the play' (*Letters* 2 610).

References

Beckett, Samuel (1949) 'Three Dialogues: Samuel Beckett and Georges Duthuit' *Transition Forty-Nine*, No. 5 (December), pp. 97–103.

Bram van Velde (1958) with texts by Jacques Putman, Georges Duthuit and Samuel Beckett, Collection Le Musée de Poche, Paris: Editions Georges Fall.

Gontarski, S. E., ed. (1986) *On Beckett: Essays and Criticism*, New York: Grove Press.

Harmon, Maurice, ed. (1998) *No Author Better Served: The Correspondence of Samuel Beckett and Alan Schneider*, Cambridge, MA: Harvard University Press.

Moorjani, Angela (1998) '*En attendant Godot* on Michel Polac's *Entrée des auteurs*', *Samuel Beckett Today/Aujourd'hui* 7, pp. 47–56.

Rainey, Lawrence (1998) *Institutions of Modernism: Literary Elites and Public Culture*, New Haven: Yale University Press.

Texts Matter

6

Editing Beckett

An extract from *Watt* massacred by the compositor, appeared
in the filthy new Irish rag *Envoy*. (Beckett to George Reavey,
9 May 1950)

It is no small irony that for a writer so punctilious about his texts
– almost notoriously so for their performance – Samuel Beckett's
work has been subject to so much inept editing and so many publication blunders that he could lament to his official biographer,
James Knowlson, 'my texts are in a terrible mess'. The innumerable printing errors introduced into early editions of his work
(the edition of *Watt* published jointly by Collection Merlin and
Olympia Press in 1953 and reprinted then both by John Calder
in the UK and Grove Press in the US being perhaps the most egregious) have still never been fully corrected, although some progress
has been made with recent editions (Grove Press, 2006; Faber &
Faber 2011). On 13 August 1992, John Banville, then Literary
Editor of the *Irish Times*, could lament in an essay for the *New
York Review of Books*, 'It is time now for *all of Beckett's works*
[. . .] to be properly edited and published in definitive and accurate
editions in order that future readers be allowed to see them for the
unique testaments that they are' (20, emphasis added). One could
hardly agree more – but Banville's call for something like textual
purity may simply be a longing for a 'paradise lost', since textual
problems are more easily recognised and ridiculed than remedied.

A spate of letters to the *Times Literary Supplement* as *Dream
of Fair to Middling Women* was published is a case in point.
What should have been a cause for celebration, the appearance of
Samuel Beckett's long-suppressed first novel of 1932, has instead
fuelled a textual controversy and led to a clash of egos. Although
Beckett wrote only one *Dream of Fair to Middling Women*, two

separate and competing editions of it, with more than a few typographical differences between them, remain in print. In his letter
to the *Times Literary Supplement* on 16 July 1993, Eoin O'Brien,
co-editor of *Dream*, dissociated himself from the second edition,
although he remains listed as its editor: 'Both the US (Arcade) and
UK (Calder) 1993 editions of this work have been printed without
taking into account the necessary corrections I, and my co-editor,
Edith Fournier, made to the proofs of the re-set text. It is of deep
concern that Samuel Beckett's work be treated in this manner. We
can be held accountable', he continues, 'only for the first edition
published in 1992 by Black Cat Press in Dublin and can accept
no responsibility for the errors in the US and UK flawed editions'
(17). But even that 1992 Dublin edition of *Dream* is not without
flaw and leaves itself open to questions of editorial policy. What
justification exists for choosing one of Beckett's two endings to
the exclusion of the other and why some silent editorial changes
(which were decidedly not corrections of error) were made to the
Dublin text remain unexplained. Let me cite just one example of
the latter. In Beckett's typescript the narrator discusses the protagonist's (i.e., Belacqua's) translation of Rimbaud's *Le bateau
ivre* into English as follows: 'You know, of course, don't you, that
he did him into the eye into English.' For some inexplicable and
undisclosed reason editors O'Brien and Fournier have decided that
Beckett's original language needed improvement, and they published the following sentence as Beckett's: 'You know, of course,
don't you, that he did him pat into English.' In the not too distant
future one might expect that *Dream* will have to be re-edited.
Much of the frustration surrounding the accuracy of Beckett's
texts is summarised by Gerry Dukes in his letter to the *Times
Literary Supplement* of 7 January 1994 in which he attacks publisher John Calder, who, along with Richard Seaver, apparently
re-edited, at least made some adjustments to, or rushed to publication before final changes were made to their, the second, edition
of *Dream*: 'Instead of clean texts, John Calder keeps providing
misreadings, misprisions, misprints and distortions of the canon.
The principal victim of these editorial and publishing eccentrici-
ties is the work of Samuel Beckett. Perhaps the Beckett estate and/
or Beckett's literary executor should take a closer interest in an
accurate publication of the work.' Dukes's sweeping attack suffers
from the usual flaws of over-generalisation, but it is not without
some merit. The Beckett Estate has indeed exercised some over-

view function in the reprinting of the Beckett canon with British publisher Faber & Faber in 2009, but the resultant texts in Faber & Faber's new uniform series remain as inconsistent, their quality as uneven, as those they replaced.

Beckett's plays have fared only slightly better, worse in some cases, often corrupted by the exigencies of commercial publication, and so even the venerable house of Faber does not escape blame. In a 1983 essay entitled 'Texts and Pre-texts of Samuel Beckett's *Footfalls*', I noted that, 'Eager to make the play available for opening night, Faber & Faber secured a typescript from Beckett before he was finally satisfied with it and set their copy from what in the sequence of typescripts Beckett called Ts. 3' of four typescripts (Gontarski 1983: 191). To their credit Faber & Faber went on to correct their text, incorporating the revisions Beckett made for his 1976 world premiere production at the Royal Court Theatre into the text published in a collected edition entitled *Ends and Odds*; but, as I point out, 'this revised text . . . remains corrupt and is even inconsistent internally. Faber indeed changed the number of May's footsteps from seven to nine in the stage directions, for instance, but left her counting her steps one through seven in the dialogue' (1983: 191). Evidently, neither Faber's in-house editors nor Beckett himself checked the revised and anthologised text of *Footfalls* as closely as one might have expected.

Such publishing inconsistencies aside, Banville's apparently simple plea for Beckett's work 'to be properly edited and published in definitive and accurate editions', laudable as it is, is considerably less simple than it appears, complicated not only by the gremlins that inhabit the publishing world but by Beckett's own practice of constant rewriting, especially as a theatrical director, and by the critical and theoretical climate of our time, both of which make references to anything like a 'definitive' text or to textual stability of any sort as suspect as references to any single performance as 'definitive'. Beckett himself tampered with his 'definitive' *Godot* at least twice after Faber printed its pronouncement in 1965, which was essentially the uncensored text Faber should have published in 1956 (two years after the uncensored American edition appeared from Grove Press). As Beckett's direct work in the theatre increased, he demonstrated a disregard for the sort of sanctity of his plays as published that others have tried to enforce – at least for his own productions. Beckett in the theatre has himself destabilised Beckett on the page.

Between 1953, when *Waiting for Godot* was first staged in Paris, and 1967, Samuel Beckett served a fourteen-year theatrical apprenticeship, moving from being a consultant in the staging of his dramatic works, to functioning as a shadow director in his years working with the Royal Court Theatre, to taking full responsibility for their staging. During his twenty-year directing career, from 1967 to 1986, Beckett staged some seventeen productions of his work in three languages, English, French and German. Each time he returned to his plays – most often to texts already in print and well established in the critical discourse – to prepare them for staging, he found himself dissatisfied. His plays seemed wordy and incompletely conceived for the stage, and so he set about revising them as he staged them. Of *Godot*, for instance, he has said on more than one occasion, 'I knew nothing about theater when I wrote it',[1] and during rehearsals in Berlin in 1967 for *Endspiel* (*Endgame*) he conceded that the play was 'not visualized' (*TN 2* xv).

By 1986 Beckett's own productions of his work suggested a repudiation of his published *oeuvre*, even those publications that were often dubbed by his publisher as 'definitive'. Beckett's *oeuvre* thus generally exists in multiple versions because he revised as he translated, revised as he directed, and so each of those encounters became something of a self-translation, became a textual transformation. Such translation, whether between or among languages or between page and stage, became not the literary equivalent of its predecessor but essentially a new and not-quite-parallel text, one that did not necessarily but often did supersede the original, which remained in print. Thus, after his work as a theatrical director, multiple versions of his texts existed, and still exist, even within a single language. Without access to Beckett's notes and revisions, critics and directors are often forced into a position of building interpretations and mounting productions not so much on corrupt or incomplete texts, such as almost all British versions of *Waiting for Godot*, but on those the author himself found unsatisfactory, incompletely conceived, too wordy, in short unfinished. As Beckett grew increasingly dissatisfied with his plays as published, he decided in 1986, after years of suggesting that theatrical directors not stage the published scripts but follow instead his directorial revisions, to authorise publication of his theatrical notebooks and what *he* called 'corrected texts' for his plays, that is, texts which incorporated the revisions he made as a director, along with the notebooks in which the rationale of those revisions was worked out. This was an extraordinary decision on Beckett's part, essentially repudiating his dramatic canon as published and available to the public, and offering instead a much more fluid and multiple series of performance texts.

The execution of that project as the four-volume series called *The Theatrical Notebooks of Samuel Beckett*, was, however, fraught with complications since each volume finally contained a single, 'corrected' text for each of the plays Beckett staged. Such a solution which bows to the conventions of commerce is somewhat misleading since it runs counter to Beckett's own practice as a theatrical director and to the critical climate of our time, much of which Beckett himself embraced. In another, more tranquil, less sceptical era, one less ideologically charged than our own, the problems of editing or correcting Beckett's works might have been achievable without a great deal of theoretical soul-searching, a matter simply of replacing those texts with which Beckett was dissatisfied, that is, those which he himself revised for production, with the rewritten texts, and then correcting obvious typographical errors, oversights and inconsistencies in the remainder of his work. Within the theoretical discourse of our age, however, an enterprise of 'correcting' literary texts – or as Stanley Fish calls them, literary documents, to emphasise that they are the physical objects of interpretation (or phenomenological intention or performance, which I treat as a 'reading') – is bound to generate theoretical and ideological debate. Moreover, traditional theories of editing threaten to resurrect the spectre of a single and stable 'correct' text, for one, and so to re-establish the authority of the text and of the author over the reader, a position which Beckett himself both embraced and repudiated.

The problem of textual authority or validity is further compounded in the theatre by the collaborative nature of the theatrical enterprise itself and the inconsistent quality of the collaborators, problems of which Beckett was quite aware and which he took into account in his own directing. In the theatre we may, on the whole, be more willing to accept the play script as an incomplete art work, something less than the final stage of a work's creation, a document which needs to be *real*-ised on stage through a set of intermediaries; that admission suggests that theatrical texts are themselves extra-literary, if by literature we mean at the very least a completed and stable work of art. In Beckett's case the value of his performance is enhanced, given authority, by the fact that the author himself has directed his play, a practice that playwrights like Pinter, Stoppard, Albee, Barker and Shepard, among others, have followed. But the relation between performance – even *author*-ised performance – and published text remains as problematic with Beckett's directing as with any other director. Quite clearly as a director approaching his work afresh after at times a substantial hiatus, Beckett continued reshaping his work, but many of his changes were not necessarily evolutionary, that is, necessarily improvements, but reflected particular circumstances. Beckett's revisions from production to production were not always consistent, not a clear progressus. Two productions of the same work directed by Beckett – even in the same language – were not necessarily, that is, could not be, identical. If they were there would have been little point mounting the second. Beckett has often re-designed a text and production for a particular set of actors playing on a particular playing space under a particular set of circumstances. In a letter to Polish critic Marek Kedzierski dated 15 November 1981, for example, Beckett was forthright about the theatrical process, which he had come to understand: 'Herewith corrected copy of *Fin de partie*. The cuts and simplifications are the result of my work on the play as director and function of the players at my disposal. To another director they may not seem desirable.'[2] Even Beckett's own revised or 'corrected' texts, then, seem something less than stable, absolute or definitive, but instead subject to the subsequent intervention of future directors or future readers. In Beckett's post-publication revision of *Play*, for instance, the note called 'Repeat' ends with the phrase, 'and so on *if* and *as* desired' (emphasis added). Presumably such textual fluidity allows for future directorial flexibility, but whose desire then are we finally staging? The challenge for the textual editor working in a late Modernist or long Modernist textual climate Beckett himself has encouraged and embraced is to reconcile the traditional demands for a single final version of a text, one version bound between boards, more often than not a commercial decision, and the theory of the incomplete, permeable or mutable text; that is, how does one reconcile the demand for a single text closest to the author's final textual intention and the late Modernist notion of textual multiplicity? Such questions of textual plurality at least foreground much of the current theoretical debate about the nature of texts, textuality, and finally meaning, particularly in the theatre. What exactly is this entity, this artefact, this commodity we want so to preserve and call a text?

Even the phrase 'corrected' if not 'definitive' texts threatens to revivify the epistemological paradigm that meaning is somehow contained immutably *within* and restricted to a text, impervious to the flux of language and the vicissitudes of culture, a notion particularly dubious in the theatre. Further, the idea of 'correct' texts suggests a linear, evolutionary model of history, particularly literary history as the work of a single author where later or subsequent versions are by definition improvements of or progress beyond the former and so supersede them. In the case of Beckett's theatrical texts (and even his translations), that is, those cases where multiple and parallel texts exist, such assumptions are dubious.

The problems of textual validity and stability are further complicated in Beckett's case by his own fundamental authorial and so textual ambivalence. On the one hand, Beckett has abandoned the author's traditional role as textual authority, the final arbiter of meaning, by steadfastly refusing interpretation of his own works. To the critic Colin Duckworth, Beckett announced, 'I produce an object. What people make of it is not my concern . . . I'd be quite incapable of writing a critical introduction to my work' (Beckett 1966: xxiv). Asked by his assistant at the rehearsals of *Endspiel* (*Endgame*), 'Are you of the opinion that the author should have a solution for the riddle at hand', Beckett replied curtly, 'Not the author of this play' (Haerdter 1967, cited in McMillan and Fehsenfeld 1988: 14). In a letter of 15 October 1956 to his American director Alan Schneider he admitted, 'Sorry I was not of more help about the play [*Endgame*] but the less I speak about my work the better' (Harmon 1998: 17). And in rehearsals for *Endgame* at the Riverside Studios in London in 1980, Rick Cluchey, who was playing Hamm under Beckett's direction, asked Beckett directly if the little boy in Hamm's narrative was actually the young Clov. 'Don't know if the little boy is the young Clov, Rick', Beckett responded, 'simply don't know' (in the presence of SEG).

On the other hand, Beckett has exercised so much direct influence over the production of his plays, even taking legal action against some forms of textual deviation, most dramatically and posthumously through his Estate against the 1994 Fiona Shaw / Deborah Warner production of *Footfalls* in London's West End,[3] that he has maintained more authorial control over his work and performances than any other writer in history – with the possible exception of James Joyce, who seems to have manipulated the early criticism of *Ulysses* and *Finnegans Wake* fairly directly. Yet despite correcting a variety of proofs for various editions, Beckett allowed obvious textual inconsistencies to stand, for instance, to the text of *Come and Go*, the English version of which has four lines missing at the opening and two at the closing. With *Come and Go* the textual variants were the result of simultaneous translation. Beckett added some six lines to the 121 words of the English version while translating the work into French and after sending John Calder a typescript for publication. All British editions were subsequently based on the incomplete Calder text while the French and German editions contain the six lines added in translation.[4] The American edition used first the later typescript that included the six lines, but then for the sake of commercial expediency Grove photo-offset the English edition for subsequent publications and thus the six lines were lost – at least for a time. Those lines were restored by the editor to the text published in volume IV of the *Theatrical Notebooks* and then again, finally in a commercial edition, in *Krapp's Last Tape and other Short Plays* (Faber, 2009). Beckett was still undecided about the final text of *Endgame* in 1987, thirty years after having written it. Going over the 'final' text, for the final time, before its final publication in the *Endgame* volume of the *Theatrical Notebooks*, Beckett was still undecided whether or not, when Clov hits Hamm with the toy dog, Hamm should retain the dog or let it fall.

Within the critical climate of rethinking the nature of texts and textuality, the goal of retrieving something like an 'original', 'definitive' or 'uncorrupted' text has been essentially discredited since it assumes that an ideal text exists somewhere outside of the process of reading it, or, in the case of theatre, outside its 'real-isation' on stage. The contemporary critical climate has undermined the editor's traditional function of recovering and presenting something like an 'original', 'uncorrupted' or 'corrected' text in its prelapsarian purity. This age of dislocation and plurality of meaning invites a concomitant plurality of texts, and textual editors may finally have to adjust their goals to embrace that plurality or multiplicity and settle for the more modest goal of the 'best recoverable text' or set of texts.

Amid the plurality of textual revisions, the question often remains, whose words exactly we are reading, hearing, performing and finally interpreting, the historical author's, his scribe's, some typesetter's, an editor's, an over-zealous theatrical director's, or an actor's re-thinking? Such questions are all too often slighted by contemporary critics and theorists. On the one hand, if the literary text is created by the reader, and so differs from reader to reader, why bother with a quest for the uniquely authorial or 'uncorrupted' document? That was certainly the spirit of the theoretical 1960s with its denigration of textual scholarship as insignificant. One might simply suggest fatalistically that textual corruptions are inevitable, another of the broad cultural forces at work on any text, and in many cases it is that same cultural imperative that generated that text through a particular historical author in the first place. The simple answer to the question 'Why bother?' is, however, that although there are innumerable kinds of hats, and noses come in an incalculable variety of sizes and shapes, a hat is not a shoe, and a nose is not a knee. How an author or editor fills the space on a page which the reader will then turn into a text in her reading remains of utmost importance. Catherine Belsey, for one, poses the dichotomy of meaning and textuality as follows:

> While on the one hand meaning is never single, eternally inscribed in the words on the page, on the other hand readings do not spring unilaterally out of the subjectivities (or the ideologies) of readers. The text is not an empty space, filled with meaning from outside itself, any more than it is the transcription of an authorial intention, filled with meaning from outside language. As a signifying practice, writing always offers raw material for the production of meaning, the signified in its plurality, on the understanding, of course, that the signified is distinct from the intention of the author (pure concept) or the referent (a world already constituted and re-presented). (Belsey 1988: 406–7)

Despite such ideological sensitivity and authorial ambiguity, the question of accurate or even complete texts, those that represent as much of the author's creative process as possible, remains a pressing theoretical and practical issue, one given renewed energy (if not method) by the publication of Hans Walter Gabler's 1984 'synoptic' edition of *Ulysses*, the 1986 Vintage 'Corrected Text' that followed from it, John Kidd's assault on the project (more on the methodology than the ideology), and now the proliferation of *Ulysseses*. The Gabler *Ulysses* (and calling it that proclaims its difference from, say, Joyce's *Ulysses*, that is, from any single edition Joyce ever wrote or read), for all its many faults in design and execution, has at least refocused attention on these issues of texts and textuality, and his 'synoptic text' offers at least one possible solution to the problems of both textual creation and textual transmission by acknowledging the plurality of texts. As Jerome McGann notes in his essay entitled '*Ulysses* as a Postmodern Text':

> By giving priority of importance to the 'synoptic' text over the 'reading' text Gabler forces us to think of *Ulysses* as something other than a given object of interpretation on the one hand (which is the traditional New Critical view), or as an *invention of interpretation* on the other (which is the common post-structural view). (McGann 1985: 291)

In Beckett's case, the problems of establishing a single, final theatrical *oeuvre* are further compounded because of Beckett's own associations, however loose they were and however suspicious he was of them, with creative and critical movements which held the traditional concepts of textual stability and literary meaning in contempt, the surrealists in particular, but also their offspring in *la nouvelle critique*. One version of a theory of an unstable (because incomplete) text is offered in a brilliant (if still neglected) work of literary theory, *L'éspace littéraire*, by Maurice Blanchot (1982). In it he argues that the work of art can never be absolutely finished. It is itself an infinity which depends on an Other, and it gains a semblance of completion only when it is read or performed. That reading (or performance), however, is only one of a multiplicity of possible readings, and hence texts.

Blanchot's view of texts and textuality is one with which Beckett in many respects was sympathetic. The infinite or impossible or perpetual or incomplete or open text has been characteristic of Beckett's work at least since *Dream of Fair to Middling Women*, published only in 1994, and, among those works published in Beckett's lifetime, *Watt*, which celebrates its own impossibility of completion. The impossible and interminable, the always incomplete text is at least a metaphor which Beckett has embraced and folded into what passes for plot in his ground-breaking suite of novels begun in French just after the Second World War: *Molloy*, *Malone Dies* and *The Unnamable*, and what may be construed as the fourth volume in that series, the thirteen texts which followed the novels and were called *Texts for Nothing*. That metaphor of the infinite, incomplete, perpetually unfolding, self-reflexive text is as useful a paradigm for reading Samuel Beckett's creative process as any other. We know from studying the manuscripts of his work, for instance, that Beckett was a tireless reviser. That observation might, of course, be made for any number of authors – James Joyce and William Butler Yeats among them. In Beckett's case the process of revision, and hence creation, continued – consciously and deliberately – well beyond publication, which was, there-fore, not always the statement of a work's 'completion', a concept which seems alien to Beckett's *oeuvre* as a whole. Once Beckett intervened in the process of performance, had become his own Other in a series of theatrical self-collaborations, and began direct-ing his own work in 1986, he took those directorial opportunities to reread and so rewrite apparently completed texts yet again. Conceptually, for Beckett, then, the process of creation, of literary composition, did not end with publication, did not end at all, or rather was always ending, yet again. Initial publication might then only be an instalment, an intermediary step in the work's continu-ous development.

But should such self-collaboration, Beckett reading Beckett, par-ticularly in the theatre, be treated differently from that of any other reader's or director's readings? Should it be given author-ity and hence prior-ity? As a director is Beckett then only another reader of his work, coming to his text as an Other and so acting as a reader whose insights might have no more validity than any other reader's? They may or may not, but they are at least worth reading and knowing, even if they are allotted no more weight, no more author-ity than any other reasonably intelligent critic's read-ings. Even the most ardent contemporary theorist must concede that all readings are not equally insightful. This is why we read Derrida, Deleuze and other critics and theorists at all. What is clear from Beckett's post-publication revisions of his texts, his theatrical notebooks, and finally his stagings of his own plays, is that Beckett is an extraordinarily adept reader of Beckett. His theatrical notebooks, for instance, contain a remarkable wealth of information, speculation and structural outlines of his work.

Despite Beckett's disclaimer of being incapable of writing a criti-cal introduction to his own work, as a director he has done pre-cisely that. Beckett's theatrical notebooks disclosed details of his work heretofore unseen by other critics. His direction is marked by a surprising amount of realistic subtext, for instance. As usual Beckett insisted in his direction of *Endspiel* on not intellectualising his text in rehearsals. He noted early on, 'I don't want to talk about my play, it has to be taken purely dramatically, to take shape on the stage. There's nothing in it about philosophy – maybe about poetry. Here the only interest of the play is as dramatic material' (cited in Knowlson 2003: 103). Beckett's admonition is not surprising, and is one that many a director has delivered to his actors early in rehearsals. In the theatre, one plays action not ideas. What is surprising, however, is that Beckett also suggested a realistic context: 'the play is to be acted as though there were a fourth wall where the footlights are'. While, on occasion, he would say, 'Here it oughtn't to be played logically', more often he would provide 'realistic' motivation. For 'Have you bled?', he told Clov, 'you see something in his face, that's why you're asking'. Examining the parasite in his trousers provides Clov with the occasion for 'What about that pee?' Hamm's 'Since it's calling you' should be choked out to prompt Clov's 'Is your throat sore?' And Clov's opening speech is motivated by some barely perceptible change that he perceives while inspecting his environment. In his Riverside Studios Notebook, Beckett writes: 'C perplexed. All seemingly in order, yet a change' (TN 4 195).

Pattern is crucial to Beckett's art and patterning dominates his theatrical notes and productions: motion is repeated to echo other motion, posture to echo other posture, gestures to echo other gestures, sounds to echo other sounds. The principle of analogy is fundamental and much of that analogy is detailed in the theatrical notebooks. In the Riverside Studios Notebook for *Endgame* Beckett says, for instance, 'analogy N's knocks on lid, H's on wall'; 'Analogy Clov-dog when trying to make it stand'; 'Analogy voice and attitude [of Hamm during his narration] with N's tailor story' (TN 4 216). The action, such as it is, is nonetheless filled with circles, arcs and crosses, from Hamm's rounds to Clov's thinking walk. The linguistic analogue to such patterning is the revision of phrases to echo each other. Even when the phrasing is not parallel, Beckett established an echo, as in the Schiller Theatre notebook where he suggests that 'Why this farce' should have the 'same quality as "Let's stop playing"' (TN 4 105). Beckett's own direction of *Endgame* approaches the fulfilment of the structure he originally proposed to Roger Blin for *Fin de partie* in 1957. 'He had ideas about the play', Blin noted, 'that made it a little difficult to act. At first, he looked on his play as a kind of musical score. When a word occurred or was repeated, when Hamm called Clov, Clov should always come in the same way every time, like a musical phrase coming from the same instrument with the same volume' (Gontarski 1986: 233). Ten years later Beckett realised this musical conception of the play. 'The play is full of echoes', he told his German cast, 'they all answer each other' (*TN 4* xxi).

Even though they are written in German, the two notebooks that Beckett prepared for his 1978 Schiller Theater production of *Spiel* (*Play*) are equally revealing. They demonstrate Beckett's near obsession with language (German in this case), structure and formal detail – all three of which are, of course, inextricably entwined. Beckett's notebooks not only comprise a motif index to his plays, they constitute as well a remarkably detailed external record of the artist's internal processes and struggles. They document Beckett's continued aesthetic and stylistic development. At the head of a series of notes he prepared for Donald McWinnie's 1976 Royal Court production of *That Time*, Beckett wrote what amounts to a one-sentence theatrical manifesto, the most succinct and explicit statement of his late aesthetics that we have: 'To the objection that visual component too small, out of all proportion with aural, answer: make it smaller, on the principle that less is more' (*TN 4* 437). As Beckett adapted the aesthetics of architect Mies van der Rohe that 'less is more', as he developed his own 'mania for minimalism', or what he punningly called a 'Process of elimination' in the *What Where* notebook (*TN 4* 437), he also seized directorial opportunities to recreate his work according to principles more in keeping with sculpture, painting or even architecture than with traditional drama, and to test the results directly on the stage.

In the *Eh Joe* notebook prepared for the second of his German productions, Beckett outlined succinctly the central thematic and theatrical conflicts of this his first teleplay. While Joe may be 'Out of sight, [and so consequently out of] reach', for example, he would not feel safe even without the assailing voice because of his 'Fear of Dark'. Beckett then outlined the ten scenes of the play as follows:

1. Out of sight, reach. Fear of dark.
2. Rupture formula – 'Best to come' (1)
3. Voices in head – behind the eyes. Mental thugee.
4. Present voice last, then his own to still, then silence till God's, unstillable
5. Clues for voice and hearer. Worse when nearly home. What if final whisper unstillable?

6. God to him 1
7. Deficient in kindness, strength, intelligence, looks, cleanliness, normality.
8. Green one. 'Best to come' 2. Duly laid
9. Same as 4.
10. Voice falling to whisper. (*TN* 4 263)

In his notebook for *Tritte* (*Footfalls*) Beckett made explicit the relationships among the imbedded characters of that play in his discussion of voices. In the dialogue within the monologues (Parts II and III), for example, the Mother's, 'What do you mean, May, not enough' of Part II should be echoed by the voice of Mrs W in Part III, 'What do you mean, Amy, to put it mildly', according to Beckett. 'Same style for both relationships', he notes (*TN* 4 337). The *Kommen und Gehen* (*Come and Go*) notebook details Beckett's preoccupation with pattern in theatre space. *Kommen und Gehen* (finally directed by Walter Asmus not Beckett) was on the programme with *Spiel* (*Play*) at the Schiller Theater Werkstatt in October of 1978. While Beckett rethought the *da capo* ending of *Spiel*, he considered adding a similar repetition to *Kommen und Gehen*. Although he outlined the pattern of what would amount to a second act to the play in his directorial notebook, he finally dismissed the possibility as 'Mathematically desirable [but] logically impossible' (*TN* 4 233).

Not all aesthetic, theatrical and finally textual issues, however, were or could be resolved during productions, the text, even in Beckett's rethinking, retaining a certain elasticity. Having worked closely with Anthony Page on the 1973 Royal Court Theatre production of *Not I* and having directed it himself in 1975 at the Théâtre d'Orsay, Beckett remained ambivalent about the dominant visual image of the play. The best advice that he could finally offer directors of *Not I* was to omit the Auditor. As he wrote to a pair of directors on 16 November 1986, 'I should have . . . advised you simply to omit the auditor. He is very difficult to stage (light – position) and may well be of more harm than good. For me the play needs him but I can do without him. I have never seen him function effectively.'[5] Beckett's final comment presumably includes the English production he supervised closely, the 1973 Royal Court production with Billie Whitelaw, directed by Anthony Page. For the 1978 French productions with Madeleine Renaud that he directed himself, Beckett omitted the Auditor all together, as did the BBC film production of the Billie Whitelaw performance, doubtless with Beckett's approval. To date, however, no published script for the play suggests that the elimination of the Auditor is a directorial option, its inclusion, a textual ingredient, more likely than not, legally enforced.

One solution then to the problems of contemporary textual multiplicity is that offered by Beckett's English-language publishers Faber & Faber and Grove Press in the series entitled *The Theatrical Notebooks of Samuel Beckett*. That series contains the theatrical notebooks Beckett kept for a particular work, published in facsimile, transcription, translation (where necessary) and with annotations along with revised texts, which accompany the theatrical notebooks and are often justified by them and are also fully annotated so that each of Beckett's changes is at least noted and often discussed. The result is something like a performance text, with an emphasis on process and transformation, which traces and documents Beckett's post-publication creative process. *The Theatrical Notebooks of Samuel Beckett* series offers then not a definitive or uncorrupted or static text, the telos of the creative process, but rather a processive text, a multiplicity or plurality of texts whose endpoint is only Beckett's latest rereading of Beckett. The revised text may place the original published text under erasure by superimposing a later stage of creative development over it but without necessarily replacing or obliterating it. By presenting the textual and production possibilities of Beckett's texts then, a critical dramatic text emerges, one which features Beckett's post-publication creative process and one which opens up reading and performance possibilities. It is admittedly an unstable text, but the instability exists within set textual limits. As a generic text, the revised texts of Beckett's plays bear similarities not to Hans Gabler's 'reading text', the one finally published as the Vintage 'corrected' *Ulysses*, but to his 'synoptic' text with all its variants, although in Beckett's case the generic text features post-publication changes exclusively. For his 'ideal' text, Gabler abandoned the traditional textual goal of retrieving the author's final intentions, and focused on the process of composition, the authorial function. As Jerome McGann notes, 'In fact, all texts are unstable to the extent that they are all processive and (in Gabler's terms) "continuous." At the same time, all are fixed within certain real, determinable limits as they assume certain specific form' (1985: 287). Traditional critics tend to overlook the former, contemporary critics the latter. One can only hope that Faber & Faber will be allowed to publish Beckett's revised and corrected texts separately and without the theatrical apparatus I have been describing, but that's a business and legal decision not an aesthetic and theoretical one.

So far, the close scrutiny of published texts that Gerry Dukes has called for has not always been beneficial to scholars and to the general reading public. For one, Beckett's heir has prohibited the separate publication of what Gabler might call 'reading texts' of the revised plays or what for Beckett we might call 'performance texts'. Those crucial critical texts are the 'synoptic' versions of Beckett's plays published in the *Theatrical Notebooks of Samuel Beckett*. The broader public of readers, scholars and theatre practitioners should have, in fact deserve, easy access to such 'performance texts' that Beckett worked with most diligently directly in the theatre. Anything less, that is, any obstacles or restrictions placed on at least access to such texts for scholarship and for performance, is historically irresponsible.

Notes

1. Conversations with the author.
2. Copy of letter sent by recipient to SEG.
3. See Mel Gussow's review in the *New York Times*, 26 March 1994, at www.nytimes.com/1994/03/26/arts/modify-beckett-enter-outrage.html (last accessed June 2016).
4. See the text established by Breon Mitchell and the discussion of his textual corrections in 'Art in Microcosm: The Manuscript Stages of Beckett's *Come and Go*' (Mitchell 1976).
5. Letter to David Hunsberger and Linda Kendall dated 16 November 1986, copy in possession of SEG sent by recipients.

References

Beckett, Samuel (1966) *En attendant Godot*, ed. Colin Duckworth, London: George C. Harrap.

Belsey, Catherine (1988) 'Literature, History, Politics', in David Lodge, ed., *Modern Criticism and Theory: A Reader*, London: Longman.

Blanchot, Maurice (1982) *The Space of Literature*, trans. Ann Smock, Lincoln: University of Nebraska Press.

Gontarski, S. E. (1983) 'Texts and Pre-texts of Samuel Beckett's

Footfalls', *The Papers of the Bibliographical Society of America*, 77:2, pp. 191–5.

Gontarski, S. E. (1986) *On Beckett: Essays and Criticism*, New York, Grove Press (second edition, London: Anthem Press, 2012).

Harmon, Maurice, ed. (1998) *No Author Better Served: The Correspondence of Samuel Beckett and Alan Schneider*, Cambridge, MA: Harvard University Press.

Haerdter, Michael (1967) *Materialien zu Beckett's Endspiel*, Frankfurt am Main: Suhrkamp Verlag.

Knowlson, James (1999) 'My Texts Are in a Terrible Mess', in Bruce Stewart, ed., *Beckett and Beyond*, The Princess Grace Irish Library Series, London: Colin Smythe, Ltd, pp. 176–86.

Knowlson, James (2003) 'Beckett as Director', in James and Elizabeth Knowlson, eds, *Images of Beckett*, Cambridge: Cambridge University Press, pp. 97–147.

McGann, Jerome (1985) '*Ulysses* as a Postmodern Text', *Criticism: A Quarterly for Literature and the Arts* 27:3, pp. 283–305.

McMillan, Dougald and Martha Fehsenfeld (1988) *Beckett in the Theatre: The Author as Playwright and Director, from* Waiting for Godot *to* Krapp's Last Tape, London: John Calder.

Mitchell, Breon (1976) 'Art in Microcosm: The Manuscript Stages of Beckett's *Come and Go*', *Modern Drama* 19:3 (September), pp. 245–60.

7

A Century of Missed Opportunities: Editing an Accurate Edition of Beckett's 'Shorts' and Other Textual Misadventures

Discussing his productions of the American Beckett Festival of Radio Plays (1986), producer Everett Frost notes, 'As is well known, Beckett had very firm convictions about what ought and ought not be done with his work' (1991: 364). The comment summarises the received wisdom on Samuel Beckett's personal oversight of his art, but the issue of Beckett's relationship to his texts is up for periodic review in this age of the after-Beckett, as we ask how directly and consistently he was involved in ensuring what we might call the integrity of his art. We know that, on occasion, Beckett intervened in what he deemed aberrant productions, usually prodded into action by others, since he almost never saw those questionable productions himself, but how generally vigilant was he about productions and, even more important, about his written legacy, his texts? How account, for instance, for the innumerable deviant productions of his plays and for persistent inconsistencies among his published works? Despite Frost's assertion, early editions of Beckett's work are replete with errors, and the English-language texts still have been neither fully corrected nor reconciled, although new editions from Grove Press (2006) and Faber & Faber (2009), on the whole and with notable exceptions detailed below, constitute major advances; in particular, the new editions of *Watt* from both houses. Surely, Beckett read proofs for each of the first three editions of *Watt*. Yet, despite his reputed vigilance and the willingness of his publishers to accommodate his desires and revisions, and despite the most recent efforts of his English-language publishers, calls for corrected and uniform texts have gone largely unheeded in the after-Beckett. A clear sign of the problems faced is Frost's asking Beckett which text of *Cascando* he should produce for the American radio festival. Beckett, unsure of the implications of Frost's question, responded self-evidently, '[t]he printed version'. He seemed shocked when Frost asked, '"Which printed version?" After Beckett made a quick check of his texts, Frost asked how far he might rely on Grove Press editions; "Not very," was the playwright's terse reply' (Brater 1994: 37), without, we might add, his assuming responsibility for what would appear to be less-than-thorough textual oversight.

Beckett himself was, perhaps too often, less than scrupulous about his texts. Such incidents as those above, as they come to light, continue to raise questions about the integrity of Beckett's texts and, in particular, his theatrical texts, which have historically presented problems less of inattention than of excessive attention; that is, Beckett was an incurable reviser, and that process of continual revision coupled with publishers eager to make the latest text available, often at productions, resulted in an inevitable proliferation of published texts, each substantially different from the others. Several versions of the same text were thus published and remained available, often in the same bookshop, and various versions of any particular text circulated among producers, directors, scholars and even publishers, without Beckett or his publishers having made any serious attempt to reconcile them. The text of *Play* is another case in point. As Beckett continued to revise his script through British and French productions in 1964, various versions of the play circulated in typescript. Prompted by questions of an impending Swedish translation, Beckett wrote to Grove Press on 17 August 1964, 'As to your MS text [of *Play*], it is less likely to be accurate [Beckett's word!] than the Faber published text for which I corrected proofs.'[1] The same letter promised further, comprehensive revisions, another version of *Play*, which would reflect more of Beckett's theatre work and thus offer improvements on the Faber text:

> [Grove editor Fred] Jordan suggested publishing in *Evergreen Review* the text *in extenso* (as played in London and Paris), i.e., giving changed order of speeches in the repeat and indicating vocal levels. This is quite a job to prepare and I suggest we reserve this presentation for Grove and let translations follow the existing text, simply correcting 'Repeat play exactly' to 'Repeat play'.[2]

Beckett seemed, here, unusually cavalier or, at least, inconsistent about both the relation between the English and American editions and about translations of his work, which presumably would become the authorised versions in any number of countries; but at the same time, he was eager to include his performance changes in anything like a final printed version of the play, at least for Grove, allowing the Faber text to stand and remain with its resultant 'inaccuracies' the text of record in the UK.

Evidence for what appears to be almost whimsical decision-making about performances and texts themselves continues to surface as scholars gain access to Beckett's written exchanges with producers, directors and publishers, but such business correspondence is unlikely to appear in the current selection of his letters in the imperfect and restricted collection, *The Letters of Samuel Beckett*, appearing from Cambridge University Press since 2009. On 26 June 1969, for example, a Professor of Music at Yale University wrote to Grove Press for permission to create something of an opera based on one of the *Texts for Nothing*: 'I am a composer on the faculty of the Yale School of Music and am interested in writing a piece for voice and electronic sounds using the words of one of Samuel Beckett's *Texts for Nothing* [. . .] the piece would be performed in a free concert.' While Beckett routinely rejected such requests, in response to Schmidt's query letter of 7 July, he wrote a simple, yes, and returned it to her. No explanation was offered; no guidelines for why this project struck his fancy and any number of other such applications for musical renderings did not. Schmidt responded to the composer with the good news: 'I sent a copy [of your letter] to Mr. Beckett and he has agreed to your setting one of the *Texts* [. . .] to music. If you are being paid for the performance, 50% of the fee should be sent to Grove Press for Mr. Beckett.' Unsolicited letters to Beckett's publishers are legion and dominated by such requests for adaptations but also with requests to 'finish' or 'complete' *Waiting for Godot* by creating its missing third act.

On the other hand, Beckett could be protective and fastidious about his texts, not infrequently requesting publishing delays to accommodate performance changes, detailed corrections or revisions decided on after submitting his typescript for publication, or corrections of errors brought to his attention, more often than not, by scholars like literary critic Ruby Cohn, for example. How closely or accurately such instructions were subsequently followed depended very much on human factors, which is to say that the final products were too often inconsistent, dependent on whichever novice employee or intern was assigned the task. And so the printed texts, particularly the theatrical texts, are, in a sense, as provisional as performance itself, both approximations of the unattainable ideal or stable text.

Texts can be improved, however, errors corrected, publications brought closer to the author's final or most recent thinking by scrupulous historical editing, but even these efforts have fallen, perhaps needed to fall, short. Beckett's English-language publishers have made concerted if inconsistent efforts at such historical editing, particularly for major, landmark publications, but they have gotten the texts wrong as often as they have gotten them right. Eager to eliminate a series of very short prose texts, none of which was selling particularly well independently, Grove commissioned me in 1995 to collect these into something they might call *Samuel Beckett: The Complete Short Prose* (1996), which I did, correcting most of the egregious errors from previous editions and adding some previously uncollected work. The Beckett Estate intervened at the very last moment, after advanced proofs had been distributed to reviewers, to insist that the volume be recalled, demanding that *First Love* not be grouped among the *Quatre Nouvelles*, since it had been published separately, so that the *Quatre Nouvelles* became, de facto, *Trois Nouvelles*. The same edict was evidently imposed on Beckett's long-time British publisher John Calder three years later, as he published, in 1999, a twelve-volume boxed set of 'shorts', one of which, number ten, is called *Three Novellas (Trois Nouvelles)*. The running head of the volume, however, remains 'Four Novellas', suggesting again a hasty, last-minute demand of a cut imposed by the Estate, and finally Calder's incomplete re-editing of the text to comply with the Estate's dictates. The fourth novella, *First Love*, was then published as number eight of a separate volume in Calder's edition.

For its *Samuel Beckett: The Complete Short Prose*, Grove was further forbidden to publish the previously unpublished short story Beckett wrote to conclude *More Pricks than Kicks*, 'Echo's Bones', in its 'complete' collection, the 1933 story published as a separate volume only in 2014, edited by Mark Nixon. Grove capitulated in 1996, to my dismay, I might add, resetting the volume, that is, unediting my text and rearranging my chronology, all at considerable expense. Grove Press went on to publish a stunning boxed set of Samuel Beckett's works in four volumes in 2006 to celebrate the 100th anniversary of his birth, each with an introduction by a prominent writer: Edward Albee, Salman Rushdie, J. M. Coetzee and Colm Toíbin. This, then, was the second uniform edition of Beckett's work published by Grove. The first, in sixteen volumes, appeared in 1970 hard upon the awarding of the Nobel Prize. The second uniform set, the Grove Centenary Edition (2006), was designed as something of an American Pléiade, as Grove's publicity suggests:

> Edited by Paul Auster, this four-volume set of Beckett's canon has been designed by award winner Laura Lindgren. Available individually, as well as in this boxed set, the four hardcover volumes have been specially bound with covers featuring images central to Beckett's works. Typographical errors that remained uncorrected in the various prior editions have now been corrected in consultation with Beckett scholars C. J. Ackerley and S. E. Gontarski.

Wonderful sentiments and intentions; they're just not entirely accurate. Chris Ackerley and I suggested a full range of corrections, some of which were accepted, but, although the text of *Watt* was substantially improved in this celebratory edition, the full textual overhaul that such a project needed was neither solicited nor effected. Too often, publishers seemed preoccupied with shelf appeal, packaging rather than the packaged, and so would rather spend money on covers than on content. The business of publishing itself, publishing as a commercial enterprise, seems to conspire against anything like a uniform or authorised text. The entire process of textual transmission – printing, correcting and subsequent reprinting of manuscripts and typescripts – is subject to inevitable human error. Theatrical texts are particularly vulnerable, since they are not infrequently released to the public, intentionally or unintentionally, while the author (or director) is still making rehearsal changes, as was the case with *Play* mentioned above. Admittedly, the publication of various versions of the same play is a publishing issue not restricted to Beckett's work, of course, nor to Beckett's publishers; but for most other publishers, the issue is not so grave, since few other authors insist on the sanctity of their written text. Publishers specialising in theatrical texts routinely publish disclaimers in the earliest editions of play scripts. Nick Hern Books, for one, regularly prints its understated disclaimer: 'This text went to press before the end of rehearsals and so may differ slightly from the play as performed.' One curious example is the publication of Tennessee Williams's

play, *Cat on A Hot Tin Roof*, the final act for which was substantially re-written by strong-willed director Elian Kazan. The
Signet Books edition of 1955, then, contains two Acts III, the one
Williams originally wrote and the one 'As Played in the New York
Production'. It was the price that Williams, who was himself a
supporter of and a financial investor in the New York production
of *Waiting for Godot*, had to pay to maintain Kazan as a director.
Beckett had no, rather would tolerate no, Elia Kazans, although
rumours abounded that the play would be rewritten for New York
by a 'play doctor', in this case Thorton Wilder. As Barney Rosset
reported to Beckett on 6 December 1955, 'Thorton Wilder was
going to write an adaptation of your play and that that would
be the one to be put on [on] Broadway' (*Letters 2* 579n5). On 2
February 1956 Beckett wrote back to accept a Broadway production of *Godot*, which Schneider and Rosset had advised against,
and to forestall what Beckett called 'unauthorized deviations'
from it in the forthcoming Broadway production with a fresh
director and cast, and a producer conscious of the play's dismal
failure in its Miami premiere. Rosset had written on 13 January
that producer Michael Myerberg would not allow a *New York
Times* journalist to see the text of the play, 'saying it was going to
be changed???????' (punctuation is Rosset's). Beckett responded
on 2 February:

> I am naturally disturbed by the thought of a new director of pro-
> duction [that is, not Alan Schneider]. And still more disturbed by
> the menace hinted at in one of your letters, of unauthorized devia-
> tions from the script. This we cannot have *at any price* and I am
> asking [London producer Donald] Albery to write [American pro-
> ducer Michael] Myerberg to that effect. I am not intransigent, as the
> [bowdlerised] Criterion production [in London] shows, about minor
> changes, if I feel they are necessary, but I refuse to be improved by a
> professional rewriter. Perhaps it is a false alarm. I do hope so. (*Letters
> 2* 600–1)

Rosset followed up on 6 February dispelling the notion of a 'false
alarm': 'Myerberg once told me on the phone that he considered the translation to be a poor one and that he would like
to have Thorton Wilder redo it. I think it entirely possible that
he may be messing around with it but I also think that a word
from Albery would stop him from doing anything without your

permission' (*Letters 2* 601n1). Myerberg had a strong connection with Wilder, having produced the Broadway premiere of *The Skin of Our Teeth* in 1942, directed by Elia Kazan, but it ran for only twenty-two performances. On the strength of Alan Schneider's revival of Wilder's play in 1955 for performances in Paris before its American tour and presentation on American TV, Wilder recommended Schneider as director for the American *Godot*. But Myerberg took the direction of *Godot* away from Schneider after the play's Miami failure, retaining only Bert Lahr from the Miami cast, and, desperate to have a Broadway run of more than twenty-two performances, engaged Herbert Berghof to direct. To his credit Myerberg had sent Schneider to Paris to see Beckett and to London to see the Peter Hall production of the play in preparation for the Broadway production and its Miami try-out. Wilder was, moreover, incalculably helpful to Schneider as they found themselves on the same ocean liner crossing the Atlantic to France. As Schneider recalls, they discussed *Godot* daily:

> The first thing Thornton did was to make sure that I understood the play. '"Godot",' he explained, is an existentialist work about '"the nullity of experience in relation to the search for an absolute".' The audience has to understand that Godot himself represented the absolute, and all of Estragon's and Vladimir's gyrations represented the nullity. If that wasn't entirely clear, a brief dip into Heidegger or Jaspers would clear it all up for me. '"Dread",' '"the leap of faith",' '"the absurd",' things like that.[3]

Wilder was thus not too far off the mark; so much so that throughout this process of a fully commercial production, the prospect of having a substantially altered version of the play open on Broadway in 1956 was very real, although Beckett's unaltered, uncensored English-language text had been available from Grove Press from 1954.

That Beckett himself was a textual tinkerer, a process writer as well as a process philosopher, a perfectionist incapable of ending the process of revision and so calling his texts final or complete, is well documented, and each return to a text – variously for productions, for reprints, for translations, for anthologies – resulted in changes by the author or in human error by those involved in the process. On occasion, the wrong edition or the wrong version found its way back into print, as an editor getting a call from his distributor that supplies of a particular title were dwindling, might lean back in his chair towards the bookshelf, pull down the copy nearest to hand, and send it on to production without looking at or through it, assuming, that is, that all published texts are equal. Writing to his American publisher on 4 November 1963 about the new tri-lingual German collection of his plays, for instance, Beckett noted, 'Have received another copy of 1st volume of the Suhrkamp trilingual edition (plays written in French). A fine job, though rather a lot of mistakes in French texts. And to my dismay they have used Faber's mutilated (Lord Chamberlain [censored]) version of *Godot* instead of [Grove's].' That is, in 1963 at least, Beckett considered the Grove edition of *Godot* to be the most accurate English-language version in print, but at the time, a decade after its premiere, various editions of *Waiting for Godot* were in circulation for performance, translation or reprinting. An acting edition of *Godot*, with details of the first production, a stage diagram, properties and lighting effects, was published in London by Samuel French (Acting Editions #510) in 1957, with significant variants from either the Grove or Faber editions, and it is still available today. Had circumstances differed slightly, this 'Acting Edition #510' might have been one rewritten by Wilder. Beckett subsequently revised the 'mutilated' *Godot* for Faber in 1965; that is, two years after Faber sent what edition it had on hand to Suhrkamp for translation and after, doubtless prodded by the blunder, Beckett revised the British text again, thereby creating an edition different from the American text, which heretofore he had preferred. Faber subsequently declared its 1965 *Godot* a 'complete and unexpurgated text [. . .] authorized by Mr Beckett as definitive', but the publisher neither withdrew nor recalled the 'mutilated' texts. Faber editions, old and new stock, remained in bookshops until they were sold. Nor did Grove, then, issue this 'definitive text', since its original 1954 edition was uncensored. Hence, by 1965, at least four substantially different but authentic and fully authorised versions of *Godot* in English were in public circulation and so used for performances.

A decade earlier, on 25 June 1953, Beckett had initially denigrated his own translation of *Godot* for Grove Press, calling it 'rushed', and noted again, on 1 September 1953, that '[i]t was done in great haste to facilitate the negotiations of [producer] Mr. Oram and I do not myself regard it as very satisfactory', Myerberg taking his cue from Beckett's own denigration of his translation.

After the French production had closed at the end of October, Beckett improved his English translation, asking his publisher, Barney Rosset, on the 14 December 1953, to delay publication in favour of a better text: 'Could you possibly postpone setting the galleys until 1st week in January, by which time you will have received the definitive text. I have made a fair number of changes, particularly in Lucky's tirade.' This Grove did, but throughout the process of revision and translation, Beckett maintained differences between the French and English texts, beginning with their titles. Fully revised, then, *Waiting for Godot* was finally published by Grove Press in April of 1954, in advance of any English-language production. By the time of the Broadway opening at the John Golden Theatre on 19 April 1956, two years after the play's publication by Grove, three decidedly different English-language texts were being performed in major cities. The British production was a special case, since the play was censored for its West End debut to comply with the Lord Chamberlain's objections. The first Faber & Faber text of 1956 was this bowdlerised version, the one Beckett called 'mutilated'. Faber's note to its first edition announced, 'When *Waiting for Godot* was transferred from the Arts Theatre to the Criterion Theatre, a small number of textual deletions were [sic] made to satisfy the requirements of the Lord Chamberlain. The text printed here is that used in the Criterion production.' One might well ask why Faber did not publish the Arts Theatre text originally? The result of such publishing timidity was that hundreds of variants existed between the Grove Press *Godot* of 1954 and the Faber edition of 1956, and apparently it was this 'mutilated' text of 1956 that Faber inexplicably sent to Suhrkamp in 1962 for translation. Faber went on to 'correct' its *Godot* in 1965, which remained substantially different from the American text, but to mark his eightieth birthday, Faber collected all of Beckett's plays into a single, celebratory volume, *Samuel Beckett: The Complete Dramatic Works* (1986), at which time it reprinted the bowdlerised text of 1956, at least in its initial, hard-bound release, where the Gozzo matriarch has 'warts' rather than 'the clap' (CDW 22). In March of 1975, a decade after 'correcting' the text for Faber, Beckett directed the play himself for the first time and, in the process, produced a substantially altered, trimmer acting text. Those changes are detailed in *Waiting for Godot*, Volume 1 of *The Theatrical Notebooks of Samuel Beckett* (1993). But the independent revisions Beckett made for the Pike

Theatre production of 1955 were not reconciled with the final acting version published in the *Theatrical Notebooks*, and to date, the Pike revisions have not appeared or been acknowledged in any publication of the play (see Dukes 1995, 2004).

Over the years, Grove Press silently revised its text, correcting most instances of 'well' for 'we'll', for instance, so that by the 1970 uniform edition in sixteen volumes, *The Collected Works of Samuel Beckett*, with which Beckett was delighted, most of the earlier typos had been corrected, at least in the American editions. For the publication of the centenary bilingual edition of Beckett's most famous play, Grove Press reunited the long separated fraternal twins, the English and French editions of *Godot*, but the American and English editions remained unreconciled. Faber, moreover, published its own bilingual edition separately and thus ensured that significant differences remained between English and American texts. In the discussion of the Eiffel Tower, for instance, Vladimir notes in the Grove text, 'We were more respectable in those days' (3). The Faber edition of 1965 has the couple more 'presentable'. And in the discussion of Vladimir's urinary difficulties, the Faber edition has the characters responding '*angrily*' two times fewer. And Vladimir 'peers' into his hat one time fewer in the British text, Beckett revising the fourth '*peers*' to a '*looks*'. Such differences remain, and one cannot help but wonder that an opportunity to develop a single English-language *Godot* in the centenary year of 2006 was lost. But perhaps such textual diversity is further testimony to the play's multiplicity not only between French and English but among English and American versions as well, the Grove text remaining closer to the spirit of Beckett's original translation. The compromise text for both publishers in English might have, perhaps should have, been the last version of the play that Beckett worked on assiduously. Beckett's most precise thinking about his theatrical texts in performance is documented in the *Theatrical Notebooks*, a four-volume series under the general editorship of James Knowlson that Beckett not only supported but financed with his royalties as well. The notebooks were published jointly by Faber & Faber and Grove Press, not without acrimony, we might add, between 1992 and 1999, and detail the changes Beckett made as a director of his works, often after 'final' publication. Sadly, they were published in luxury, boxed editions at high prices, which have since escalated among collectors, putting the volumes out of reach for rank-and-file scholars and theatre practitioners. For Beckett, his 'definitive' 1965 Faber *Godot* was substantially less than definitive when he brought his director's eye to bear on the text a decade later. This revised acting text of *Waiting for Godot* published in Volume 3 of the *Theatrical Notebooks* series (1994) represents Beckett's final thinking about his most famous play and might have been published in 2006 as the closest we are likely to come to something like a definitive text, as Beckett's latest thinking about a performance text, or as the uniform text for the bilingual *Godot* of 2006. That textual rapprochement was vetoed by the Beckett Estate for reasons that continue to elude the scholarly community.

Useful as a bilingual *Godot* is, or rather a pair of bilingual *Godot*s, those of Grove and Faber both published in 2006, Mark Scroggins, in his blog *The Culture Industry*, expresses some justifiable reservations about the celebratory bilingual edition, as he raises questions, and rightly so, about the market forces at work on the project. Of the bilingual Grove *Godot*, Scroggins writes:

> The cynic in me, I fear, smells marketing here. Why only *Godot*? Why not *Godot* and *Endgame*, Beckett's other dramatic masterpiece originally written in French? (And for that matter, since Beckett's English-to-French translations are as much creative acts as his French-to-English efforts, why not throw in *Happy Days* and *Krapp's Last Tape*?) There's certainly space here: the 2006 Grove bilingual *Waiting for / En attendant Godot* clocks in at 357 pages; that in comparison to only 509 pages in the complete *Dramatic Works* of the GCE [Grove Centenary Edition].
>
> I guess it's a matter, in terms of typography, of feast or famine. In the GCE, *Waiting for Godot* occupies only 87 pages, but they're rather packed pages: fairly narrow margins, stage directions pressed right up against speeches, speakers' names hived off into the left margin. Turning to the 2006 *Godot* (where the English text takes up 174 pages) is like going from the cramped Oxford World's Classics edition of the King James Bible to a big, airy presentation volume. Margins are vast; speakers' names (in all caps) rest atop speeches; stage directions have paragraphs all to themselves. Really, I can't help feeling, there's *too much* space. Even as I revel Ronald Johnsonianly or Susan Howeishly [poets both] in the tracts of white space, I gotta suspect that Grove is stretching things out to make a substantial volume of this.
>
> And as welcome as the bilingual edition is, I'm also a trifle exasperated with what I've called (in reference to the GCE) the '"black

box" nature of the textual editing'. The 2006 *Godot* has a teasing introduction by Beckett scholar & textual editor S. E. Gontarski that makes much of the text of this new issue, without ever really showing what's been changed. Gontarski goes over the play's textual history from the first Grove edition of 1954; he spends a good deal of time excoriating Faber & Faber for publishing a 'mutilated' version of the play in 1956, and reprinting that text (censored at the behest of the Lord Chamberlain) in 1986, even though they had access to a 1965 Grove edition [Faber, actually] that Beckett considered 'definitive'; & he draws attention to 2 further revised versions of 1975 and 1955.

In the 2006 *Godot*, Gontarski, gloats somewhat anticlimactically, 'Grove Press has not only reunited the long separated fraternal twins, the English and French *Godot*, but has brought British and American texts closer to harmony'. Er – meaning *what* precisely? Show me the textual notes, guys. You've got over 350 pages to play with here; 15 or 20 pages of textual notes and variants at the end would have been far more welcome than a lot of that beautiful white space in which Didi & Gogo's back-&-forthings echo like Laurel & Hardy in the Sahara. No Shakespeare editor could get away with this.

Similarly, a reviewer of this edition on Amazon in 2008 noted, 'We have here in this introduction only the barest of bones of some textual variants, with a very brief bibliography', but he (or she) quickly adds, 'Yet not much more is needed.'[4] I accept such admonitions, although Scroggin's commercial reservations are simultaneously apt and misplaced as far as those of us involved in the project are concerned, since much of the white space was a deliberate publishing decision to keep the French and English passages parallel, so that when substantial portions of the French text were excised or English text was added, the corresponding space remained blank. Moreover, the length of the introduction was a financial decision; when a commercial house like Grove Press (or Faber, for that matter, but more of that anon) calls and asks one to write a 1,000-word introduction to a planned bilingual *Godot* and to do so over the weekend, no less, the answer has to be, 'Yes, of course', despite the restrictions and one's personal reservations. I, for one, already know that I will be able at least to double the allotted word count. I would love to have been commissioned to write a full textual history of the play, the variorum edition that Scroggins seems to call for, but the work would either not have been published or not have been published yet. To the criticism, I respond that the 'barest of bones' was mandated and that we are all – author, publisher, critic and reader – part of a commercial enterprise we call publishing. If the public were inclined to buy variorum editions, Grove and Faber would doubtless publish them. And again, the *Theatrical Notebooks*, a project teetering on collapse at each new costing, was made possible only by Beckett's full cooperation and participation – and his substantial subvention – and still it was published at some $150 per volume.

Much of what I have been documenting may fall under the rubric of opportunities lost or opportunities thwarted by economic or legal forces, the Estate's refusing to allow the reprinting of the *Theatrical Notebooks* in cheaper paperback format or the separate publication of the revised texts contained therein, for example. But in the post-centenary year of 2008, another opportunity to improve Beckett's texts arose when British publisher John Calder lost control of the publishing venture he had run since 1949. While Grove Press has published all of Beckett's work in North America since 1953, English and Commonwealth rights were divided between the venerable Faber & Faber, which wanted only the theatre works at first, and John Calder, a new and more adventurous publisher in the 1950s, who accepted the remainder, that portion which, at the time, was called 'Calder's folly' (quoted in Ackerley and Gontarski 2004/2006: 79). In the aftermath of Calder's economic collapse in 2008, Faber & Faber took control of all of Beckett's work in English outside of North America. In a press release of 25 May 2007, Faber's poetry editor, Paul Keegan, proudly announced that: 'We hope editorially to pay renewed attention to Beckett's words, in ways that reflect his own devotion to them and intentions for them. And [. . .] to ensure that the prose works [. . .] are recognized alongside the works for theatre [. . .].' Publishers' press releases are routinely full of such high purpose – in this case, pledging textual care and faithful restoration – and Faber followed up by launching an ambitious project, a complete reprinting of the Beckett canon, reorganised into seventeen soft-covered volumes, each in the hands of a different, and mostly capable, editor. This would be Britain's first uniform edition of the Beckett canon and an overt repudiation of the Calder texts, but the differences between the high purpose of the press release and the ground rules for the project emerged quickly. To begin with, while work on each

volume and each genre would be essentially the same – depend-
ing, of course, on the number of historical problems presented
by each work or collection – Keegan sought to lower editorial
expectations, announcing in an email to the volume editors that
the term '"Preface" rather than "Introduction" would be used for
the front-matter of these Faber editions', and that those scholars
working on the prose texts would be called editors even as precious little editing was to be done on most of the fiction. But for
the de facto 'editors' of the drama, no such designation would be
permitted, Faber being keen, apparently, to avoid any suggestion
that its texts needed editing or had been edited, even as some
of the theatre works were substantially and judiciously revised.
Keegan was straightforward with the editors and – what to call
those of us working on the drama, prefacers? – about restrictions on the content, the information we could provide, the limits
imposed by the property owner. He noted that the Estate insisted
that prefatory material be short, prominent, and without interpretation! To borrow a barb from Scroggins, 'Er – meaning *what*
precisely?' A number of prefaces were subsequently turned back
for, well, offering too much information or interpretation; some,
like my own, were hacked at and truncated – indiscriminately, to
my mind. On the matter of changes to the dramatic texts, Keegan
sent a note directed primarily to those of us lobbying for the past
decade for the release of the 'corrected' or 'revised' acting editions
from the *Theatrical Notebooks* pointing out that he had been
obliged by the Estate to retain the texts as originally published
by Faber. The opportunity, then, of offering a distinctively new
anthology of Beckett's 'Shorts' by publishing, as the lead text, the
version of *Krapp's Last Tape* that Beckett revised for his productions and urged other directors to follow for theirs was ended
before it could be proposed. The same restrictions would apply
to the *Endgame, Happy Days* and *Waiting for Godot* volumes
of this 'new' series. The Estate, and thereby the publishers, have
consistently resisted the release of the 'corrected' or 'revised'
acting editions, even though they qualify as texts published by
Faber, and the texts represent Beckett's final intentions for them.
The Estate thus seems to consider theatre a second order of art,
derivative and so inevitably a corrupt and inferior version of
some sort of pure, ideal, inviolable original, which it insists all
productions follow, even as such a single text is inexistent. This
is a policy, a prejudice, I would venture, that Beckett himself did

not share, since his correspondence with publishers is filled with requests for publication delays so that production changes could be incorporated into the published texts. I took as my position in editing, or unacknowledged editing, or prefacing the volume that Faber calls *Krapp's Last Tape and Other Shorter Plays*, the Scroggins admonition 'Show me the textual notes, guys'. And Keegan left the door ajar for such edits with the statement that despite the textual restrictions imposed by the Estate, Faber would accept historical revisions, corrections proposed on the basis of the print (not performance) history.

The first shock came with receipt of the proofs for the volume's front matter; they were a travesty. In what amounted to final proofs, the volume was attributed to another scholar, J. C. C. Mays, listed as 'Editor' thus:

> Samuel Beckett:
> Krapp's Last Tape
> and Other Shorter Plays
> Edited by J. C. C. Mays

Moreover, I provided Faber with two separate essays, one called, as requested, not 'Introduction' but 'Preface', and another called 'Notes on the Texts', which I conceived of as something of an appendix, afterword, or post-face and not part of the introduction. What I received as a proof was an incoherent series of fragments from my preface, ineptly edited, about 50 per cent of the original essay now conjoined to my textual notes, which had nothing to do with the theses in the preface. Moreover, much of my preface to the *Krapp's Last Tape and Other Shorter Plays* volume contained an argument for a different title, noting that:

Beckett himself dubbed [. . .] [his] later works *shorts* to his English and American publishers. What had been the more prosaic '*Short . . . Pieces*' in *Cascando and Other Short Dramatic Pieces* (Grove, 1968), became simply '*Shorts*' in *Breath and Other Shorts* (Faber, 1972) and *First Love and Other Shorts* (Grove, 1974). The '*Short*', Beckett's preferred designation for what Faber continues to call *Short Plays*, became a discrete theatrical genre in Beckett's hands, those designated for theatre in particular at once more and less than the traditional one-act play [that is, there are narrative 'shorts' as well, the designation that Calder gave his twelve-volume boxed set of 1999].

Faber published the argument but ignored its implications, retaining the title *Krapp's Last Tape and Other Shorter Plays*, to my mind reducing the generic innovation of these later works to mere brevity, shorter versions of one-act plays. Even the title *Krapp's Last Tape and Other Short Dramatic Pieces* would have been preferable, since it would have retained more of the sense of Beckett's theatrical innovation with these works, maintaining the theatrical pun of *Piece of Monologue* or *Piece for Theatre*. From the first, Grove Press called its volume *Krapp's Last Tape and Other Dramatic Pieces* (1958). But Faber seems to have been driven by consistency, by analogy with *Collected Shorter Plays of Samuel Beckett* (1994), a collection which Grove thereafter merely photo offset.

Worse, Faber moved the textual notes into the preface, producing an inelegant mash-up. This gave the notes greater prominence, but the texts themselves as published in the volume did not always follow the changes described in the notes. This was especially true regarding a significant series of changes to the text of *Come and Go*, especially changes outlined in the final paragraph of my notes to that play. Similarly, the notes submitted for the changes to the text of *Play* were in keeping with Beckett's final version of the play, produced for the Grove Press magazine *Evergreen*, which revisions he had called '*in extenso*'. These revisions were especially important to publish in 2009, more than forty years after Beckett made them, because when Grove published *Play* in book form in *Cascando and Other Short Dramatic Pieces* (1968) it printed not its own best and newly revised text but the incompletely revised Faber edition instead. Beckett certainly read proofs for that volume, but somehow he either ignored or failed to notice the revisions he had made to an earlier text of *Play*, and he apparently missed the omissions to the text of *Come and Go* and the fact that the corruptions of the text of *Cascando*, about which he had complained to Frost, had not been addressed. In a single volume, Grove thus published three corrupt, incompletely revised texts: *Play*, *Come and Go*, and *Cascando*. Most surprising of Beckett's omissions, perhaps, is that he did not notice the absence of the first four lines of *Come and Go*, when John Calder, to whom the play was dedicated, published it originally, nor again, when Faber reprinted the Calder edition; and, although the lines appeared in the first American edition of 1968 and in the French and German translations, subsequent English texts by Faber, including the

Collected Shorter Plays of Samuel Beckett (1984) and *Samuel Beckett: The Complete Dramatic Works* (1986) were based on the 1967 Calder and Boyars text, so lacked the fugitive opening lines. In effect, the first four lines of *Come and Go*, which are included in the Grove Press editions, have been missing from all Faber editions until the *Krapp's Last Tape and Other Shorter Plays* volume. Faber has now published my notes as to what a historically edited text of *Come and Go* should look like, but they have not made the full and appropriate changes to the text offered in the same volume, perhaps because it is the text that appeared in the fourth volume of *The Theatrical Notebooks of Samuel Beckett: The Shorter Plays* (1999), which texts are apparently being officially shunned. Curiously, the changes *did* appear in the Suhrkamp trilingual edition, even in the English text published there, which was apparently based on some Faber text it itself did not publish. I say 'apparently', because I assume that the Faber decision not to include the full revisions of *Come and Go* called for in the 'Preface' was conscious, but the possibility exists that the omissions were further evidence of editorial laxity at chez Faber – else, why not reconcile the notes and the text? We might note here as well that the first printing of the Faber edition of *The Unnamable* in this 'new' series contains a confusion of gatherings, the novel jumping from page 26 to 59, then from 74 to 43, pages 59 to 74 then repeated while pages 26 to 43 are missing altogether. Such a blunder was subsequently caught, but not before many corrupt, unreadable texts were distributed and remain for sale somewhere. Such inattention to detail is less unusual than one might expect even from so storied and venerable a publisher. But then again when Faber published *The Faber Companion to Samuel Beckett* in 2006 (what was, in 2004, *The Grove Companion to Samuel Beckett*), someone at Faber decided to declare the *authors* of the volume, Chris Ackerley and me, to be 'editors', although we had written all 700,000 words of the original typescript and there was no sign of the term 'editor' in the Faber copy text (i.e., the Grove Press volume, where we were rightly listed as authors). Since Faber never sent proofs of *their* volume to Ackerley or to me, the error was irreversible. The proof of *Krapp's Last Tape and Other Shorter Plays* I received from chez Faber had me listed thus:

S. E. Gontarski has edited *The Faber Companion to Samuel Beckett: A Reader's Guide to His Life, Works, and Thought* (Faber 2006), together with volumes IV (*Shorter Plays*) and II (*Endgame*) of *The Theatrical Notebooks of Samuel Beckett* (Faber 1993, 1999); he has also edited *Samuel Beckett: The Complete Short Prose* (Grove Press 1995).

That error was fortunately caught by the volume's 'Editor', rather 'Prefacer', in proofs and altered to:

S. E. Gontarski is co-author, with C. J. Ackerley, of *The Faber Companion to Samuel Beckett: A Reader's Guide to His Life, Works, and Thought* (Faber 2006), and has edited volumes IV (*Shorter Plays*) and II (*Endgame*) of *The Theatrical Notebooks of Samuel Beckett* (Faber 1993, 1999) as well as *Samuel Beckett: The Complete Short Prose* (Grove Press 1995).

Witness as well the further inconsistency of Faber's refusing to use the designation 'editors' for the volumes of drama, when the Faber webpage for *Krapp's Last Tape and Other Shorter Plays* used precisely the forbidden language, 'Edited by S. E. Gontarski'.

The good news, however – to return to the question of revisions to the published texts – is that a version of *Play*, corrected in light of documentation that wasn't available in the mid-1990s when volume 4 of the *Theatrical Notebooks* was published, has now finally appeared in 2009 in the Faber *Krapp's Last Tape and Other Shorter Plays*, and that alone is reason enough to own the volume. General readers and theatre professionals interested enough in these issues can now craft a completely revised *Come and Go* by marking into the text of the play the revisions called for in the notes on the text, or in the second half of the preface. This revised text will certainly be more readily available than that in the English strand of the trilingual German edition mentioned earlier. Furthermore, since the best texts for *Footfalls* and *What Where* are those now only available in volume 4 of *The Theatrical Notebooks of Samuel Beckett*, readers can photocopy those, if they can be found in a university library, and paste them into the new *Krapp* volume as well. Finally, the most scrupulous of readers, those who want the volume as edited, can cross out the last seven characters of the title and replace them with an 's' to produce this EDITOR's preferred title, *Krapp's Last Tape and Other Shorts*. In this way, what Faber have provided contemporary readers with is an interactive exercise: with a little knowledge of arts and crafts and a handy pot of paste readers can build their own volume of Beckett's theatrical shorts in the versions he wished them published and performed.

Despite the costly efforts of both English-language publishers and the labours of textual scholars during and just after Beckett's centenary year, Beckett's texts have improved only incrementally and inconsistently. It will doubtless be some time before another such effort to correct Beckett's texts is undertaken, perhaps not before 2089, the centenary of his death, or 2106, the bi-centenary of his birth. For those impatient scholars, theatre practitioners and general readers who don't want to wait, an alternative is available. They can turn to the texts in *The Theatrical Notebooks of Samuel Beckett*, if they can find and in finding afford them, while those who want accurate and affordable versions of Beckett's 'Shorts' can now cut and paste their own volume from the latest inconsistent efforts of chez Faber.

Notes

1. All unreferenced quotations from letters are from the Barney Rosset/ Grove Press Archives.
2. See full details in Gontarski 1999: 442–55.
3. The text quoted here is from an excerpt of Alan Schneider's autobiography *Entrances* (1986), published in *The New York Times Magazine*, 17 November 1985, at www.nytimes.com/1985/11/17/mag azine/waiting-for-beckett.html?pagewanted=all (last accessed June 2016).
4. See http://www.amazon.com/Waiting-Godot-Bilingual-Samuel-Beck ett/dp/0802144632 (last accessed June 2016).

References

Ackerley, Chris and S. E. Gontarski (2004) *The Grove Companion to Samuel Beckett: A Reader's Guide to His Life, Work, and Thought*, New York: Grove.

Ackerley, Chris and S. E. Gontarski, eds [!] (2006) *The Faber Companion to Samuel Beckett: A Reader's Guide to His Life, Work, and Thought*, London: Faber & Faber.

Beckett, Samuel (1953) *Watt*, Paris: Olympia.

Beckett, Samuel (1956) *Waiting for Godot*, London: Faber & Faber.

Beckett, Samuel (1956) *Watt*, Paris: The Traveller's Companion Series, Olympia.

Beckett, Samuel (1959) *Watt*, New York: Grove.

Beckett, Samuel (1963) *Watt*, London: Calder.

Beckett, Samuel (1965) *Waiting for Godot*, London: Faber & Faber.

Beckett, Samuel (1970) *The Collected Works of Samuel Beckett: Watt*, New York: Grove.

Beckett, Samuel (1993) *The Theatrical Notebooks of Samuel Beckett, Vol. 1, Waiting for Godot*, ed. James Knowlson and Dougald McMillan, London: Faber & Faber; New York: Grove Press [1994].

Beckett, Samuel (1999) *The Theatrical Notebooks of Samuel Beckett, Vol. 4, The Shorter Plays*, ed. S. E. Gontarski, New York: Grove; London: Faber & Faber.

Beckett, Samuel (2006) *The Selected Works of Samuel Beckett*, Vols 1–4, The Grove Centenary Edition, New York: Grove.

Beckett, Samuel (2006) *Waiting for Godot*, bilingual ed., introduction by S. E. Gontarski, New York: Grove.

Beckett, Samuel (2006) *Waiting for Godot*, bilingual ed., London: Faber & Faber.

Beckett, Samuel (2009) *Krapp's Last Tape and Other Shorter Plays*, Preface and Notes by S. E. Gontarski, London: Faber & Faber.

Beckett, Samuel (2009) *The Unnamable*, ed. Stephen Connor, London: Faber & Faber.

Beckett, Samuel (2009) *Watt*, ed. C. J. Ackerley, London: Faber & Faber.

Brater, Enoch (1994) *The Drama in the Text: Beckett's Late Fiction*, New York: Oxford University Press.

Dukes, Gerry (1995) 'The Pike Theatre Typescript of Waiting for Godot: Part 1', *Journal of Beckett Studies* 4:2, pp. 77–92.

Dukes, Gerry (2004) 'Englishing Godot' in Anthony Uhlmann, Sjef Houppermans and Bruno Clement, eds, *After Beckett / D'Apres Beckett, Samuel Beckett Today / Aujourd'hui*, Amsterdam: Rodopi, pp. 521–32.

Frost, Everett (1991) 'Recording Samuel Beckett's Radio Plays', *Theater Journal* 43:3, pp. 361–76.

Gontarski, S. E. (1999) 'Beckett's *Play*, in extenso', *Modern Drama* 42:3, pp. 442–55.

Schneider, Alan (1986) *Entrances: An American Director's Journey*, New York: Viking.

Scroggins, Mark (2011) 'More Beckett', The Culture Industry (blog), 26 December 2008, at http://kulturindustrie.blogspot.com/2008_12_01_archive.html

8

Still at Issue After All These Years: The Beckettian Text, Printed and Performed

Since Samuel Beckett lamented to his official biographer, James Knowlson, that his 'texts are in a terrible mess', much attention has been paid to the issues of textual accuracy and fidelity, much written about textual variance in the Beckett canon, and many attempts made and considerable money spent to remedy such variation and publishing inconsistencies, many the unavoidable result of simultaneous but separate publishing processes, issues leavened by publishers' eagerness to launch Beckett's new work, especially for the theatre, even as he was often still developing the piece in rehearsals. Add to such creative issues something of a general slovenliness, inattention, oversights, and blunders by everyone involved in the process of publication, and we have the current state of the Beckett texts, still apparently 'a terrible mess'. For those of us involved with such issues these past forty (or so) years (see preceding chapters, 6 & 7, for instance), an unacceptable level of textual variance and inconsistency persists even as concurrent and persistent calls for an adherence or return to the Beckettian text resound. The retort has often been to ask, 'Which Beckett text?', or rather, where might one find '*the* Beckett text'? Is one publisher more faithful, more attentive, more reliable, more scrupulous, say, than another, for instance? In the theatre especially the question can be reframed more theoretically to ask whether '*the* text' is located on the page or on the stage, literary scholars tending to favour the (semi)stability of the former at the expense of the latter, performance specialists favouring the energy and vitality of the latter, often at the expense of the former, Beckett himself somewhere in between, neither vacillating nor undecided but attracted to the possibilities of each position. Either answer, however, draws us towards plurality, towards textual multiplicity, towards the slippery issue of what is a text anyway? Apparently, the purity or stability of the Beckett text, its sanctity and inviolability, may be a remnant of an earlier age persisting as one of the great fictions or myths of twentieth- and twenty-first-century literature and theatre performance. It might be more useful to consider texts and textuality as mobiles rather than stabiles, mutable rather than immutable, variable rather than stable. That apparently was a, if not the, central issue as early as *Watt*, at the cusp of Beckett's linguistic, aesthetic shift.

Much of the shift to a theoretical level of textuality is abetted by massive cultural shifts in communication and its technologies, from Modernism to Late Modernism, from Modernism to Postmodernism, in the final quarter of the previous century, thence to the post-Gutenberg world of twenty-first-century electronic publishing where text has become a verb. In these early years of the present century, despite the morass cited above, much remains to celebrate in Beckett scholarship and explorations of textuality. The most exciting may be the development of the Beckett Digital Manuscript Project (BDMP), which is not only making primary documents available (via subscription just now) but thereby raising a host of theoretical issues, emphasising the process of composition. But even on the level of print there is at least as much to celebrate as to decry, most stunningly perhaps are two long-overdue and now recently published volumes, *The Collected Poems of Samuel Beckett* and a scholarly edition of the short story 'Echo's Bones', both from Faber & Faber in the UK and Grove Press in the US, both published to excellent reviews. Writing in *The Telegraph* on 5 January 2015, in a piece prosaically entitled '*The Collected Poems of Samuel Beckett*, ed. by Seán Lawlor and John Pilling: review', Robert Douglas-Fairhurst celebrates (with the usual reviewerly reserve) this 'comprehensive (if not complete) edition of Beckett's poems. On the plus side, the editors have done an excellent job in providing corrected texts of poems previously available only in slightly dodgy versions, unpicking their tangled textual histories, and supplementing them with a generous selection of notes.' Douglas-Fairhurst may seriously simplify Beckett's creative process as he notes that 'collecting so many poems into a single volume makes it much easier to trace the patterns that are worked into Beckett's imaginative DNA', a metaphor of inevitable and linear unfolding that has tempted many an early critic of Beckett's work but one which some of us might have hoped critics had outgrown by now. What reservations Douglas-Fairhurst has about the volume are those that we might share in that we would have liked an even longer volume that includes poems and drafts teasingly cited but omitted. Similarly, on 3 July 2014, Dwight Garner, writing in the Book Review supplement to *The New York Times* in a piece called 'A Castoff Joins a Master's Canon: "Echo's Bones", a Beckett Short Story Rediscovered', strains to find a reservation, in this case the 'Crrrritic' carping about the amount of scholarly apparatus included in the volume:

> Eight decades later [i.e., after the story's initial rejection], Grove, Beckett's stalwart American publisher, is issuing 'Echo's Bones' for the first time. This is a handsome book, and a well-padded one. The 49 pages of Beckett's story are tucked, and nearly lost, inside acknowledgments, an introduction, a note on the text, a scan from the original typescript, a selection of letters from Prentice to Beckett, a bibliography and 57 pages of (excellent) annotations from this volume's editor, Mark Nixon.

Garner fails to acknowledge that much of what appears to be savvy and historical insight in his own essay is garnered from just such scholarly apparatus.

The two reviews seem to represent the poles of popular reviewing of scholarly publications: in the case of 'Echo's Bones', too much; in the case of the *Collected Poems*, too little. Each reviewer, furthermore, perpetuates myths and misconceptions about Beckett and his work that will not die: that Beckett's work has a DNA in Douglas Fairhurst's case or that James Joyce was Beckett's 'mentor' in Garner's case. At least Garner did not call Beckett Joyce's secretary. As curious is the labelling of 'Echo's Bones' as a 'Rediscovered' text since it has been hiding in plain sight in the Dartmouth College and Harry Ransom Center archives and was even included in the final proof version in 1995 of *Samuel Beckett: The Complete Short Prose* before the Beckett Estate demanded its elimination from a text that had already been set thus rendering *The Complete Short Prose* instantly incomplete (although something of the same might be said for Faber's *The Complete Dramatic Works*, which fails to include *Eleutheria* but does include a work not by Beckett, *The Old Tune*). With print editions of the Beckett Digital Manuscript Project appearing regularly if slowly, most recently *The Making of Samuel Beckett's L'Innommable/The Unnamable* (2014) by Dirk Van Hulle and Shane Weller, and the promise of more such scholarly editions to come, we may be on the winding road to Damascus. The Reading Beckett archive has recently added major new material to its public collection: a long sequestered *Murphy* manuscript, and the Billie Whitelaw archive. Finally, the Beckett letters project, flawed as it is in comprehensiveness, inconsistent in its annotations, belabouring the obvious and ignoring central literary connections, continues to emerge, if limpingly.

On the theatrical side of the canon the issues are further complicated by ideological resistance, material possession and economic investment. Differences, often substantial, have existed not only among performances, as one might expect, and not unexpectedly between French and English texts (or other translations) of what are presumably the same work, but among English texts themselves, and such disparity is simultaneously astounding and inexplicable. Currently, not only are two major and different English texts available for *Waiting for Godot*, one American and one British, but several versions of the play in various stages of correction and revision circulate in bookshops and online sites in both the US and UK. Is '*the* Beckett text' then just the one we happen to pull off the shelf of a new or used bookshop, its authority implicit only in the fact of its publication? Apparently, that is how reprints have been approached historically, sometimes with embarrassing results. There are parallels on the prose side, of course.

Beckett experienced difficulties with the stylistic and typographical innovations implemented in *Watt*, writing on 15 December 1949 to John Ryan, editor of the short-lived Irish journal *Envoy* about the corrected punctuation of the proofs to an extract from the novel, 'I have restored my punctuation which I still prefer to that of your compositor' (Pilling 2004: 10). When the journal appeared Beckett was less gentle in a letter to George Reavey, 9 May 1950: 'An extract from *Watt*, massacred by the compositor, appeared in the filthy new Irish rag *Envoy*' (*Letters* 2 202). Even today, at least four very different versions of *Watt*, each with substantial typographical variations and inconsistent corrections, are currently on sale in English. In the US, the standard edition has now been largely replaced by the (semi?) corrected edition published in the Grove Centenary Edition of 2006, but the 'uncorrected' copies have not been recalled; both versions are currently for sale in American bookshops, although the former are being phased out. In Britain Faber & Faber has now published a more fully corrected *Watt* (2009) to replace the standard Calder edition, generally viewed as the least reliable of the texts of *Watt*, even as Beckett read proofs for it, but currently both Faber and Calder editions are commercially available in the UK. If we add to the mix issues of adaptation and performances of the prose works, most recently well-received stage adaptations of *Watt*, the issues are further compounded. Is such staging a text? Similar arguments could be made for the stagings of *Three Novels*, *Texts for Nothing*, *All Strange Away*, and perhaps the most frequently adapted and performed (even by this critic), the novels of *Nohow On*.

Moreover, translations proliferate as Beckett's work is increasingly a global phenomenon; but from which language, from which base or authorised text are translations made? Curiously, Beckett himself often paid scant attention to this issue, especially with regard to translations in languages not central to his milieu. Over the last decade and a half, moreover, a flurry of interest in Beckett's work has occurred in South America. Brazilian artists and scholars in particular have been retranslating Beckett's work into a Brazilian Portuguese, so that much major work now exists in two Portuguese versions, some translated from French texts, some from English, the more recent versions complete with fuller scholarly apparatus. Fábio de Souza Andrade, Professor Doutor em Teoria Literária e Literatura Comparada (USP), for instance, introduces the second edition of his translation of *Endgame* with a full scholarly essay, 'Matando o tempo: o impasse e a espera' (Beckett 2002). On a grander scale, China's appetite for things Western continues to develop with a considerable interest in literature that includes a Chinese translation of *Finnegans Wake* in 2013. Currently, *The Complete Works of Samuel Beckett* are in the process of being translated into Chinese, scheduled for publication by the Department of Foreign Literature of the Hunan Literature and Art Publishing House, Changsha (publication supported by the National Press Foundation of China) in 2016. Consultations with the Chinese translator of Beckett's short plays often reveal intractable points, the translator commenting that this expression or that wording, usually Beckett's slang phrases, often religious phrases, or his Irishisms, simply cannot be translated into Chinese.[1]

In the theatre the issues, while more complicated and more pressing, are even more interesting, since while Beckett's work as a theatrical director is still undervalued and so under-researched, the possibilities for such research have multiplied exponentially over the last two decades of the post-Gutenberg age of YouTube. From *Godot* onward, rehearsals would extend Beckett's creative process, and, as a director, pre-production preparations and rehearsals would extend the creative and composition process. At times Beckett's complete vision would be realised only well after the original publication when as a director he turned a fresh eye on his text. Directing himself would allow him to implement and refine a personal creative vision. Beckett evolved, from a playwright, to an advisor on productions of his work, to a shadow director, before assuming full responsibility for its staging, during which process the boards grew to be an extension of his writing desk, a platform for self-collaboration through which he reinvented his own theatrical output in more decidedly embodied, performative terms. But does it really matter whether or not we have a theatrical text that represents Samuel Beckett's latest if not last thinking about a work, since no production of any play follows any text exactly in every performance? Actors change moods, delete words, add, slip, forget, especially when the director is no longer hovering and offering post-performance notes. Such exigencies historically have been the strongest argument for discounting performance. What we hear in the theatre is never what we might read in a text, even if the texts were consistent. On the other hand, the text any reader selects or happens upon may not be the one that the director or producer happened upon, and so a performance may be closer to some idealised Beckett text than the paper copy. Yet again, performance is a mediated art; that is, something is, or various entities are, interposed between reader and text – actors are an additional, a new medium. The texts of Beckett's plays, then, present special issues.

Some variations are matters of inattentiveness or ineffectual even inept editing, like American and British editors trying to make corrections to *Finnegans Wake*; the most egregious of these may be junior editors insisting on adding an apostrophe to *Finnegans*. Beckett's *Watt*, too, has suffered its share of overcorrection witness Beckett's harsh response to the revised punctuation published in 'An Extract from *Watt*' (*Envoy*, January 1950, 11–19) cited above. Less conspicuous are the English texts of *That Time* where C's speech, which begins 'till you hoisted your head', has a repetition in the ending phrase in both Faber & Faber and Grove Press editions called *Ends and Odds*, 'who it was was there at your elbow' (Beckett 1976: 30; 1977: 24–5). For the collected editions of both publishing houses (*Collected Shorter Plays*), the Grove version merely a photo-offset from the Faber & Faber text, the repeated 'was' was evidently deemed superfluous, an error, and so was omitted, as it was from the German text as well. In the Grove and Faber *Collected Shorter Plays* (1984) and the Faber *Complete Dramatic Works* (1986), two further deletions occur. In B's fragment which begins 'stock still side by side', the 'too' has been dropped from what was in both editions of *Ends and Odds*, 'and all around too all still' (1976: 34; 1977: 27), the 'too' apparently syntactically incomprehensible to some editor. Another repetition in C's fragment, 'the Library that was another another place another time' was altered (1976: 36; 1977: 30), the repetition of 'another' deleted in the collected editions. These last two corrections, deletions or omissions, however, remained part of the last English text of the play which Beckett reviewed and revised, the English portion of the Suhrkamp trilingual edition (1976) which Beckett used for his staging of *Damals* in 1976, and so these last two have been restored to the original English text, but only in one edition. To some, such corrections may seem slight, trivial or inconsequential, but each effects the poetic rhythm of the dialogue, each effects performance, and thus each effects impact, affect and meaning. These corrections have now been made to the Faber edition *Krapp's Last Tape and Other Shorter Plays* (2009), but that is probably not the edition that most scholars or directors reach for when citing or staging this text.

Other Beckett plays seemed also to have suffered either from editorial overcorrection or neglect. *Rockaby*, too, seems to contain some anomalies with at least two lines dropped from the Grove Press first edition, *Rockaby and Other Short Pieces* (1981). Of the sequence 'another living soul / one other living soul / at her window' (Beckett 1981: 13), the second phrase, 'one other living soul', does not appear in the Faber first edition, *Three Occasional Pieces* (1982). Similarly, in the sequence 'went down / down the steep stair / let down the blind and down' (Beckett 1981: 19–20), the middle phrase, 'down the steep stair', is missing from the Faber first edition, and both are missing in all the collected editions. Compelling evidence for the restoration of those lines was deemed insufficient by the publisher, so that the Faber text of *Krapp's Last Tape and Other Shorter Plays* has remained without the two missing or revised lines.

But even productions that Beckett did direct did not always result in permanent changes to the printed text. Occasionally, local revisions were made by Beckett to respond to the process of collaboration or to the nature of a particular theatrical space, or changes were contemplated which were never dutifully incorporated into any text or production. In his notebook for *Damals* (*That Time*) that he directed along with *Footfalls* at the Schiller Theater in 1976, for instance, Beckett offered an alternate staging of the play that might have increased its verisimilitude. If Listener's hand were to be seen at full light, it should be clutching a sheet around his neck. The tension of that grip should then increase during the silences. That detail, that revised image of the play, that added detail to the play's limited palette suggests that *That Time* could be seen as an experiment in perspective. We perceive the Figure as if we were watching him from above as, perhaps, he lay in a bed. Furthermore, in the annotated text for his second German production of *Eh Joe* at the Süddeutscher Rundfunk studios in Stuttgart in 1979, Beckett altered the closing fade by cutting '*Image fades, voice as before*' just after 'In the *stones*', and in the margin he wrote 'Hold image to end of voice +5' before fade' (Beckett 1999: 270). But that revision was also never made to any of the English texts. The German text also ends with a second 'He Joe', which is omitted even in the facing English of the German text Beckett used. But such changes remain central to the performed and recorded text, which one might argue gives them a certain priority especially since the production is readily available on YouTube for readers and directors to consult.[2]

Other revisions that Beckett never got around to making to the final English text were clearly part of his developing conception of the play. In his three productions of *Footfalls* in three languages (with Billie Whitelaw at the Royal Court Theatre in London in 1976, shortly thereafter with Hildegard Schmahl on the bill with *That Time*, and finally with Delphine Seyrig at the Théâtre d'Orsay in 1978), for instance, Beckett revised the English script in detail, changing, for example, the number of May's pacing steps from seven to nine. Most texts now contain this revision. Beckett also made some fundamental changes to the lighting that, however, he never incorporated directly into the English texts, changes that were central to and consistent in all three of his productions. For each of his productions Beckett introduced a '*Dim spot on face during halts at R [right] and L [left]*' so that May's face could be seen during her monologues. Beckett further introduced into his stagings a vertical ray of light as if it were coming through a partially opened door, this to balance the horizontal beam on the floor. In addition to being part of all three of Beckett's productions, these lighting changes were incorporated into the French translation. These changes may not be readily evident in Beckett's production now available on YouTube, but they are central to Walter Asmus's various re-stagings of Beckett's reconception.[3]

On the other hand, even recorded performances are not immune to textual variance or deviation and so raise another set of textual issues. One case in point is the silent self-censoring of Beckett's second radio play, *Embers*. Having written the play in 1957, Beckett had some hesitations about its quality and so did not send it to the BBC until February of 1959, where it aired on the Third Programme on 24 June 1959, the production directed by Donald McWhinnie. That BBC production was decidedly, if discreetly, bowdlerised, however, and this only a year after Beckett's firm stand against censorship in the Saorstát. In 1958, Beckett responded to the anti-intellectual climate of his homeland when a planned adaptation of James Joyce's *Ulysses* and a new play by Sean O'Casey, *The Drums of Father Ned: A Mickrocosm of Ireland*, were withdrawn from the Dublin International Theatre Festival of that year because of objections from the Archbishop of Dublin. Beckett responded swiftly, withdrawing his own contributions to the festival: 'After the revolting boycott of Joyce and O'Casey I don't want to have anything to do with the Dublin Theatre "Festival" and am withdrawing both mimes and *All that Fall*' (Knowlson 1996: 401). In the BBC version of *Embers*, then, Holloway on the hearthrug is *not* 'trying to toast his arse' (*CDW* 255), nor is the young Henry a 'sulky little bastard' (256). Moreover, at least four possibly offensive religious expletives, 'to Christ', 'to God', 'Jesus' (256), and just 'Christ' (263), are deleted from the BBC production, although two other mentions of 'Christ' (263) are retained.[4] Such deletions may alter the tone, mood and affect of the play only slightly, but alter it they do. The text in the *Complete Dramatic Works*, moreover, is itself less than letter perfect. In both American and English first editions, the phrase 'better off dead', which follows 'sulky little bastard', is repeated in both the BBC and NPR productions and the first British and American editions. The *CDW* text, however, inexplicably drops the repetition (256). Yet another curiosity of the BBC *Embers* is that Kathleen Michael as Ada expanded all of Beckett's contractions. The change is most apparent when we lose the connection between Henry's 'Don't' (*CDW* 260) and Ada's picking it up a few lines later in 'Don't stand there gaping.' Kathleen Michael's 'Do not' breaks that link.

Moreover, even in our age of mechanical reproduction such bowdlerising and inadvertent alterations in performance are not easy to remedy once cultural restrictions loosen. When the Gate Theatre Dublin's Samuel Beckett Festival played at the Barbican Theatre Centre in September 1999, the BBC rebroadcast its 1959 *Embers* (with a new introduction by Martin Esslin), but the bowdlerised 1959 production was the one broadcast. What the BBC rebroadcast made clear was that *Embers* is very much a production of its time and not a production for all time. The American re-make, directed by Everett Frost with Barry McGovern as Henry, Billie Whitelaw as Ada, and Michael Deacon as Riding Master and Music Master, and which was broadcast at various dates across the US in 1989 on National Public Radio as part of the Beckett Festival of Radio Plays, is not only more textually faithful, it is in many respects a superior version overall, but not the performance that comes to mind for scholars and not the one easily available in our age of YouTube.

Any number of other examples of inconsistencies among Beckett's dramatic texts might serve at this point. To the issue of *Embers* we might add those of *What Where*, but those have been detailed in the fourth volume of *The Theatrical Notebooks of Samuel Beckett* (1999). And the text of *Come and Go* has been partially (but only partially) corrected by Faber in its *Krapp's Last Tape and Other Shorter Plays* (2009), but no follow-up has been effected in the *Complete Dramatic Works*, which is the text most frequently referred to and cited by scholars as if it represented *the* authoritative Beckettian texts. Suffice it to say at this point that textual inconsistencies persist and that those issues are not likely to be resolved in the near future, even as progress, at times glacial, is being made. That said, we can point to some publishers' interest to offer corrected, scholarly or full variorum editions, although the market for them remains small. That path continues only if the public (particularly Beckett scholars) buys such books. However, our post-Gutenberg world holds the potential for the most dramatic change in research – textual, genetic and performative – with the Beckett Digital Manuscript Project, on the one hand, and YouTube on the other, the latter an apparently irrepressible feature of our world, which, among its vast offerings, makes easily available both authorised and deviant performances of Beckett's work not only to fresh audiences (and, of course, that is our collective future) but to scholars interested in researching the Beckett *oeuvre* and issues of performance, and thus creates something of a performance archive online, performances thus constituting and so *featuring* multiplicity and variation. Such electronic change makes print publication easier (and cheaper) as well, and so offers the potential for nothing short of a revolution in the study of not only Beckett's theatre, but of all his texts, as texts themselves develop into something of an archive, research thus becoming excavatory, archaeological, but with an emphasis on what Beckett's texts might be or become rather than what they were or might have been. Finally, and perhaps most importantly, the attitude towards textuality has to change among scholars and serious readers of Beckett's work. Scholars need to write with a consciousness of textual variability and multiplicity in Beckett's printed and performed oeuvres, to plumb the depths of and finally to accept what simply is: textual variation and even inconsistency, and to make such plurality and multiplicity, texts as process, performance as change, part of the discourse in Beckett Studies.

Notes

1. Dr Liu Aiying, the translator referred to here, has also written one of the first books in English on Samuel Beckett's theatre published in China (PRC): *Samuel Beckett: The Body Matters*, Shanghai: Shanghai Foreign Language Education Press, 2012.
2. See the intense close up and final, slight, almost tentative smile in Beckett's 1966 German production, at https://www.youtube.com/watch?v=g6N35OjDQyo (last accessed June 2016).
3. Beckett's staging is available in parts, at https://www.youtube.com/watch?v=RGvwqERVkFw&list=PL40AF889C7EE0204C (last accessed June 2016).
4. See https://www.youtube.com/watch?v=_wp0MDYuaQU (last accessed June 2016).

References

Beckett, Samuel (1965) *Krapp's Last Tape and Embers*, London: Faber & Faber.

Beckett, Samuel (1976) *Ends and Odds: Eight New Dramatic Pieces*, New York: Grove Press.

Beckett, Samuel (1977) *Ends and Odds: Plays and Sketches*, London: Faber & Faber.

Beckett, Samuel (1981) *Rockaby and Other Short Pieces*, New York: Grove Press.

Beckett, Samuel (1999) *The Theatrical Notebooks of Samuel Beckett, Volume 4, The Shorter Plays*, ed. S. E. Gontarski, New York: Grove Press; London: Faber & Faber.

Beckett, Samuel (2002) *Fim de Partida*, tradução e apresentação de Fábio de Souza Andrade, São Paulo: Cosac e Naify.

Blin, Roger (2012) 'Blin on Beckett', in S. E. Gontarski, ed., *On Beckett: Essays and Criticism*, London: Anthem Press, pp. 167–74.

Knowlson, James (1996) *Damned to Fame: The Life of Samuel Beckett*, London: Bloomsbury.

Pilling, John (2004) *A Companion to Dream of Fair to Middling Women*, Tallahassee, FL: Journal of Beckett Studies Books.

Performance Matters

9

'That's the Show':
Beckett and Performance

'Oh but the bay, Mr Beckett, didn't you know, about your
brow.' (*Dream* 141)

We call the whole performance off, we call the book off, it tails
off in a horrid manner. [. . .] The music comes to pieces. The
notes fly all over the place [. . .] all we can do [. . .] is to deploy
a curtain of silence as rapidly as possible. (*Dream* 100)

Narrative and Performance

The idea of performance preoccupied Samuel Beckett well before
he began to explore its potential directly in the theatre. Its roots
are in the doubling if not multiplication of being or the self that
is already implicit in the idea of a representation and in the quasi-
Cartesian idea of the 'pseudocouple' that Beckett would hone into
his fiction and drama alike. A character named 'Mr Beckett', for
instance, appears as the obscure narrator in 'TWO' of *Dream of
Fair to Middling Women* (the novel written between 1931-2),
'thanks Mr Beckett' (69), returns as a belaurelled poet at the
conclusion of the short chapter called 'Und', 'Oh but the bay, Mr
Beckett, didn't you know, about your brow' (141) (in 1931 laurels
for the young author were, of course, very much a fiction), and
reappears in 'THREE', 'Behold, Mr Beckett (186). He is briefly
reprised for a thank you in the residua of the novel in the short story
'Draff': '(Thank you Mr Beckett)' (Beckett 1970: 175). At such
points of unveiling the author no longer stands entirely outside his
work and so loses his or her privilege, he or she folded instead into
and so become part of the narrative, an inside and outside simultaneously, author as narrator a part of and apart from the narrative. Such fictionalising and multiplication of a self, narrated and

narrator overlapping if not one, followed hard upon Beckett's one and only direct stage appearance. He was persuaded to appear as Don Diègue in three performances of Trinity College's 'Cornelian nightmare', *Le Kid*, at Dublin's Peacock Theatre between 19 and 21 February 1931 (Knowlson 1996: 126). Later in the 1930s Beckett would write a twenty-three-line poem in French, 'Arènes de Lutèce', in which he explored more fully the fractured, doubled or multiple self, what Lawrence Harvey referred to as the experience of *dédoublement* (Harvey 1970: 202–7). In his pseudonymous 1934 essay 'Recent Irish Poetry', Beckett would refer to such multiplication as the crisis of the subject. What we read as the narrative of *Watt*, moreover, has apparently already been performed (or at least rehearsed) for an audience, a character named 'Sam', who then re-presents the tale (with the inevitable modifications of any *metteur en scène*) to a second audience, the reader. The model for such fictionalising and performance of the self may have been Beckett's beloved Dante, and perhaps Proust as well, whose 'Marcel' relates what becomes *Remembrance of Things Past*. The idea of the author as a fiction performing in his own work appeared most directly finally, if fleetingly, as a descriptor in *That Time*, where voice 'B' (Beckett?) was referred to at one point as 'something out of Beckett', a convention carried over from 'Three Dialogues', where 'B' is (roughly) Beckett, 'D' (roughly) Georges Duthuit. Ruby Cohn prevailed upon Beckett to excise the self-reference before publication and performance (Cohn 2001: 332; 404n10), but such self-reflection invites us to read Mr Beckett, Sam, or Samuel Beckett as, at least potentially, a series of voices in and for performance, in short as a text himself. For the most part, however, Beckett learned to heed the advice he gave himself about Dante in the *Whoroscope Notebook* (University of Reading Ms. # 3000) as he was writing *Murphy*, 'keep whole Dantesque analogy out of sight'; the advice would, on the whole, apply equally to one 'Mr Beckett', even in his thin disguises as 'I' in the opening of 'Ding-Dong' and the first sentence of *Mercier et Camier*.

With two stage works written amidst the three post-war French novels, Beckett would explore the crisis of the subject, its doubling if not multiplicity, on stage and page. The second of the two plays, *En attendant Godot*, written between *Malone muert* and *L'Innommable*, was the first (finally) to be staged, in January of 1953 by Roger Blin at the Théâtre de Babylone. Beckett had high hopes for its predecessor and companion, *Eleutheria*, as well. On

15 August 1947 he wrote to confidant Thomas MacGreevy, 'My play in French was almost taken by Hussenot-Grenier (playing at the Theatre Agnes Capri) but only almost. They were very nice about it. And recommended it to Jean Vilar, who has it at present' (*Letters 2* 60). On 4 January 1948 Beckett reported, again to MacGreevy, 'Jean Vilar is taken with the play and nibbling' (*Letters 2* 71), and some two months later, on 18 March, he noted, '*Eleutheria* is hithering, thithering and beginning to be spoken of a little. I think it will see the boards in time if only for a few nights. But never those of the Gate [Theatre in Dublin]' (*Letters 2* 75). In a long letter to Georges Duthuit on 11 August 1948, Beckett discusses *Eleutheria* at considerable length, disclosing candidly its centrality to his thought, work and his sense of being, and commenting on Duthuit's efforts to have it staged:

> You know I really have no wish to be set free, nor to be helped, by art or by anything else. Young people after reading *Eleutheria*, have said to me, but you are sending us away discouraged. Let them take aspirin, or go for long walks, before breakfast. Nothing will ever be sufficiently against for me, not even pain, and I do not think that I have any special need for it. I say confusedly what comes uppermost, like Browning [echoed by Winnie in *Happy Days*]. [. . .] Victor [Krap] (name to be changed incidentally, I need Nick something instead) is utterly defenceless, he too can be heard from afar, what he has to say, in order to have the right to be silent, is in the end the old nonsense, he is afraid, he says Mr Inspector sir, he seems to be telling them off, in reality he is licking their boots, talking to them is sucking their arses. Georges my old friend, don't go to any more trouble over it. I mean trying to get it put on, we will have a better laugh another way, we will dig out, somewhere else, well away from there, a better kind of seriousness. (*Letters 2* 97–8)

From there Beckett grows quite philosophical, discussing ideas I have elsewhere deemed decidedly Bergsonian: time, space, knowing and motion (Gontarski 2015).

And yet, and yet, with the success of *Molloy*, nominated for the Prix des Critique in 1951, Beckett began to grow uneasy about *Eleutheria*, Suzanne Deschevaux-Dumesnil writing to French publisher Jérôme Lindon on 25 May, 'About *Eleutheria*. B. is more and more worried about this work, But he thinks that there is perhaps a way of reshaping it'; nonetheless, she asked him to pass on a copy to Charles Bensoussan, which Lindon did on 16 May. Bensoussan then seemed eager to mount either *Eleutheria* or *En attendant Godot* (*Letters* 2 254, 254n2). By 8 May 1951, Beckett writes Mania Peron, 'I have told messier Bensoussan not to count on *Eleutheria* for the autumn' (*Letters* 2 277). He wrote to Mania again on 6 September 1951, 'Eleutheria: the Bensoussan man wanted to put it on, but I was unwilling. I am not sure altogether why. I did not like the tone of his message. And it is not a work that greatly attracts me' (*Letters* 2 288). With the staging and success of *Godot* in 1953 by Roger Blin, Beckett sequestered the autobiographical *Eleutheria* (published only in 1995 and never officially staged) to his trunk, as indeed perhaps too personal, and turned his development of performance in another direction, another mode. To translator Christian Ludvigsen, who had just translated *Godot* into Danish, Beckett wrote on 23 April 1956, 'Since *Eleutheria* was announced for publication I have changed my mind and decided that it can be neither produced nor published as it stands. I may try to revise it some day, but I think this is unlikely' (*Letters* 2 616). (For publication details see my 'Introduction' to the American translation (1995), which picks up the story in 1986.)

Soon after writing his two longest plays, Beckett would explore the performative in a personal, serio-comic, aesthetic commentary, 'Three Dialogues: Samuel Beckett and Georges Duthuit', which he published in the newly revived, post-war *Transition* magazine in 1949, as *Eleutheria* and *Godot* were circulating among producers and as he was wrestling with the last of his three French novels, *L'Innommable*. In the self-deprecating critical piece, Beckett exploited the performative and travestied both aesthetic debate and the philosophical dialogue favoured by Plato.

The philosophical tradition through which Beckett was working included Denis Diderot (1713–84) and Bernard Le Bovier de Fontenelle (1657–1757), the latter a French polymath and sceptic who was associated with Diderot in the making of the *Encyclopédie* (1751–72). Beckett's rendering of Fontenelle's 'De mémoire de rose on n'a vu que lui [le même jardinier]' from *Entretiens sur la Pluralité des mondes* (1686) was cited in the *Dream Notebook* (reference no. 581 in Pilling's 1999 edition). Beckett's source appears to have been one of Diderot's three philosophical dialogues, *Le Rêve de d'Alembert* (1769, published in 1830), in which d'Alembert's dream is discussed by his *amie*, Mlle. de l'Espinasse, and Doctor Bordeu:

Mlle. de l'Espinasse: Doctor, what is this sympathy of the eternal?
Bordeu: That of a transient being who believes in the immortality of things.
Mlle. de l'Espinasse: Fontenelle's rose, saying that within the memory of the rose no gardener has been known to die.
Bordeu: Precisely; that is graceful and profound.

Beckett used the 'graceful and profound' image in the short story 'Echo's Bones' (Beckett 2014: 19), 'the words of the rose to the rose', and punned on it in *Dream* where the aged gardener broods 'over the fragility of all life' (174). That fragility is most poignantly expressed at the conclusion of 'Draff', the tenth and final story of *More Pricks than Kicks*, as a conversation, with emphatic punctuation, among roses on the topics of time and immortality, 'No gardener has died, comma, within rosaceous memory' (Beckett 1970: 191), the conceit there associated with his father's death. (The quotation remained on Beckett's mind as late as 14 September 1977 when he wrote it out for Anne Atik, a note she reproduced in facsimile in her memoir, calling it 'his own beautiful translation' [Atik 2001: 87]). As interesting as theme and image are, Beckett admired the dialogue format that both Diderot and d'Alembert favoured for philosophical, literary and aesthetic discourse, particularly Diderot's philosophical dialogue, *Le Neveu de Rameau* (1760). Set in a Paris café with two interlocutors, 'Moi' and 'Lui', it offered a model for 'Three Dialogues', the 'Exit weeping' of the second perhaps playing against Diderot's final 'Rira bien qui rira le dernier' (roughly, one who laughs last laughs best).

Beckett also knew George Berkeley's (1685–1753) decidedly less dramatic *Three Dialogues between Hylas and Philonous*, echoes of which reappear in *Fin de partie* (*Endgame*) that he began writing, in fits and starts, shortly after the Duthuit dialogues. Hamm's neo-Romantic dreams of fertility beyond the immediate sterility and decay, for instance, echo Hylas' admonition of Philonous' scepticism of the senses: 'Philonous – Look! Are not the fields covered with delightful verdure? Is there not something in the woods and groves, in the rivers and clear springs that sooths, that delights the soul?' Hamm understands that Philonous' profound scepticism leads to madness, like that of the 'painter – an engraver' whom Hamm apparently visited in the asylum (*Endgame* 44). Hamm's persistent hopes ('Let's go from here, the two of us! South!' and 'But beyond the hills? Eh? Perhaps it's still green. Eh? . . . Flora!

Pomona! ... Ceres!' [34, 39]) keep him, for better or worse, from the asylum. British publisher John Calder thought 'Three Dialogues: Samuel Beckett and Georges Duthuit' dramatic enough to stage as part of what he announced to Beckett as 'an evening devoted to your work' (25 June 1965). Beckett's response, on 30 June, was polite but adamant, 'Whatever you like, but please not the Duthuit dialogues. We can always find something to replace them' (copy of the letter in the Rosset archive).

Writing *Eleutheria* (which he began on 18 January 1947) and *Godot* (which he began on 9 October 1948), Beckett folded the idea of performance into both texts as meta-theatre or plays within plays (an 'Audience member' and 'Stage-box Voice' interrupting the action in Act III of *Eleutheria* and Lucky's monologue and his *performance* of the tree in *Godot*, most obviously). Beckett then began to extend the idea of performance in his fiction to new levels, developing a form of dialogic monologue with a consciousness of audience that would eventually find its way to the stage with *Krapp's Last Tape* in 1958 and dominate the short, late theatre thereafter. Thus we have Auditor's echo of the spectator, of an audience that makes him (her?) so critical to the performance of *Not I*, for example. Similarly, Listener mirrors the audience and so adds to the multiplicity of *Ohio Impromptu*. In *Mercier et Camier* (written in 1946, under contract to Bordas in October 1946 [*Letters 2* 45] but only published in 1970 and in English translation in 1974), the eponymous duo, whom Beckett called a 'pseudocouple' in his subsequent fiction (*Three Novels* 297), feel the presence of another, or an other, an audience of some sort:

> I sense vague shadowy shapes, said Camier, they come and go with muffled cries.
> I too have the feeling, said Mercier, we have not gone unobserved since morning.
> Are we by any chance alone now? said Camier.
> I see no one, said Mercier. (Beckett 1974: 19)

> Strange impression, said Mercier, strange impression sometimes that we are not alone. You not?
> I am not sure I understand.
> Now quick now slow, that is Camier all over.
> Like the presence of a third party, said Mercier.

Enveloping us. I have felt it from the start. And I am anything but
psychic.
Does it bother you? said Camier.
At first no, said Mercier.
And now? Said Camier.
It begins to bother me a little, said Mercier. (Beckett 1974: 100)

'Pseudocouple' would become the critical term of choice for
Beckett's paired characters (like Vladimir and Estragon, Hamm
and Clov, Nagg and Nell, among others) who often seem to be features of a single character, a multiple presentation of what might
have been a single being. In *Molloy* of 1951, the first of Beckett's
Three Novels, the sucking stones episode is prefaced by suggestions of a performance, perhaps even a magic show complete
with audience that the narrator addresses, 'Watch me closely',
before exercising some prestidigitation, 'I take a stone [. . .] I take
a second stone [. . .]' (*Three Novels* 97). In *The Unnamable*, published as *L'Innommable* in Paris by Les Éditions de Minuit in
1952, Beckett imbedded the dialogic within a monologue and,
more important, folded the sense of an audience into what was
becoming a dramatic narrative:

Well I prefer that, I must say I prefer that, that what, oh you know,
who you, oh I suppose the audience, well well, so there's an audience,
it's a public show, you buy your seat and wait, perhaps it's free, a free
show, you take your seat and you wait for it to begin, or perhaps it's
compulsory, a compulsory show, you wait for the compulsory show
to begin, it takes time, you hear a voice, perhaps it's a recitation, that's
the show, someone reciting, selected passages, old favourites, a poetry
matinée, or someone improvising, you can barely hear him, that's the
show, you can't leave, you're afraid to leave, it might be worse elsewhere, you make the best of it, you try and be reasonable, you came
too early, here we'd need Latin, it's only beginning, it hasn't begun,
he's only preluding, clearing his throat, alone in his dressing-room,
he'll appear any moment, he'll begin any moment, or it's the stage-
manager, giving his instructions, his last recommendations, before the
curtain rises, that's the show, waiting for the show [. . .] (*Three Novels*
381–2)

That final comment, 'that's the show, waiting for the show', is as
much a nod to Dada and surrealist performance as it is a gloss on

En attendant Godot. Subsequently, much of the late drama, like *A Piece of Monologue*, became, almost inevitably, nearly indistinguishable from the late prose fiction. 'From an Abandoned Work', for example, was initially published as a theatre piece by Faber & Faber after it was performed on the BBC Third Programme by Patrick Magee on 14 December 1957. Although 'From an Abandoned Work' is anthologised with Beckett's short fiction, Faber initially collected it among four theatre works in *Breath and Other Shorts* (1971), which grouping highlighted its debut as a piece *for performance*. Beckett was so enthusiastic about it as a monologue for performance that he wrote to Schneider on 29 January 1958, 'I think Magee's performance is very remarkable' (Harmon 1998: 33). That performance set Beckett to work almost immediately (20 February 1958) on another monologue, this overtly for the stage and called at first 'Magee Monologue' but ultimately *Krapp's Last Tape*. Beckett even suggested to Schneider that 'From an Abandoned Work' might be used to fill out the evening with the American premiere of *Krapp's Last Tape*. As we see that narration itself became a mode of performance for Beckett, we more readily understand not only the late drama but the impulse of so many theatrical directors to stage, to perform, the prose fictions.[1] The 1980 novel *Company* alone has been staged by some six major theatre companies.[2] The key to the late texts, prose and theatre, where narrative dominates – what we might call 'non-dramatic theatre' or 'narrative theatre' – is then Beckett's earliest fiction and poetry. In both, identity is very much the spectacle.

Performance as creation

As Beckett explored the implications of performance fully in the mid-1950s, he began to understand its necessity to his theatrical creative process. As he wrote to an American friend Pamela Mitchell on 28 September 1956, 'The new play [*Fin de partie* but which at this point he thought to call simply *HAAM*, 'a label – like the novels'] is now as finished as is possible *before rehearsals*' (*Letters* 2 657, emphasis added). He was perplexed about the work and didn't know what to think 'really until I start hearing it and looking at it – not of course even then'. The full embrace of performance would come shortly thereafter with the Royal Court Theatre production of *Krapp's Last Tape*. Writing to his American publisher, Barney Rosset, on 20 November 1958, Beckett was unrestrainedly enthusiastic about Magee's performance, which he oversaw so closely that some have claimed he directed it, although the director of record was Donald McWhinnie:

> Unerringly directed by McWhinnie Magee gave a very fine performance, for me by far *the most satisfactory experience in the theatre up to date*. I wish to goodness that Alan [Schneider] could have seen it. I can't see it being done any other way. *During rehearsals we found various pieces of business not indicated in the script and which now seem to me indispensable*. If you ever publish the work in book form I should like to incorporate them in the text. [... .] The BCC are doing extracts from the *Unnamable*, read by Magee, in January [1959], with learned discourse by Cronin who did the *TLS* article [. . .] (*Letters 3* 176–7, emphasis added)

The following day Beckett sent almost the identical letter to Schneider:

> I am extremely pleased with the results [of the *Krapp's Last Tape* production] and find it hard to imagine a better performance than that given by Magee both in his recording and his stage performance [. . .] In the course of rehearsals *we* established *a certain amount of business which is not indicated in the script and which now seems to me indispensable*. If Barney ever brings out the work in book form I shall enlarge the stage directions accordingly [... (Rosset did, Beckett did not)] The most interesting discovery was the kind of personal relationship that developed between Krapp and the machine. This arose quite naturally and was extraordinarily effective and of great help in the early stages whenever the immobility of the listening attitude tended to be tedious [. . .] At the end [. . .] we had a fade-out and the quite unexpected and marvellous effect of recorder's red light burning up as the dark gathered [. . .] (Harmon 1998: 50–1, emphasis added)

By the mid-1950s, then, Beckett was already talking and working like a director, committed to the lexicon and processes of performance. In a letter to Rosset's editorial assistant, Judith Schmidt, on 11 May 1959, Beckett referred to the *staging* of *Krapp's Last Tape* as its 'creation'.[3] The Irish journalist Alec Reid reports a similar attitude towards performance when he noted that Beckett 'will speak of the first run-through with actors as the "realization" of the play, and when it has been performed publicly he will say that it has been "created"' (Reid 1986: 12).

Beckett's exploration of performance would culminate in a second career that spanned the last twenty years of his life. That career was almost forced upon him as his awareness grew that dramatic works were, needed to be, created on stage. Such a revelation threw into high relief fundamental problems inherent in the idea of productions 'of' a text, that is, stagings 'of' a pre-existing work, ostensibly a completed script. The revelation that scripts produced in the study, no matter how finely honed, remained skeletal, incomplete until realised on the stage, would drive Beckett reluctantly into the semi-public posture of a theatrical director. As Beckett began increasing his role first as advisor to productions, then as a shadow director, mostly at the Royal Court Theatre, then to directing himself fully beginning in 1967, staging became a full extension of his creative process – not only for new plays but for those already published and well established as part of the theatrical repertory but not fully explored by him on the boards.

But theatre had its own frustrations. Rehearsing a revival of *En attendant Godot*, what Beckett called an 'exhumation', while trying to complete what became *Happy Days*, he complained to American director Alan Schneider: 'Had a hard time here with *Godot* rehearsals in absence of [director Roger] Blin and [producer Jean-Marie] Serreau rehearsing Raimbourg's [as Vladmir] part till a week before opening. But we made out and it is now doing very well' (*Letters* 3 411). In the same letter to Schneider, Beckett would go on to comment on the nature of the writing process: 'You could go on laboring forever on these things but the time comes, and I think it has come here, when you have to let them go. You won't find much difference [in *Happy Days*] from the script you read – got the hubby in both acts and think the song will be the Valse duet (*I love you so*) from the *Merry Widow* [. . .]' (*Letters* 3 411).

Once he had grown deeply involved in performance, he found it difficult 'to let them go' without theatre work and made such clear to his publishers repeatedly, that no final text could or should go to press before he had worked on the piece with actors. Writing to Grove Press about *Happy Days* on 18 May 1961, for instance, he said, 'I should prefer the text not to appear in any form before production and not in book form until I have seen some rehearsals in London. I can't be definitive without actual work done in the theatre' (letter inexplicably omitted from *Letters 3*; quoted from version in the Rosset Archive). Grove Press editor Richard Seaver acknowledged Beckett's request on 30 June 1961, simply repeating Beckett's instructions for clarification, 'You asked that the book [i.e., *Happy Days*] not go into production until you had a chance to work with the script in the theater.'

On 24 November 1963 Beckett wrote to Rosset that his wife was disappointed with the world premiere of *Play*, the German *Spiel*, reiterating his position on the relationship of performance to publication, repeating his comments to Alan Schneider two days later but without comments on publication: 'Suzanne went to Berlin for Deryk's [Mendel] second production and did not like it. But when I saw Deryk himself on his return he was very pleased. It seems in any case to have been well received' (*Letters 3* 583). Her major objection was that 'there was little visible beam' to the interrogating light, which is a character in this play, as Beckett reaffirms: 'The man on the light should be regarded as a fourth player and must know the text inside and out', and the light 'should not involve auditorium space. Light, W1, W2 and M belong to the same separate world'. Beckett went on to detail the Mendel twenty-five-minute production, 'everything for the sake of speed, if you adopt the da capo' (584), to Schneider with drawings of the urns, touching each other and too short in the Mendel production. On the amount of expressive emotion generated by W2's two laughs, Beckett was still unsure since, 'I simply can't know until I work on it in the theatre' (584). And to Schneider, Beckett expressed the principle of creation as a continuum, that finality has degrees: 'I shall send you this week the latest "final" text' (584), but to Rosset two days earlier, in a letter neither included nor summarised in *Letters 3*, Beckett laid out crucial theatrical and publishing principles more generally and in more detail:

> I realize I can't establish definitive text of *Play* without a certain number of rehearsals. These should begin with [French director Jean-Marie] Serreau next month. Alan's text will certainly need correction. Not the lines but the stage directions. London rehearsals begin on March 9th [1964, Beckett will appear at rehearsals on 14 March].

In fact, even after having read 'final' proofs for *Play*, Beckett halted its publication mid-production so that he could continue to hone the text in rehearsals, as he confirmed to Seaver on 29

November 1963: 'I have asked Faber, since correcting proofs, to hold up production of the book. I realize I can't establish text of *Play*, especially stage directions, till I have worked on rehearsals. I have written to Alan [Schneider] about the problems involved.' On 25 February 1964, Beckett expressed his continuing doubts about the play, at least about its 'final' state, to Judith Schmidt, in the process laying out a comprehensive view of theatre:

> I don't know what to think of <u>PLAY</u> myself. It seemed to function on my dim mental stage when I did it, enough at least to justify my letting it go. And I felt it had something the others had not, nothing to do with the writing (no attempt at writing there) or with more or less compassion or humor, but simply in the way of theatrical contrivance and attitude. (*Letters 3* 593)

These issues surrounding *Happy Days* and *Play* would become standard, if often frustrating, procedures between Beckett and at least his English-language publishers, much of it as rooted in a theory of theatre as in textual theory. The texts that Beckett was working towards, those that reflected much of what he learned serving an apprenticeship at the Royal Court Theatre and then through his staging of his plays, have, however, never been published in versions generally available to the public, even the *Krapp's Last Tape* he promised to revise for the Grove Press publication, which he does only with his own direction. To date, then, the 'Purple nose' of the original published script of *Krapp's Last Tape* remains a detail that Beckett revised out for the 1958 London production and which he systematically eliminated in private copies to anyone discussing the play with him, yet it remains, almost half a century on, part of every text of the play, in French and English, except that in the third volume of *The Theatrical Notebooks* where a fully revised performance text appears.[4]

The sheer complexity and fluidity of Beckett's creative vision, theatre and performance as part of the creative process, even as his changes were not all subsequently incorporated into a published text, has often puzzled some critics, forcing some into retreat, others into critical denial. Beckett's textual revisions were admittedly often made in response to the exigencies of production, and therein lies much of the problem, at least according to critics like Colin Duckworth. Commenting on the video version of *Waiting for Godot*, part of the *Beckett Directs Beckett* series, Duckworth admits that with Beckett's revisions, 'we can now have a clear insight into his own view of his most famous play a third of a century after he wrote it' (1987: 175), but he finally recoils from exactly that insight, concluding that 'It is difficult to explain this textual vandalism, perpetrated on some of the most magical moments of the play' (190). 'It makes one wonder', he continues, 'whether authors should be let loose on their plays thirty-odd years later' (191). Duckworth's argument is based primarily on the fact that Beckett did not fully direct the San Quentin Drama Workshop production, the result of which is finally almost a mirror image of Beckett's 1975 Schiller Theater production. Much of the preliminary work for the San Quentin production was done in Chicago in December of 1983 by Beckett's assistant at the Schiller Theater production in 1975, Walter Asmus, who began rehearsals by reviewing Beckett's Schiller production. Duckworth seems puzzled that although the new cuts and changes were made by Beckett in 1975 they were never incorporated into the German or any other revised text, and so he takes these to be less than authoritative changes. He quotes the actor Rick Cluchey (hardly a textual authority) as saying, 'Beckett will not impose any of these cuts on the published editions of this play.' Cluchey goes on to quote Beckett's ambiguous phrase, 'The text is the text' (Duckworth 1987: 185), to which we might add but it is neither static nor even stable. Since four very different English language texts of *Godot* were in print and available in bookshops at the time of Beckett's comment (two separate British and two very different American editions), which text 'is the text' was very much an open question even then. In 1985, then, Beckett authorised publication of a new text for *Godot*, one based on the revisions made in his two productions, and it appeared in 1993 as part of a series of acting texts included with publication of the theatrical notebooks. Beckett preferred that text, and all his revised texts, to the originals, but those texts, Beckett's preference, have never been published separately, have never been made commercially available.

To suggest, as Duckworth does, that the San Quentin Drama Workshop production of *Godot* is far from a definitive production is not exactly news, and if this were his fundamental point one might agree with him. No one who spoke to Beckett about his productions could come away from those conversations thinking that he had a very high regard for the acting abilities of the San Quentin Drama Workshop. Friendship with its founder, Rick

Cluchey, the only true San Quentin alumnus in this group, kept Beckett working with them.[5] 'The possibility of a definitive production of the play', continues Duckworth,

> analogous to the definitive version of a text that every scholarly editor wants to bring out, seems vitiated by two factors: first, the frame of mind of the writer-director during any given set of rehearsals [but of course, this charge could be made of any production of any performance at any time, and so Duckworth's position boils down to an attack on performance itself]; and secondly the fact that Beckett was having to work with and through the temperaments of actors whom he had not hand picked (as he had in the case of the Schiller Theater production). (1987: 178)

In an age of late modern textuality and performance such neo-Romantic yearning for definitive productions or even a 'definitive text' seems at best anachronistic.

The critic Michael Worton, in a high-profile publication in the *Cambridge Companion to Samuel Beckett*, has similarly argued that Beckett's direct work in the theatre is contingent and so should be dismissed as irrelevant to any critical evaluation. Worton too is bent on devaluing performance by dismissing Beckett's work as a director, work Worton considers more impulsive than deliberative: 'we should focus on the text itself and not seek to make our interpretations fit with what the dramatist may have said at any particular moment' (Worton 1994: 68). But the theatre notebooks from which Beckett worked were the product of the writing desk in advance of any rehearsals. They thus represent a textual rethinking. Moreover, such textual rethinking and revision brings to the fore questions about what exactly (or even approximately) is 'the text itself' or which of the multiple texts available is 'the text'. Furthermore, 'any particular moment' presumably refers to Beckett's twenty-year directing career, which Worton would simply dismiss as irrelevant to textual production and so to critical discourse. Worton finally seems more than a little confused about what constitutes 'text' in general and, in the theatre in particular, about the status of an art work that is performed, and so he takes text to mean simply material script, which, by implication, freezes and is static on first publication. Worton does, however, isolate the crux of Beckett's work in the theatre when he suggests that 'What Beckett says outside the text of his plays is undoubtedly worth considering, but when he comments on either texts or productions, he is just another critic, just as eligible for sceptical examination as any other interpreter' (1994: 68). Those interpretations, Beckett's or those of any other director, must be judged on the amount of insight they bring to the art work, and it matters little who is bringing that insight, another director or Beckett. But where Worton goes most wrong is in treating the published work as sacrosanct, immutable, finished and so static, and so ignoring the fact that Beckett continued to 'create' his theatre works on the stage.

Rarely does one find such overt critical resistance to performance as that displayed by Duckworth and Worton, where the critics seem to set themselves up as final arbiters, protectors of a sacred text, that sanctity defined by (often initial) publication. Both critical positions seem, however, to contain contradictions about the nature of performance. Performance cannot be both the ultimate achievement of dramatic art and simultaneously critically irrelevant since it is subject to compromise, collaboration and theatrical contingencies – that is, since it is a performance. Duckworth finally makes a reluctant concession in his ultimate sentence, that Beckett's revisions of his own work were 'an incomparable barometer of the evolution of the Beckettian world view over thirty years' (1987: 191). All that is missing is the admission that such evolution is the central creative process in theatre. As we continue to evaluate the relationship between the literary text and its performative realisation, and the playwright's relationship to both, the case of Samuel Beckett's acting simultaneously as theatre artist staging a play and author revising it, a unique instance of self-collaboration in the late modern (and Modernist) theatre, may force us to re-evaluate the centrality of performance to the literary field of drama. For Beckett's drama, performance would stand as the principal text. The results of that direct theatrical process, his fastidious attention to the aesthetic details of the artwork, need to enter our critical and performative equations if we are not to underestimate and so not distort Beckett's creative vision, and his own theoretical and unique contributions to the Modernist theatre.

The actual accommodation of performance (the whole show) into the critical discourse, however, is not easily achieved. As he began increasingly to work directly on stage, to use the stage as an artistic canvas, as a theatrical laboratory, to trust his direct collaborations with actors and technicians, Beckett did not, unfortunately, always immediately record those insights or revise his texts accordingly, as Duckworth rightly points out. For some productions Beckett simply never got around to making the full and complete revisions to his texts, that is, never committed his revisions to paper other than in letters to friends and colleagues, revisions which were clearly part of his developing conception of the play. Instead he was willing to let the production stand as the final text. The most obvious and stunning example is the movement piece, ballet, or mime called *Quad* in English. Beckett's final version of the work, the production for German television, broadcast on 8 October 1981, is called *Quadrat I & II*, a title that suggests two acts – if not two plays. Near the end of the taping of *Quad*, Beckett created what amounted to an unplanned second act. When he saw a replay of the original taped production on a black and white monitor, he wanted that version too and decided instantly to create a second act, *Quad II*, at slower speed and without colour. The result was the performed *Quad I & II*. Beckett's printed text (in any language) was, however, never amended to accommodate this remarkable revision. The Faber & Faber *Collected Shorter Plays* (1984) and *Complete Dramatic Works* (1986) offer only a concessionary acknowledgment: 'This original scenario (*Quad I*) was followed in the Stuttgart production by a variation (*Quad II*). (5)'--that is, four cycles of action in *Quad I*, but only one circuit of the quad, number 5 in total, constitutes *Quad II*, and it should run, presumably, for five minutes at the slow tempo, 'series 1' only, or 1 series only (Beckett 1984: 293; *CDW* 453). No printed version of the play then reflects the full text for or contains a complete description of *Quad II*, that is, no accurate text exists in print, one that includes Beckett's theatrical insights and revisions. Beckett's own videotaped German production remains his final word on that work, the only accurate text for *Quad*, I and II. For *Quad*, then, as well as for all the works that Beckett staged himself, the work on stage, the performance, 'that's the show'.

Appendix: Samuel Beckett as Director

In Paris

Va et vient (Come and Go) and Robert Pinget's *L'Hypothèse* at the Odéon Théâtre de France, 28 February 1966 (uncredited for his own work)

La dernière band (Krapp's Last Tape) at the Théâtre Récamier, 29 April 1970

La dernière band (Krapp's Last Tape) with *Pas moi (Not I)* at the Théâtre d'Orsay (Petite Salle), April 1975

Pas (Footfalls) with *Pas moi (Not I)* at the Théâtre d'Orsay, April 1978

In Berlin at the Schiller Theater (Werkstatt)

Endspiel (Endgame), 26 September 1967

Das letzte Band (Krapp's Last Tape), 5 October 1969

Glückliche Tage (Happy Days), 17 September 1971

Warten auf Godot (Waiting for Godot), 8 March 1975

Damals (That Time) and *Tritte (Footfalls)*, 1 October 1976

Spiel (Play), 6 October 1978

Krapp's Last Tape in English at the Akademie der Künste with the San Quentin Drama Workshop, rehearsals 10–27 September 1977

In London

Footfalls at the Royal Court Theatre, May 1976

Happy Days at the Royal Court Theatre, June 1979

Endgame with the San Quentin Drama Workshop at Riverside Studios, May 1980

Waiting for Godot with the San Quentin Drama Workshop; rehearsals began at the Goodman Theater in Chicago from early November 1983 to January 1984 under the direction of Walter Asmus. Beckett joined the group at the Riverside Studios, London on 2 February 1984 and rehearsed the actors for ten days. Production premiered at the Adelaide Arts Festival, 13 March 1984.

Teleplays

He Joe (Eh Joe), at Süddeutscher Rundfunk, Stuttgart, directed March 1966 (with Deryk Mendel and Nancy Illig), broadcast 13 April 1966 (first theatrical event to credit Beckett alone as director)

Geistertrio (Ghost Trio), at Süddeutscher Rundfunk, Stuttgart, directed May–June 1977 (with Klaus Herm and Irmgard Foerst), broadcast 1 November 1977

Nur noch Gewolk (... but the clouds ...), at Süddeutscher Rundfunk, Stuttgart, May–June 1977 (with Klaus Herm and Kornelia Bose), broadcast 1 November 1977

He Joe (Eh Joe), second version at Süddeutscher Rundfunk, Stuttgart, directed January 1979 (with Heinz Bennent and Irmgard Först), broadcast September 1979

Quadrat I & II, at Süddeutscher Rundfunk, Stuttgart, directed June 1981 (with Helfrid Foron, Juerg Hummel, Claudia Knupfer and Suzanne Rehe), broadcast 8 October 1981

Nacht und Traüme at Süddeutscher Rundfunk, Stuttgart, directed October 1982, broadcast 19 May 1983

Was Wo (What Where) at Süddeutscher Rundfunk, Stuttgart, directed June 1985, broadcast 13 April 1986

Notes

1. For further elaboration on this point see Chapter 2.
2. *Company*'s interlocutory nature has encouraged several dramatic readings and theatrical adaptations, beginning with Patrick Magee's reading on BBC Radio 3 in July 1980, and John Russell Brown's version for the National Theatre, London, in September that year, featuring Stephen Moore. Another London version was staged by Tim Piggot-Smith and produced by Katherine Worth, with Julian Curry (1987); it was seen at the Edinburgh Festival and in New York (1988). There had been two earlier American stagings. In 1983 Frederick Neumann directed the play for Mabou Mines, with Honora Ferguson; and in 1985 my production at the Los Angeles Actors' Theater with Alan Mandell was the English premiere of Pierre Chabert's adaptation, which had opened 15 November 1984 at the Théâtre du Rond-Point in Paris, a version with which Beckett had been closely associated. For further details on my staging of *Company* see Chapter 11.

3. Surprisingly, this letter to Judith Schmidt on the significance of performance, dated 5 May 1959, is not published or referenced in *The Letters of Samuel Beckett*, volume 3, although a long letter to Barney Rosset of the same date is included. The Schmidt letter is cited here from the letters to Barney Rosset and the Grove Press staff, part of the Barney Rosset/Grove Press archives now at the George Arents Research Library at Syracuse University and the John J. Burns Library, Boston College. All material is used with the permission of the principals.

4. These performance texts are available, however, in the *Theatrical Notebooks of Samuel Beckett*, four volumes of which were published jointly under the General Editorship of James Knowlson by Faber & Faber in the UK and Grove Press in the US: Volume 1, *Waiting for Godot*, ed. Dougald McMillan and James Knowlson (1994); Volume 2, *Endgame*, ed. S.E. Gontarski (1992); Volume 3, *Krapp's Last Tape*, ed. James Knowlson (1993); and Volume 4, *The Shorter Plays*, ed. S. E. Gontarski (1999). A prototype volume, *'Happy Days': Samuel Beckett's Production Notebooks*, ed. James Knowlson, was also published by Faber & Faber and Grove Press in 1985 in a different format that was never brought into conformity with the subsequent four volumes.

5. See, for example, Gontarski 1992 for further discussion of this issue.

References

Atik, Anne (2001) *How It Was: A Memoir of Samuel Beckett*, London: Faber & Faber.

Beckett, Samuel (1970) *More Pricks than Kicks*, New York: Grove Press.

Beckett, Samuel (1974) *Mercier and Camier*, New York: Grove Press.

Beckett, Samuel (1984) *Collected Shorter Plays*, London: Faber & Faber.

Beckett, Samuel (1995) *Eleutheria,* trans. Michael Brodsky, New York: Foxrock Books.

Beckett, Samuel (2014) *Echo's Bones*, ed. Mark Nixon, New York: Grove Press.

Cohn, Ruby (2001) *A Beckett Canon*, Ann Arbor: University of Michigan Press.

Duckworth, Colin (1987) 'Beckett's New *Godot*', in James Acheson and Kateryna Arthur, eds, *Beckett's Later Fiction and Drama*, London: Macmillan, pp. 175–92.

Gontarski, S. E. (1992) 'Beckett Directs Beckett: *Endgame*', *Journal of Beckett Studies* 2.2, pp. 115–18.

Gontarski, S. E. (2015) *Creative Involution: Bergson, Beckett, Deleuze*, Edinburgh: Edinburgh University Press.

Harmon, Maurice, ed. (1998) '*No Author Better Served': The Correspondence of Samuel Beckett and Alan Schneider*, Cambridge, MA: Harvard University Press.

Harvey, Lawrence (1970) *Samuel Beckett, Poet and Critic*, Princeton: Princeton University Press.

Knowlson, James (1996) *Damned to Fame: The Life of Samuel Beckett*, London: Bloomsbury.

Pilling, John, ed. (1999) *Beckett's 'Dream' Notebook*, Reading: Beckett International Foundation.

Reid, Alec (1986) 'Impact and Parable in Beckett: A First Encounter with *Not I*', *Hermathena: A Trinity College Review*, ed. Terence Brown and Nicholas Grene, CXLI, pp. 12–21.

Worton, Michael (1994) '*Waiting for Godot* and *Endgame*: Theater as Text', in John Pilling, ed., *The Cambridge Companion to Beckett*, Cambridge: Cambridge University Press, pp. 67–87.

10

Reinventing Beckett

'I don't know whether the theatre is the right place for me anymore.' (Beckett)

... the bourgeoisie will recuperate [the avant-garde] altogether, ultimately putting on splendid evenings of Beckett and Audiberti (and tomorrow Ionesco, already acclaimed by humanist criticism). (Roland Barthes, 'Whose Theater? Whose Avant-Garde?')

Samuel Beckett's creative life (and personal life, for that matter) was marked by a series of transformations and reinventions. In the process of re-making himself, over and again, from donnish academic to avant-garde poet, from Joycean acolyte to post-Joycean minimalist, from humanist to post-humanist, perhaps, most certainly from poet to novelist to playwright, to theatre director, Beckett was simultaneously reinventing every literary genre he turned his attention to. In the midst of remaking narrative in the wake of the Second World War, for example, he began simultaneously the reinvention of theatre, writing the ground-breaking (but still unproduced) *Eleutheria* between *Molloy* and *Malone meurt*, and *En attendant Godot* between *Malone meurt* and *L'Innommable*. Almost as soon as he began to experience some recognition, most notably in the theatre, however, he began to recoil from it as well, as if it represented a threat, the desired attention he had struggled so hard to achieve barbed with threats to his art (and even perhaps to his self-image). Enthusiastic about his anti-boulevard play, *Eleutheria*, and eager for its publication and performance, for example, he would finally repudiate it, withdrawing it from publication after the staging of *Godot*, finding it in later years impossible either to revise or to translate even for his long-time publisher, Barney Rosset, refusing again to have it published,[1] at least in his lifetime, and finally, if fundamentally by proxy, prohibiting any staging, apparently in perpetuity. It was, however, a play central to Beckett's theatrical reinvention as it, almost literally, swept the stage clear of both boulevard and naturalistic debris and so bared the stage for what would become, in English, *Waiting for Godot*. British critic and staunch Beckett advocate Harold Hobson may have privileged Beckett's second full-length play in the following description, but his comments are equally apposite to *Eleutheria*, the restriction to 'the English theatre' excepted. *Godot*, he noted,

> knocked the shackles of plot from off the English drama. It destroyed the notion that the dramatist is God, knowing everything about his characters and master of a complete philosophy answerable to all of our problems. It showed that Archer's dictum that a good play imitates the audible and visible surface of life is not necessarily true. It revealed that the drama approximates or can approximate the condition of music, touching chords deeper than can be reached by reason and saying things beyond the grasp of logic. It renewed the English theatre in a single night.

Joyce may have celebrated 'Ibsen's New Drama', noting that 'the long roll of drama, ancient or modern, has few things better to show' (Joyce 2000: 49), and Shaw accepted the role of heir in 'The Quintessence of Ibsenism', but for Beckett no such lineage; Ibsen's new theatre smacked of didacticism and 'explicitation' from which Beckett recoiled: 'All I know is in the text.' He wrote to his American director, Alan Schneider, on 16 October 1972 in relation to the staging of *Not I*, '"She" [Mouth in this case] is purely a stage entity, part of a stage image and purveyor of stage text. The rest is Ibsen' (Harmon 1998: 283).

Godot would not, of course, be Beckett's sole or final theatrical reinvention. At the dawn of a new century, it has become the most 'recuperated' of Beckett's plays, high-profile performances often celebrated by waves of bourgeois nostalgia. By 1963, however, a decade after the French premier of *Godot*, Beckett would repudiate the character-based drama on which he had, thus far, made his theatrical reputation, and focus instead on shaping and reshaping, as author and stage director, an iconic theatre of sculpted images. The composition and performance history of *Play* beginning in

1963 not only altered stage space, blurring distinctions between then and now, between exterior and interior, between story and image, it triggered an increase in Beckett's direct involvement in stagecraft as well, since it demanded a level of technical sophistication and precision unknown in his earlier work, and the demands of staging *Play* finally forced a reluctant and private Samuel Beckett to assume full, public, directorial responsibility for his own works. With *Play*, then, Beckett reinvented the theatre again, moving it yet further from Ibsen, if not more broadly from humanism itself, as his art moved beyond, even denied, character and plot, mainstays of traditional theatre, and shifted the theatrical (and theoretical) ground from corporeality to the incorporeality of what we call (perhaps too glibly) Beckett's late theatre, a shift from the body, say, to voice, from materiality to consciousness, from matter to memory, to echo Henri Bergson, often detached from ground, that is, memory untethered and with no discernible or recognisable receptacle or reservoir. After 1963 Beckett's became a theatre of immateriality, of ghosts, his work itself the ghost or afterimage of not only the commercial theatre, but of his own earlier work. It became more overtly a theatre of images and the enigmas of their perception. His theatre would become, in many respects, a recuperation of the Bergson he had lectured on in his short, conflicted career as a university don. Moreover, as a man of the theatre, he began not only directing much of his new work, but also revising, and thereby reinventing, his previous *oeuvre*, his own canon, even those works firmly established within the theatrical repertory.

Beckett's transformation from playwright to theatrical artist was thus a seminal development, a final blow perhaps to early modernist or Ibsenist theatre, a shift beyond textuality since most of the late works are unreadable, and yet it is slighted in the critical and historical discourse that continues to privilege print over performance, the apparent stability of text over the vicissitudes of theatre. Such neglect of the impact of Beckett's direct staging of his plays distorts the arc of his creative evolution or creative involution (to coin a phrase) as it undervalues his emergence as an artist committed to the performance of his drama as its creation and continual re-creation. Beckett would finally embrace theatre not just as a medium through which a preconception was given its accurate completion but as *the* process through which the work of art was realised, was created anew. As Beckett evolved from being a playwright offering advice to directors and actors, to functioning as a shadow director, to taking full charge of staging his plays, practical theatre offered him the opportunity for self-collaboration through which he might continually reinvent himself as an artist as he found the means to subvert his own texts. Denial of the evolutionary or involutionary vitality of performance continues to mark much of Beckett criticism today, and avoidance of Beckett's direct theatrical creations delimits a dynamic process of becoming (or creation) at an arbitrary point, publication. Such emphasis on stability, arbitrary as it might be, has become the core ideology of the protectors of Beckett's reputation into the after Beckett. The Beckett Estate, the legal extension of the author, remains committed to the decidedly untheatrical ideology of invariant texts in the face of overwhelming evidence to the contrary. The Estate seems determined to stop the process of self-subversion that is the hallmark of vanguard art, blunting its political edge, and domesticating Samuel Beckett and his work into bourgeois acceptability. Theirs is an argument for an homogeneous Beckett. Such recuperation of the revolutionary has, of course, become the hallmark of late capitalism as patronage of even our most radical art has come from the bourgeoisie, from investors, from global capitalism, from what is called neo-liberalism, and the Beckett Estate is following suit if only by insisting on the completeness of its property rights. What most grates, perhaps, is the exercise of those rights under the banner of aesthetic purity and authorial protection designed to save Beckett from his own self-subversions.

Embracing the Performative

Reluctant as he may have been at the onset, Beckett embraced the volatility of performance as *the* theatrical art. The transition was gradual, growing from his involvement in staging *En attendant Godot* from 1950 to its opening in January of 1953, and then through his apprenticeship at the Royal Court Theatre during the George Devine years. Jean Martin, who was the first Lucky, recalls Beckett's being passive at rehearsals in the closing weeks of 1952: 'I rehearsed for only about three weeks in all. Sam said practically nothing while we were putting it on. You see he was extremely shy and very, very discreet. [. . .] He relied entirely on Roger Blin [his French director, who also played the role of Pozzo]. But he came to rehearsals every day. And Suzanne came very often too. But they didn't offer any advice' (Knowlson and Knowlson 2006:

117). Beckett's letters to Roger Blin belie Martin's observations, however. As early as 19 December 1950, Beckett wrote to Blin, 'I have an idea for the set. We ought ['Il foudrait', must?] to meet. Could you call in at our place one day this week? [. . .] Or else suggest a time and place for us to meet outside, if that suits you better' (*Letters 2* 209). In spirit, though, Martin's observation represents Beckett's public posture, his advice almost always rendered privately. What diffidence or reluctance existed began to assuage with the staging of Beckett's next play, *Fin de partie (Endgame)* in both French and English at the Royal Court Theatre in 1957, but the year of near total transformation from author to director committed to performance was 1966. Beckett was preparing (with Marin Karmitz and Jean Ravel) a film version of Jean-Marie Serreau's June 1964 Paris staging of *Comédie (Play)*. He rushed off to London to oversee the taping of *Eh Joe*, with Jack MacGowran and Siân Phillips, his first teleplay (nominally directed by Alan Gibson and broadcast on BBC 2 on 4 July 1966). He supervised two vinyl recordings for Claddagh records: *MacGowran Speaking Beckett* and *MacGowran Reading Beckett's Poetry*, the former accompanied by music, Schubert's Quartet in D minor, Beckett himself playing gong in a family trio that included John and nephew Edward. He then rushed back to Paris to oversee Jean-Marie Serreau's series of one-acts at the Odéon, Théâtre de France, including a reprise of *Comédie*, *Va et vient*, and his own staging of Robert Pinget's *L'Hypothèse* with actor Pierre Chabert. Beckett wound up taking over full responsibility for staging this theatrical evening at the Odéon, but without programme credit. The first of his works for which Beckett received full directorial billing was the 1966 Stuttgart telecast of *He Joe*, broadcast by SDR on Beckett's sixtieth birthday, 13 April 1966.

By 1967, after almost a full year of non-stop theatre, Beckett would lament to his American publisher 'Forget what writing is about',[2] but he went on to accept an invitation from the Schiller Theater to direct a play. He chose *Endspiel*. The monumental decision would commence a systematic reinvention of nearly all of his theatre works over the next two decades. He prepared a *Regiebuch*, a director's notebook, for each production, and those notebooks, with their meticulous outlines of the play's actions and internal parallels, would characterise his approach to directing. In February of 1969 Theodor Adorno wrote to relay an offer for Beckett to direct *Waiting for Godot* in Hamburg. In his reply to Adorno on 15 February 1969, Beckett politely declined, citing the amount of work it would take: 'it is a very big job and health is not grand'. But he noted as well, 'I have promised to do *Das letzte Band* [*Krapp's Last Tape*] with Martin Held at the Schiller (Werkstatt) this summer.'[3]

As crucial as Beckett's re-intervention into his published texts is the almost simultaneous development of his radical imagistic aesthetics that would come to dominate his theatrical work. That minimal imagism may be most evident, of course, in the thirty-five-second playlet called *Breath*. When Ruby Cohn asked Beckett in the summer of 1968 whether or not he had a *new play* in the offing, 'He answered, almost angrily, "New? What could be new? Man is born – vagitus." Then he breathes for a few seconds, before the death rattle intervenes.' He then wrote out the entire play called *Breath* for Cohn on the paper table cover of a café (Knowlson and Knowlson 2006: 129). That spirit of abstraction and contraction, captured most succinctly and fully in the image of and for *Breath*, would inform the whole of his directing career.

Beckett's directorial changes, then, represented – and still do for that matter – his 'latest word' on his plays, yet that latest word has, more often than not, been ignored – by theatre directors, scholars, and most important, by his guardians and heirs. Theatre directors and some scholars have themselves often been suspicious of the implications of Beckett's own productions, fearing that Beckett's 'latest word' might freeze text and performance possibilities. The pressing issue for these scholars and theatre practitioners quickly became what relationship existed between Beckett's creative interventions, his self-subversions in his own meticulously directed works, and future performances. Are Beckett's productions now the standard, from which no deviation should obtain? This is roughly the position of the Estate that sanctions, in both senses of that self-contradictory term, performances. Oddly, the Estate also rejects the texts that are the products of that final intervention. That is, they too have rejected the revised texts, arguing that they are localised variations on an invariant text as originally published (with minor subsequent corrections). The revised texts are thus merely versions of a published original, but all texts, reaching back to the earliest drafts, are merely versions – and each was deemed a stage that the author considered final, until the next intervention, the next version. The revised texts are then that next version. Whether or not the creative process comes to a halt at publication is a much contested point, especially in theatre and theory, but even the most conservative of Beckett scholars do not accept a doctrine of textual invariance. But that essentially is the position of the Beckett Estate, and it has caused something of a crisis in the theatrical community. More than a few directors have refused to work with Beckett's material (Herbert Blau and Lee Breuer, chief among them), while others have been prohibited, at least temporarily, from doing so (Deborah Warner and JoAnne Akalaitis, among them). Admittedly, some of the tension between Beckett's theatre and the international community of directors was established and aggravated during Beckett's lifetime. Beckett was less than happy with André Gregory's 1973 *Endgame*, for which the audience was seated within wire-meshed chicken coops.[4] In Robert Brustein's review of the Beckett/Schneider letters in the *New York Times* (31 January 1999), he identified Beckett's American director, Alan Schneider, as a self-interested conspirator, quoting Schneider's condemnation of his competitor, Gregory: 'the André Gregory troupe [. . .] was "inclined to use text for own purposes"' (Harmon 1998: 253), and his later reporting, in a long letter, on how 'the production takes such liberties with your text [. . .] and with your directions', calling it a 'self-indulgent travesty, determined to be "different" for the sake of being different' (Harmon 1998: 301). Beckett intervened to stop a European tour of Gregory's production on Schneider's advice and request. But it was JoAnne Akalaitis's staging of *Endgame* at the American Repertory Theater in December of 1984 that prompted Beckett to intervene fully and forcefully to try to halt the performance. Hours before the opening lawyers were still negotiating the textual alterations. Akalaitis's crimes were that she had set her production in a subway station with an abandoned subway car as backdrop, adding music by her ex-husband, Philip Glass. (We might recall, *en passant*, that Peter Hall's 1955 London premiere of *Waiting for Godot* used a fragment of Béla Bartók to set the mood, to which Beckett objected.) Beckett was convinced, with much goading from Schneider, that the production was an unacceptable alteration of the text, particularly the stage directions, which for Beckett, as we know, are not ancillary but integral to and inseparable from the text. He further objected to the increasingly common American theatrical practice of colour-blind casting, black actors here in two of the roles. A final compromise allowed the production to open but with Beckett's disclaimer printed in the playbill: 'A complete parody of the play. Anybody who cares for the work couldn't fail to be disgusted.'

In addition to Akalaitis's 1984 *Endgame*, high-profile conflicts surrounded De Haarlemse Toneelschuur's all-female *Waiting for Godot* in 1988. Through the Société des Auteurs et Compositeurs Français, Beckett took legal action to prevent the Dutch company from staging its all-female production. Gildas Bourdet's 'pink' *Fin de partie* for the venerable Comédie Française, also in 1988, met overwhelming resistance as well. Beckett and his French publisher, Jérôme Lindon, forced the Comédie Française to withdraw certain alterations of, and additions to, the prescribed setting and costumes from the production, leading to Bourdet's decision to remove his name from the credits. The performance went on but with the pink set draped in black. The Beckett Estate, then controlled by the French publisher, saw as its duty such continued monitoring and enforcement. Susan Sontag's radical *Godot* in war-torn Sarajevo in 1993 erred by the introduction of multiple cast members,[5] but Sarajevo was evidently beyond the reach of western European law; Deborah Warner did not fare as well in her 1994 London production of *Footfalls* at the Garrick Theatre, which was denied permission to tour Europe after being viewed by Edward Beckett. But Katie Mitchell's 'peripatetic' evening called (provocatively perhaps) *Beckett's Shorts*, for the Royal Shakespeare Company in 1996, where several productions were shown simultaneously, was ignored by the Estate's lawyers. Unsurprisingly, Akalaitis and Warner have had difficulties returning to Beckett's work since their 1984 *Endgame* and 1994 *Footfalls*, respectively. Akalaitis noted in 2002, 'I don't think I'd be allowed the rights.'[6] But she was, as was Debra Warner; both did return, and triumphantly at that, both in 2007, Warner with *Happy Days*, again featuring Fiona Shaw,[7] and Akalaitis with 'Beckett Shorts' at the New York Theatre Workshop with Mikhail Baryshnikov.[8]

Some theatre artists with close connections to Beckett received the dispensation of benign neglect, however. The itinerant Hungarian theatrical director George Tabori, for one, who studied in Germany until 1933 before emigrating to England where he was a journalist for the BBC. He then worked with Brecht in America, returning to Germany after the Second World War. Fascinated by Beckett's work, Tabori directed many of the plays, situating himself within the debate between directorial originality and fidelity to Beckett's vision. His search for a subtext to Beckett theatre assumed radical forms in a series of productions of what he called 'dangerous theatre' in the 1980s. 'Beckett Evening I' in 1980 took place in the Atlas-Circus in Munich, with circus artists and animals denoting the state of being captured and tamed, whips and whistles suggesting the Holocaust. The actors were to take Beckett's work literally, find their personal subtext, and pursue the concrete experience behind the image. His production of *Breath* was simply recited, stage directions and all; *Not I* presented a young actress tied to a wooden wall with knives fixed all around her by a knife-thrower. The Auditor was an elephant on which the woman, set free by the elocutionary act, rode triumphantly from the arena. *Play* was performed by three actors walking about restlessly, *seeking* the limelight to tell their part of the story.

Beckett's reaction to Tabori's excesses was restrained. When Tabori staged *Le Dépeupleur* Beckett wished him 'the best of agonies', but did not restrict a bizarre interpretation that combined Auschwitz with being improperly born, naked bodies, black plastic pipes, a carp in a large aquarium, and the subtext of the human condition in a scorched landscape bereft of love. Tabori's 1984 *Waiting for Godot* was much acclaimed, but it horrified Beckett. The characters were refugees, intellectuals, foregrounding Beckett's activities in the Resistance during the war. The play was set in the round with production crew on stage to suggest the evolution of an imaginary rehearsal, with scenes of hatred and compassion, despair and tenderness, played out as interludes in the ritual of waiting. His *Happy Days* of 1986 was even more *outré*, with Winnie's mound replaced by a bed, Beckett's 'woman about fifty' acted by the attractive, young Ursula Höpfner, in plunging *décolletage*. The subtext was to imbue the metaphysical with concrete human experience, that of a tense human relationship; but casting the physically handicapped Peter Radtke as Willie, in a performance incorporating Karl Böhm's rehearsal comments about *Tristan und Iseult*, and groans and whistles of whales to accompany Willie's agonised craving for Winnie, was a curious mix (Feinberg-Jütte 1992: 95–115). Through it all Tabori's hope was to liberate Beckett's texts from dogmatic models, a hope shared by many subsequent directors, Gildas Bourdet, JoAnne Akalaitis and Deborah Warner among them.

Beckett himself thus often assumed a moderate, flexible approach during his lifetime, modulating such antinomies of production. He was far from consistent in this respect, of course. For all that he believed in authorial control, in practice, when it came to 'alternative' productions, 'it made a tremendous difference if he liked and respected the persons involved', as biographer James Knowlson notes (1996: 608). On the issue of gender change, however, he remained steadfast. Writing to his American publisher and theatrical agent, Barney Rosset, on 11 July 1973, he noted: 'I am against women playing *Godot* and wrote Miss [Estelle] Parsons to that effect. Theatre sex is not interchangeable and *Godot* by women would sound as spurious as *Happy Days* or *Not I* played by men. It was performed once in Israel, without our authorization, by an all-female cast, with disastrous effect.' But in February of 2006, amid celebrations of the Beckett centenary, the headline in the *Guardian* read: 'Beckett estate fails to stop women waiting for Godot':[9]

> before his death in 1989, the Nobel Literature prizewinner had objected to previous attempts to use women in the production. They also cited a ruling in Paris in 1992, when a director was refused permission to use female leads after a judge said it was 'violation of Beckett's moral rights'.
>
> The Pontedera theatre counter-claimed, saying that although sisters Luisa and Silvia Pasello were playing the parts, the characters remained totally male. There had been no attempt to alter Beckett's work, they said.

Even with the Pontedera victory for human rights, however, the position that Beckett himself had taken with regard to Akalaitis's 1984 ART *Endgame* is the one still currently holding sway internationally. Simply stated, it is the author who would be the sole authority on and arbiter of the theatrical works, a position accepted and extended by his Estate and buttressed by international law. In other words, the process of reinvention that had been the hallmark of Beckett's creative life has apparently come to an end, Beckett's theatre rapidly becoming part of the quid pro quo of bourgeois commerce, a system he struggled so hard to unmask. One consequence of such re-positioning is that the climate in which scholars and theatre practitioners investigate the complexities of Beckett's theatrical *oeuvre* and his theatrical career has been chilled. The inevitable question that arises in the early years of the twenty-first century, sixty-plus years after the premier of *En attendant Godot*, in the twenty-eighth year of the after Beckett, is whether Beckett is thus rapidly becoming theatrically irrelevant. Put another way, will the year of celebrations of Samuel Beckett's work in the centenary year of 2006, including innumerable productions, presumably all authorised, be its headstone as well. Put yet another way, is there a future for Beckettian performance? Can it be re-invented again, and if so what might such reinventions look like given the restrictions on performance imposed by the legal heirs to the work, heirs who function with all the *droits de l'author*, but none of his flexibility. Must the avant-garde accept its own impotence, as Roland Barthes asked, or worse bring about its own death? (Barthes 1972: 69). In addition to their most publicised interventions into performance, the Executors have all but kept from the public the principal work of the final two decades of Beckett's creative life, his continuation of the creative process, his full revisions of his dramatic texts. These revisions are, of course, available in a limited capacity, in the very expensive editions of *The Theatrical Notebooks of Samuel Beckett*, which Beckett himself not only authorised but financed as well, but their expense restricts their availability. Even libraries resist such expenditure under current budgets. The Estate has refused permission to publish the revised or acting texts separately or to re-issue the *Notebooks* in affordable, paperback editions.

Admittedly, part of the rationale for the Estate's position is the difficulty of determining authorial intent off the page. Which of the revisions in Beckett's productions are meant for the local contingencies of particular actors or a particular stage? As Beckett wrote to Polish director Marek Kędzierski on 15 November 1981, 'Herewith corrected copy of *Fin de partie*. The cuts and simplifications are the result of my work on the play as director and function of the players at my disposal. To another director they may not seem desirable' (copy of the letter sent by the recipient to the author). What Beckett sent Kędzierski, however, is simply not readily available to other directors, except in the *Theatrical Notebooks*.[10] Moreover, Beckett did not direct and revise each of his plays, and so not every text has been systematically reinvented. That is, Beckett's work on productions did not always result in permanent changes to a printed text. Occasionally, local revisions were made by Beckett to respond to the process of collaboration and to the nature of a particular theatrical space, or changes were contemplated and even used in production but were never formally incorporated into any text or production. In his notebook for

Damals, the German translation of *That Time*, which he directed along with *Tritte* (*Footfalls*) at the Schiller Theater in 1976, for instance, Beckett offered an alternate staging of the play, one that might increase its verisimilitude. If Listener's hand were to be *seen* at full light, it should be clutching a sheet around his neck. The tension of that grip should then increase during the silences. That detail added to the play's limited frame suggests that *That Time* is something of an experiment in perspective. We perceive the Figure as if we were watching him from above as he lay in a bed.

In addition, for his television production of *What Where* Beckett revised the German text extensively, but he never fully revised the stage directions of the original English text. This was due in part to the fact that Beckett continued to work on the visual imagery of the play all through rehearsals. By this stage of his directing career he had developed more confidence in or grown more trusting of the creative collaborations that theatre entails, and he was creating his theatre work in rehearsals, directly on stage (or in this case on the set), although he made a pre-production notebook for the performance as well. As his technical assistant, Jim Lewis, recalls:

> If you want to compare this production [of *Was Wo*] with the others for television, there's one major difference. And that is his concept was not set. He changed and changed and changed [. . .] I've never experienced that with him before. You know how concrete he is, how precise he is. Other times we could usually follow through on that with minor, minor changes; but this time there were several basic changes and he still wasn't sure. Many things, different things. (Quoted in Fehsenfeld 1986: 236)

Lewis's observation suggests the single most salient element in Beckett's evolution into a theatre artist: his commitment to the idea of performance and his acceptance of a variety of possible outcomes. In practical and literary terms such a commitment meant that nothing like a final text of his work could be established before he worked with it directly on stage, and not even then. Writing to Alan Schneider in response to his American director's queries about staging *Play*, Beckett expressed what had become obvious to him: 'I realize that no final script is possible until I work on rehearsals.'[11] Almost simultaneously, after Beckett has just seen a rough cut of *Film* in 1964, he argued quite clearly against a slavish fidelity to the script. Beckett wrote to Schneider on 29 September 1964, shortly after viewing *Film*:

> generally speaking, from having been troubled by a certain failure to communicate fully by purely visual means the basic intention [as outlined in the script, presumably], I now begin to feel that this is unimportant and that the images obtained probably gain in force what they lose as ideograms [or referentially, we might add] [. . .] It does I suppose in a sense fail with reference to a purely intellectual schema [. . .] but in so doing has acquired a dimension and a validity of its own that are worth far more than any merely efficient translation of intention. (Harmon 1998: 166)

The ultimate sentence above suggests if not a theory of theatre in general, certainly a commitment to the vicissitudes and validity of performance. Moreover, textual variants among the published texts testify to the fact that Beckett's plays do not exist in a uniform, static state. Legally, a director can follow any of these various published texts and still conflict with Beckett's recorded intentions. Most English editions of *Krapp's Last Tape*, for instance, still depict Krapp with a clown's nose and wearing white boots, and the play is often performed thus. Arguments about staging a *Godot* respectful of Beckett's wishes are frequently based on the assumption that a single authoritative script exists. In the general editor's preface to the *Theatrical Notebooks*, James Knowlson has noted that 'whole sections of [Beckett's texts] have *never* been played as printed in the original editions' (vii). And I myself have noted in the *Endgame* volume of the *Theatrical Notebooks*, 'critics and directors [are] forced into a position of building interpretations and mounting productions of Samuel Beckett's work not so much on corrupt texts such as almost all English versions of *Waiting for Godot*, but on those the author himself found unsatisfactory, unfinished' (Beckett 1993: xxv). The response of the Estate has its own compelling logic. Edward Beckett has argued that 'There are more than fifteen recordings of Beethoven's late string quartets in the catalogue, every interpretation different, one from the next, but they are all based on the same notes, tonalities, dynamic and tempo markings. We feel justified in asking the same measure of respect for Samuel Beckett's plays.'[12] He suggests that since musicians, however freely they may 'interpret' a piece of music, do not deviate from the composer's notes, why should a director depart from Beckett's dialogue or directions? The analogy is intriguing. What we know of a score is that it is not music, as a play script is not theatre. Both printed versions are approximations. But, of course, Edward's analogy is imperfect in other respects. Theatre, as Beckett spent much of his career demonstrating, is as much a visual as an aural art form, at least as much gesture and plastic imagery as poetry. Theatre is not a music CD. The more apposite analogy may be with opera, and there the analogy breaks down. Most operas have been staged in a myriad of what strict interpretationists might consider outlandish versions, and the music has survived, as would Beckett's unique music. But the Estate has been adamant and so Beckettian performance in the twenty-first century may be approaching a creative impasse, although the number of performances shows no sign of letting up.

Kenneth Tynan's *Breath*

The power of tragedy, we may be sure, is felt even apart from representation and actors. (Aristotle, *The Poetics*)

Perhaps the most egregious violation of Beckettian law – the sort of thing that Beckett's works apparently need protection from into the after Beckett, according to those in the business of such protection – occurred during Beckett's lifetime. The result was both a travesty of Samuel Beckett's intention and, ironically, Beckett's most successful, or at least most popular, theatre piece. *Breath* has been problematic since its conception. In fact Beckett seems to have had reservations about its being performed at all. Rosset's assistant, Judith Schmidt, wrote to Beckett on 27 August 1970, a full year after *Breath* had been playing as part of *Oh! Calcutta!*: 'Do you want *Breath* to be performed [that is, at all]? If so, I'll release rights when I receive inquiries such as attached.' Beckett's affirmation was written on Schmidt's inquiry, a simple, 'Yes. S.B.'

For many a director the problem of mounting Beckett's shortest play, but not slightest I will insist, has been less how to stage so short a piece (the options for a characterless, thirty-five-second playlet are really quite limited) than in what context it might be offered. Although Beckett called it a 'farce in five acts', it is something less than an evening's theatre. The play is simplicity itself, an anonymous life cycle reduced to its fundamental sounds – birth cry and death groan, which, according to what text there is, sound identical. A debris-littered stage with 'No verticals', a brief cry and inspiration as lights fade up for ten seconds; a hold for five more; then expiration, 'immediately cry as before', and slow fade down of light. The recorded voices and lighting fades, up and down, are identical and have the simple symmetry of Pozzo's poignant observation: 'They give birth astride of a grave, the light gleams an instant, then it's night once more' (CDW 83). There seems very little a director can do to muck it up. Its most memorable performance was its first,[13] as the opener, called 'Prelude', to the Jacques Levy directed and Kenneth Tynan conceived sextravaganza, Oh! Calcutta!, the dominant image and title derived from the painting by Camille Clovis Trouille, called on occasion the master of middle-brow or the priest of bad taste. His posterior odalisque includes a pun on the French 'O quel cul tu as', said 'cul' prominently displayed.[14] As an opener to an evening of shorts, by Beckett or a variety of artists, as was the case with the Tynan-Levy production and as it is most frequently performed, the play is inevitably lost. Tynan drew attention to the playlet by adding three words to the opening tableau. Beckett wrote, 'Faint light on stage littered with miscellaneous rubbish', to which Tynan added, 'including naked people'. Leading off with Beckett, Oh! Calcutta! premièred at the Eden Theater in New York City on 17 June 1969. After a cautious opening with thirty-nine previews, it opened, moving to the Belasco Theater on Broadway on 26 February 1971 where it ran, and ran, and ran, with only slight interruption, until 6 August 1989. Finally, 85 million people saw 1,314 performances, making it, uncontestedly, the most viewed Beckett play ever, a record unlikely to be broken. Top ticket prices were an astounding $25.00, 'unprecedented even on Broadway', according to Bruce Williamson, who introduced the work for a 'Pictorial essay' in Playboy, billed as 'A Front-Row-Center Look at Oh! Calcutta!' (October 1969, pp. 166–71). Calcutta!, known by some wags (so to speak) as Jingle Balls, 'Is the only show in town that has customers piling into front row-center seats armed, by God, with opera glasses', according to Williamson. But Tynan was called a literary pimp, and his stable of authors, Beckett included, 'a pack of whores'.

As the Playboy feature suggests, the musical spawned something of an industry reflecting the era's sexual revolution and its commodification of sex. A book version of the play was issued by Beckett's American publisher, Barney Rosset of Grove Press, who published the play *as performed* in an illustrated edition in 1969, attributing to Beckett alone the playlet – with Tynan's erotic alterations. While only the earliest playbills identified authors,[15] Rosset's volume listed them under a traditional Table of Contents. The musical was subsequently issued in an LP, was made into a Hollywood film, and is still currently available in CD, VHS, and DVD formats. The enterprise may have been Beckett's sole entry into the Age of Aquarius, and certainly his only appearance in *Playboy*. Despite such phenomenal success and unprecedented exposure, drama reduced to its bare necessities, one might say, most respectable critics have generally joined Beckett in the condemnation of at least his contribution to the production. John Calder has argued that 'the American edition of *Oh! Calcutta!* has completely changed the atmosphere of sterility and indeed the message itself by changing the stage directions [. . .]' (Calder 1969: 6). Grove responded by restoring Beckett's text as written, and the editor, Marilyn Meeker, wrote to Beckett on 16 June 1970, 'Under separate cover I'm sending two copies from the second printing of *Oh! Calcutta!* which has your corrected text.' What Meeker actually sent Beckett is difficult to determine since we have no record of Beckett's reply – perhaps a second printing hard copy – but the Grove paperbacks even through the fourth printing still contain the Tynan emendations, 'including naked people'. Such publication blunders, errors and inconsistencies have historically been part of Beckett's textual history, especially with his English language publishers (see more on this issue in Chapters 6, 7 and 8).

One might argue, finally, that 'the atmosphere of sterility' Calder refers to remains amid the detritus, but Tynan's revision does raise an additional issue, as it makes explicit the possibility of regeneration amid the brief seconds between life and death, a possibility already implicit in Beckett's text if the opening 'vagitus' is identical to the closing 'cry as before', hence possibly as much 'vagitus' as death thrall. Moreover, Beckett's characterless drama was never completely so, as the stage is always inhabited by at least ghosts of the past, of plays and actors, images of which and of whom decorate the walls and so at very least actors, playwrights and plays persist in at least afterimages of performances, even in their absence. When actors are not present, memory and ambient images provide their ghostly presences, in *Breath* no less than in *Godot* or *Hamlet*. Tynan's production merely re-projects, re-directs those implicit images onto the heap of staged rubbish.

Breath's association with the infamous *Oh! Calcutta!* has, however, been ignored in early publications, particularly in Grove Press's catchall volume, *First Love and Other Shorts*, published in 1974. The production was finally acknowledged in the *Collected Shorter Plays* of 1984 and the *Complete Dramatic Works* of 1986. Like Calder, Beckett was appalled by Tynan's alterations, but his contract forbade immediate interference, and so the play continued as re-written – at least in the United States. Beckett successfully suppressed his contribution in British and subsequent productions. But Tynan's production uncovers a haunting subtext and as such it is a production worthy of re-examination, especially if we accept the necessity of periodic reinvention of Beckett's *oeuvre* that Beckett himself seems to have embraced.

Gontarski's *Breath,* or After Tynan

It was the clamour over Tynan's excesses that kept me thinking about how a director might solve the problems of staging *Breath*. My solution was not to 'stage' it at all; that is, not to perform it in a theatrical space, but I also wanted a performance closer to Beckett's rather than Tynan's *Breath*, and to present it as an independent entity not as part of an evening's theatrical sequence. Moreover, I wanted to foreground what I still consider the play's avant-garde potential, its power to subvert or defy conventions and expectations, to foreground the play of memory, and to shock an audience into thinking, at very least, about performance itself. That was what Deborah Warner wanted with her *Footfalls* that so invoked the ire of the Beckett Estate, after all. I needed something other than a theatrical venue for the sort of performance I had envisioned. I kept in mind as well Beckett's comments to his favourite actress, Billie Whitelaw, while they were rehearsing *Footfalls*: 'I don't know whether the theatre is the right place for me anymore', Beckett told her. 'He was getting further and further away from writing conventional plays', Whitelaw observed; 'And I know what he meant. I thought, well perhaps he should be in an art gallery or something. Perhaps I should be pacing up and down in the Tate Gallery' (Kalb 1989: 235).

My opportunity presented itself in December of 1992 when I was invited to participate in an evening of visual art and performance at Florida State University Gallery and Museum. The evening would be built around the electronic satellite reception of a piece of hypertext, *Agrippa (A Book of the Dead)*, from novelist William Gibson. *Agrippa* was scheduled for simultaneous broadcast to nine sites around the world, immediately after which the piece would be distorted and destroyed by its own viruses. It was in such a fragile and ephemeral artistic environment that I had sought for a presentation of *Breath*. The overall plan for the evening was to use the gallery as a decentred theatre space. Events would be performed in several venues of the gallery, and the audience would roam or drift from one to the other with only the slightest prompting. Rather than adopt the structure of an outdoor fair where simultaneous performances are offered to a roaming audience, the gallery evening would feature sequential performances without overlap. The evening then would comprise readings, other theatrical performances and environments among the gallery's various nooks and rooms. My offering was then in keeping with the hypertext theme, or rather would present versions of digital or telereality. I decided that *Breath* like all of Beckett's short plays needed a frame, and since the traditional proscenium arch was unavailable in the gallery, I would create my own. Rather than construct a proscenium, however, I built an oversized prop television, through the absent screen of which *Breath* would be performed 'live', if that's the word, or at least the pile of 'miscellaneous rubbish' would be physically present in the gallery. In the printed programme I called the performance 'A Simulated Television Production', but the heap of 'miscellaneous rubbish' was of a piece with other installations in the gallery so that Beckett's 'play' was for many indistinguishable from other art objects on display (or from the gallery's refuse outside the service entrance, for that matter). Mine, or rather Beckett's, was simply framed by an almost clownish simulated television screen. To my mind this was the continued development of a hybrid art that I take to be Beckett's late theatre, an art of icons, images and afterimages, ghosts of memories – as closely related to sculpture as to what we have traditionally called theatre.

The performance of *Breath*, as opposed to the gallery's other sculptures, was 'announced' by the light's fading up on the set, that is, on the heap of rubbish some ten feet behind the television screen, as the gallery lights simultaneously (but only slightly) dimmed. The brief cry (vagitus) and amplified inspiration would sound for some ten seconds, and after the prescribed five-second pause, the expiration and identical cry of some ten seconds. Fade down the stage; fade up the gallery.

Breath was repeated several times during the evening, interspersed amid other performances. I had hoped that such repetition might suggest the regenerative element I saw as implicit in the play (and which the theatre-savvy Tynan made explicit). Since I had deliberately chosen to associate Beckett's 'play' with sculpture by the very fact of offering the performance in an art gallery, I was not surprised that the audience never seemed to understand that it was watching what I would consider live theatre, since the performance lacked what had heretofore been deemed an essential ingredient of theatre, actors. The audience, deprived of its standard ambience and cultural cues, failed to applaud at the fade down, but neither did they applaud the viewing of other sculptures as they departed, even when the gallery lights dimmed as they did to announce another *Breath*. And, of course, there was no curtain and so no curtain call – whom would we have called, after all. I took that lack of response as a measure of the success of this production which had blurred the distinction among artistic forms, which became, almost, invisible theatre; but while I may have saved the play from being lost amid a sequence of other plays as planned, I may have lost it to a neo-dadaist revival of found sculpture. I returned to the issue of invisible theatre in December of 2011 when I conceived and staged another variation on *Breath*, *Breath—Text—Breath*, with Jon McKenna at The Calder Bookshop and Theatre in London on The Cut. A recorded reading of *Breath* was used as a frame, performed on either side of a vagrant's discovery amid the rubbish and the subsequent piece-mealed reading through of *Text* 13.[16]

Atom Egoyan: *Steenbeckett*

One dynamic possibility for the future of performance is that offered by the Egyptian-born Canadian film maker Atom Egoyan, who directed a traditional production of *Krapp's Last Tape*, starring John Hurt, for the Beckett on film series, the ambitious attempt in 2000 to record the Gate Theatre's much toured and touted Beckett festival during which all nineteen stage plays were performed. Egoyan subsequently used the completed film as a centrepiece for his own personal art work, an installation at London's Museum of Mankind, the entry dominated by massive marble pillars. The installation folded continuous showings of the film, in altered, antithetical perspectives, into a larger, environmental exhibit of recorded memory that Egoyan called *Steenbeckett*. Egoyan's work – like Beckett's – focused on memory, its preservation and evocation. Participants entered the now all but deserted Museum of Mankind, walked past stacks of nineteenth-century diaries that obsessionally documented a diarist's every meal, say, or every journey, every bed slept in, or every partner slept with. It was the obsessive recording of what, unrecorded, might be deemed incidental, and it seemed to be the exhaustion of such documentation that appealed to Egoyan, as it did to Krapp and presumably Beckett. Spectators walked through a darkened warren of passages, up stairs, through tunnels, past discarded typewriters, phonographs, disks, 'spoooools', photographs, to a makeshift projection room where the commercial film of *Krapp's Last Tape* was screened for a restricted audience, ten to twelve at a time, sitting on a makeshift bench no more than six feet from the film projected on the opposite wall. The film's grainy images were a massive 12 to 18 feet high, and so they dwarfed the spectators, who had discovered or stumbled upon another discarded cultural object. From there spectators ambled or stumbled to another room, some not waiting for the film to end, others sitting through it more than once. In the next room a mass of film, 2,000 feet of it according to the programme, ran continuously and noisily along rollers, up and down, back and forth, in and around the room, floor to ceiling, wall to wall, over and over again, and finally through an antique Steenbeck editing table at the far end of the room, where the film was visible in miniature and seen through the cat's cradle of noisily rolling film. Obsolete, the Steenbeck editing machine was the equipment that Egoyan deemed right for editing his film of *Krapp's Last Tape*. The analogue device had all the look of a clumsy antique, the look Egoyan was apparently trying to achieve in his film. As important as the film itself, both its materiality and the giganticised and miniaturised images it provided, was the material editing machine itself, central to Egoyan's reinvention of *Krapp's Last Tape* and the centrepiece of his installation, as the material tape recorder may be to Beckett's. The play *Krapp's Last Tape* was thus another deteriorating relic, a museum piece, say, Beckett frozen in time, and simultaneously a stunningly fresh work of art (see also Barfield 2002).

Adriano and Fernando Guimarães: *Todos Os Que Caem*

The treatment of a Beckett text or its performance as a found object, as it appears in Egoyan's *Steenbeckett*, is central to the aesthetics of the Guimarães brothers, visual artists based in Brasilia, Brazil, who have maintained an ongoing and evolving dialogue with and exploration of Beckett's work since their first show, *Happily ever after*, which included various versions of *Happy Days*, *Come and Go*, *Play* and *Rockaby*, and which ran, in a variety of venues, almost all in Brazil, from 1998 to 2001. The approach of Adriano and Fernando Guimarães is to combine theatre, performance pieces, music, visual arts and literature into a hybrid, composite art form, and to collaborate with major contemporary artists. For *Happily ever after* they worked with plastic artist Ana Miguel, who designed costumes and stage props, with photographer and lighting designer Dalton Camargos, with museum curator Marília Panitz, and with guest actresses Vera Holtz as Winnie in *Happy Days* and Nathalia Thimberg as the 'Woman in chair', W, in *Rockaby*. A second instalment of their work *We were not long . . . together*, which ran in a variety of configurations during 2002–3, was built around *Breath* and featured four other pieces: *Catastrophe*, *Act without Words, II*, *What Where* and *Play*. The third incarnation of their dialogue with Beckett was built around *All That Fall*, again interspersed with their own videos, photographs, objects and performance pieces, and featuring as well *Rockaby*, *Not I*, *Rough for Theater II* and *A Piece of Monologue*. These three anthologies performed over a six-year period constituted a multimedia trilogy of spectacles in a variety of manifestations that connected Beckett's theatre works to larger public spaces beyond theatre. It was thus in conception and execution the very opposite of the Beckett on film project taking shape at almost the exact same period in Europe. No two manifestations of the Guimarães brothers project were ever the same. Theirs was an art that resisted being reduced to homage, the goal of the film project, presumably.

As the art critic Vitória Daniela Bousso writes, 'The transition between the visual and the theatrical constitutes a hybrid space, a territory of complexities ruled by experimentation in the work of Adriano and Fernando Guimarães' (Panitz 2004: 97). As their work focuses on the human body, they engage directly the cultural games of regulation and control that are played upon it. For the Guimarães brothers, the body is less ancillary than it might generally be in Beckett, say, and instead becomes the seat of the struggle of power relationships – if not overtly expressed certainly a subtext in Beckett's work as well. The body is here foregrounded, according to the art historian Nicholas de Oliveira:

> The body interprets or plays the part of a character but simultaneously represents itself, affirms itself as a recipient of the unconscious, in other words, the body interprets that role, in the installation, that gives access to what is unstable and ephemeral. The body's unpredictable action always offers a condition for rupture or destabilization in the postmodern work. (Bousso 2004: 98; see also Oliveira 2001: 12)

Beckett's works are thus treated as ready-mades by the brothers Guimarães and hence in no need of serious revision or renovation since they are already afterimages of Beckett's texts – preceded and followed, as they are, by images of the Guimarães brothers' re-imaginings of Beckett. Their performances are thus less critiques of Beckett's work than reconstitutions, reinventions of it, its afterimages. What power and affect is elicited from Beckett is as much the result of their installed environments as it is an intrinsic part of the works themselves, and thus Beckett's works move, unadulterated, into a new poetic space, become part of a new poetics. The Guimarães brothers thus create their own Beckett archive, Beckett in or as a cabinet of curiosities, a Beckett made up of cultural shards.

Their antiphonal use of Beckett's works and words is a case in point. Their treatment of the play *Breath*, for example, is presented in conjunction with an installation that they call '*Breath +*'. Although performed along with other, better known plays, *Breath* here takes on the role of a featured work, one version of which features a live, naked actor in an embryonic sack that harkens back to Tynan's *Breath*. Their image, then, foregrounds the regenerative potential of the embryo. Corollary productions, the *Breath* +, feature an actor (or actors) submerged in water who responds to an authoritarian and apparently arbitrary bell that commands and controls his (or their) submersions and re-surfacings, hence it controls his (or their) breath. In one version actors immerse their heads in buckets of water at the bell's command. In another, a single fully clothed actor is fully submerged in a massive fish tank, the duration of his submersion regulated by the bell. In a third image, submerged actors, again fully clothed, are grotesquely contorted in a bathtub and viewed from above. In each case the actor's breathing appears subject to or is regulated by an arbitrary, external force, in this case a bell or buzzer, but it might be as well the whistle or prod in the two 'Acts without Words', or the piercing bell in *Happy Days*, works which the brothers have staged as part of this ongoing dialogue. Much of their work then spills out of the theatre into gallery space or out of the gallery back into the theatre. The extension of the playing space emphasises the idea of expressive space, something other than theatrical space used as a backdrop.

Another performance is called '*Light – '*. Here power (much of it in the form of electrical power) is transferred to a participating audience where spectators turn light switches on and off to control the pace of action in performance. In this case the light switches are often dummies, the light controlled by a remote switch, so the regulatory system of control is itself diffused, often mysterious, frustrating both actors and audience, and so the body of the audience, or the audience's bodies, are folded into the performance and into the power struggle. *Double Exposure* is an installation composed of four environments with the words of several of Beckett's short plays projected onto walls, windows and transparent boxes. Beckett's words themselves are presented within boxes, cabinets of curiosities (*Wunderkammer*), the eighteenth-century forerunner of what we today call museums (Oliveira 2001: 12):

> Along the whole length of the gallery's entrance glass doors there are texts by Samuel Beckett. Upon entering, the spectator finds himself in the first environment: an almost dark rectangular foreroom, outlined by glass panes, on which fragments from texts have also been written. At each end of this room there are life-size pictures of the character that appears throughout the exhibition. The photographs are almost identical, but they reveal the character under the action of two contrasting lights: one that is excessively bright and one that is too dark. Both make its image evanescent. (Panitz 2004: 103)

That is, what we see as apparently life-like is decidedly an image (as Bergson has been reminding us at least since his *Matter and Memory*), or afterimage, its appearance or disappearance regulated by light which in turn is regulated by (electrical) power, which in turn is regulated (apparently) by spectators. If '*Breath +*' emphasised the materiality and machinery of the body, '*Light –*' foregrounded its ethereality. The focus is thus on the fact that all perception is imagistic if not imag(e)inary. The second environment is a house, a rectangular prism made of exposed brick along which Beckett's texts continue. Along its outer walls spectators can look through peepholes and see real time-videos (again images) of the gallery from a variety of angles through a set of security cameras. The interior lined with dark panes is the third environment. Here the audience watches black-and-white video of a character closing windows to stop a flood of light entering that threatens to extinguish his own image since he is only a projection of light. When vapour lamps are turned on in the room the character's image disappears and the spectator 'encounter[s] his or her own reflection on the walls'. They (as subjects) have thus *replaced* what appeared to be the 'character' or object. The fourth environment consists of a glass scale model of the house sitting on a table. Projected images are then reflected on the model's glass and on the room's walls. In another section of the installation the audience is encouraged to deposit objects, usually, but not exclusively, photographs, of sentimental value – but of course only to themselves. The audience moves through the installation, lingers, examines, reads those images on the walls or Beckett's words on or in boxes as a preface or postlude to the performances of those plays that are on display, so that the play itself, once performed, is already an echo, a double, an afterimage.

The Future of Beckett Studies and Beckett Performance

Amid the restrictions on performance imposed by the Beckett Estate – its attempts to restrain if not subdue the recalcitrant art work by its insistence on faithful and accurate performances, a faith and accuracy no one seems able to define – a resilient and imaginative set of theatrical directors and artists continues to re-invent Beckett by developing a third way, through radical acts of the imagination, by folding the authorised object, like a ready-made in a gallery, into another context, like storefronts or museum installations. They thus assert the heterogeneity of Beckettian performance without violating the dictates of an Estate-issued performance contract. 'Here, precisely, is the Beckett that will hold the stage in the new century', notes Fintan O'Toole, discussing the issue of fidelity to Beckett's texts in another context: 'The merely efficient translations of what are thought to be the great man's intentions will fade into dull obscurity. The productions that allow their audiences to feel the spirit of suffering and survival in our times will enter the afterlife of endless re-imaginings' (O'Toole 2000). The Guimarães brothers, Atom Egoyan and others offer approaches to the re-imaginings necessary to a living art. The alternative is that Beckett's work is often presented as what it may indeed have already become, a curio in a box of curiosities, a museum piece preserved, without deviation (except perhaps for deterioration), exactly as written (at least in some hypothesised version), but, even so, as I have been suggesting, even such a presentation could be re-imagined and altered radically in a new environment, an alternative space. If the Beckettian stage space has become a battleground of political and legal contention, a squabble over property rights more than artistic integrity or aesthetic values, those directors who have taken their cue from Beckett's own comments on theatre and the developing aesthetics of his late plays have found their freedom of expression, a liberation of their imaginations, by abandoning or spilling out of that contested space we call theatre into a more expressive one. They have developed a hybrid art, sweeping Beckett along with them, moving it to where he always thought it belonged, among the plastic arts, and accomplishing yet another reinvention of Beckett's theatre.

Notes

1. The full details are available my 'Introduction' to *Eleutheria* (Gontarski 1998: vii–xxii).
2. Letters to and from Rosset throughout are part of the Rosset Archive at the University of North Carolina, copies in Rosset's personal archive, and are used with the permission of the publisher and of the Beckett Estate.
3. Frankfurter Adorno Blätter III (Herausgegeben vom Theodor W. Adorno Archiv edition text + Kritik), 59. *Das letzte Band* opened at the Schiller Werkstatt on 5 October 1969, on a twin bill with Ionesco's *Der neue Mieter*. Beckett's own direction of *Godot* would not take place until March of 1975 at the Schiller-Theater in Berlin.
4. Gregory's production opened at New York University School of the Arts on 8 February 1973.

5. Good discussions of these productions appear in Oppenheim 1994 and, for Sontag's *Godot*, in Bradby 2001: 164–8.

6. Interview, *The Boston Phoenix*, 5–11 March 2004, at www.boston-phoenix.com/boston/events/theater/documents/03644284.asp (last accessed June 2016).

7. See www.theguardian.com/theguardian/2007/jan/23/features11.g21 (last accessed June 2016).

8. See www.nytimes.com/2007/12/19/theater/reviews/19beck.html?_r=0 (last accessed June 2016).

9. See www.theguardian.com/world/2006/feb/04/arts.italy?CMP=share_btn_tw (last accessed June 2016).

10. Most of these changes are also outlined in Beckett's letter to Blin of 3 April 1968, as Beckett notes, 'I strongly recommend to you the following simplifications.' The letter is printed in Oppenheim's *Directing Beckett* (1994: 299), in Oppenheim's translation.

11. For further details, see my 'De-theatricalizing Theatre: The Post-*Play* Plays' (Beckett 1999: xv–xxix).

12. *The Guardian*, 24 March 1994, p. 25.

13. The British premiere was given at the Close Theatre Club in Glasgow in October 1969, produced by Geoffrey Gilham, according to John Calder's note in *Gambit*, where the play is first published in its unadulterated form.

14. Another curiosity with Grove Press's publication of *Oh! Calcutta!: An Entertainment with Music* (1969) is the censoring of the French pun and even its English translation. On the back cover to the paperback and inside the dust jacket of the hardcover the pun is presented thus: 'Oh! Quelle _ _ _ t'as and Oh! And What a lovely _ _ _ you have'. Grove, of course, made its reputation as a publishing house crusading against censorship. In addition to bungling the Beckett text, then, the venerable publisher, a decade after it had won the *Lady Chatterley's Lover* case and so overturned the US's Comstock Laws, seems to have had something of a failure of courage with the cover copy for *Oh! Calcutta!*

15. Those for productions at the Eden Theatre and published at first by 'Evergreen Showcard', a division of Grove Press, and then by 'Playfare'. With the move to the Belasco Theater, the programme was published by 'Playbill', with Beckett's name still prominently displayed on the credits at least until 1972. Once the production moved to the Edison Theater and touring companies were created, the programme went to a large, fully illustrated format, and Beckett's name was no longer listed among the contributors.

16. See https://www.youtube.com/watch?v=FxnTzeCtdOo (last accessed June 2016), as something of a 'prequel' to the production.

References

Barfield, Steve (2002) 'In Ghostly Archives Keener Sounds', *The Beckett Circle / Le Cercle de Beckett: Newsletter of the Samuel Beckett Society* 25.1, pp. 1–2.

Barthes Roland (1972) 'Whose Theater? Whose Avant-Garde?', in *Critical Essays*, trans. Richard Howard, Evanston: Northwestern University Press.

Beckett, Samuel (1992) *The Theatrical Notebooks of Samuel Beckett, Vol. 2, Endgame*, ed. S. E. Gontarski, New York: Grove Press.

Beckett, Samuel (1994) *The Theatrical Notebooks of Samuel Beckett, Vol. 1, Waiting for Godot*, ed. James Knowlson and Dougald McMillan, London: Faber & Faber; New York: Grove Press.

Beckett, Samuel (1993) *The Theatrical Notebooks of Samuel Beckett, Vol. 1, Krapp's Last Tape*, ed. James Knowlson, New York: Grove Press.

Beckett, Samuel (1999) *The Theatrical Notebooks of Samuel Beckett, Vol. 4, The Shorter Plays*, ed. S. E. Gontarski, New York: Grove; London: Faber & Faber.

Bousso, Vitória Daniela (2004) 'Interstice Zone', in Adriano and Fernando Guimarães, *'Todos Os Que Caem' / 'All That Fall'*, catalogue published by Centro Cultural Banco do Brasil (April), pp. 97–9.

Bradby David (2001) *Beckett Waiting for Godot*, Cambridge: Cambridge University Press.

Calder, John (1969) 'Samuel Beckett's New Play', *Gambit: An International Theater Review* 4:16.

Fehsenfeld, Martha (1986) 'Beckett's Reshaping of *What Where* for Television', *Modern Drama* 29:2 (June).

Feinberg-Jütte, Anat (1992) '"The Task is Not to Reproduce the External Form, But to Find the Subtext": George Tabori's Productions of Samuel Beckett's Texts', *Journal Of Beckett Studies* 1:1 & 2.

Gontarski, S. E. (1995) 'Introduction' to Samuel Beckett, *Eleutheria*, trans. Michael Brodsky, New York: Foxrock.

Guimarães, Adriano and Fernando (2004) *'Todos Os Que Caem' / 'All That Fall'*, catalogue published by Centro Cultural Banco do Brasil (April).

Harmon, Maurice, ed. (1998) *No Author Better Served: The*

Correspondence of Samuel Beckett and Alan Schneider, Cambridge, MA: Harvard University Press.

Joyce, James (2000) *Occasional, Critical, and Political Writing*, ed. with an Introduction and Notes by Kevin Barry, Oxford: Oxford University Press.

Kalb, Jonathan (1989) *Beckett in Performance*, Cambridge: Cambridge University Press.

Knowlson, James (1996) *Damned to Fame: The Life of Samuel Beckett*, New York: Simon & Schuster.

Knowlson, James and Elizabeth Knowlson, eds. (2006) *Beckett Remembering, Remembering Beckett: A Centenary Celebration*, New York: Arcade Publishing.

Nicholas de Oliveira (2001) 'The Space of Memory', *Happily Ever After / Felizes Para Sempre*, ed. Adriano and Fernando Guimarães, catalogue published by Centro Cultural Banco do Brasil (January).

Oppenheim, Lois (1994) *Directing Beckett*, Ann Arbor: University of Michigan Press.

O'Toole, Fintan (2000) 'Game Without End', *The New York Review of Books* (20 January), at www.nybooks.com/articles/2000/01/20/game-without-end

Panitz, Marillia (2004) 'Double Exposure' and 'Multimedia Installation Composed of Four Environments', in Adriano and Fernando Guimarães, *'Todos Os Que Caem'* / *'All That Fall'*, catalogue published by Centro Cultural Banco do Brasil (April), pp. 99–105.

Staging Beckett: Voice and/in Performance (*Company*, *What Where* and *Endgame*)

> I of whom I know nothing, I know my eyes are open because of the tears that pour from them unceasingly. In know I am seated, my hands on my knees, because of the pressure against my rump, against the soles of my feet? I don't know. My spine is not supported. I mention these details to make sure I am not lying on my back, my legs raised and bent, my eyes closed. (*The Unnamable*)

> Use of the second person marks the voice. That of the third that cankerous other. Could he speak to and of whom the voice speaks there would be a first. But he cannot. He shall not. You cannot. You shall not. (*Company*)

Voice, at once or alternately seducer and assailant, comforter and adversary, has been stageable since its dramatic appearance in *Molloy*, where in some respects it remained constrained, unembodied on the page if not performed in the imagination. It made its escape, its liberation *en plein air*, with the radio play *All That Fall* in 1957 and *Embers*, written in 1957 as well but performed by the BBC only in 1959 (both now regularly performed as stage works, the former recently staged by Out of Joint in 2015–16 as 'A theatrical journey into darkness', with audience members blindfolded). Almost concurrently Beckett began a further technological exploration of voice on stage as the recorded voices of Krapp-past in 1958. From 1957 onward, then, Voice moved freely from page to stage, the line dividing Beckett's prose narratives from his radio texts and stage monologues grew fainter, was at times imperceptible, as Beckett began to explore the performative possibilities of Voice as thoroughly as he had explored its fictive possibilities in the post-war suite of novels, *Molloy*,

Malone Dies and *The Unnamable*, and such experiments would continue through *Rockaby*, *That Time* and *What Where* as well as in the television plays. Liberated from whatever restrictions the page imposed, Voice would never again be content to sit mute, and it makes appearances again in the last two theatrical projects that sustained Beckett's interest: the adaptation of the novella *Company* to the stage and his revisions of *What Where*, first for television, and then again for the stage, and yet again for television, but it comes to the fore in Beckett's own stagings, as early as 1967, for his *Endspiel* (*Endgame*), as well.

As late as 17 June 1970, Beckett seemed adamant. Asked by Grove Press's Judith Schmidt whether or not he would consent to a staging of *Eh Joe*, a work written for television, Beckett replied with a blanket rejection in an autograph note on Schmidt's query: 'No stage production of *Embers*, *Words and Music*, *Eh Joe*, *Cascando*. [. . .] You may refuse without consulting me all future proposals for stage productions of sound-radio and TV plays.'[1] Beckett's prohibition of adaptations 'of sound-radio and TV plays' did not, evidently, extend to prose works, however. Surprisingly, then, Beckett's own position on keeping his 'genres more or less distinct'[2] softened as he became less resistant to what Ruby Cohn alliteratively called 'jumping [. . .] genres' as numerous theatrical forays into the prose had been if not sanctioned at least not resisted. E. T. Kirby and his Projection Theatre, for instance, adapted *Molloy* in 1969. Joseph Dunn and Irja Koijonen of the American Contemporary Theater adapted *The Unnamable* in 1972. Mabou Mines explored and staged a variety of texts, beginning with *The Lost Ones* in 1972, *Mercier and Camier* in 1979, *Company* in 1983, *Imagination Dead Imagine* in 1984, a work the group originally planned to adapt in 1972, and *Worstward Ho* in 1986, which Mel Gussow in his *New York Times* review dubbed 'a dense introspective monologue'.[3] Moreover, JoAnne Akalaitis somehow received permission to stage one of the 'sound-radio' plays, *Cascando*, in 1976 for Mabou Mines, with music by Philip Glass, and she would go on to stage one of the 'TV plays', *Eh Joe*, and brilliantly at that, in 2007, which followed Atom Egoyan's production to celebrate the Beckett centenary in 2006. For her 1976 staging of *Cascando*, Akalaitis was awarded an Obie for 'Best Direction'.[4] Joe Chaikin and Steve Kent would combine portions of *Texts for Nothing* and *How It Is*, in consultation with Beckett in 1981 but over his objections, as *Texts*. And Gerald

Thomas has staged two versions of *All Strange Away*, both in New York in 1984, one at La Mama, ETC (Experimental Theater Company), and another at the Samuel Beckett Theater. Thomas has also worked with actor Ryan Cutrona on a radio version of *Fizzles*, but the stage version of three of the tales, with the same actor, was directed by Liz Diamond in 1984. My own entry into what had become an increasingly crowded field in the 1980s was an adaptation of *Company* that opened at the Los Angeles Actors' Theater's Half-stage, a black-box theatre, in February of 1985, with Alan Mandell as the sole Figure. This *Company* was the English-language version of *Companie* directed by Pierre Chabert at the Théâtre du Rond-Point, which opened 15 November 1984, and had the distinction of being the only adaptation of his prose work that Beckett himself had a hand in directly, sitting in, at Chabert's request, on rehearsals.

Certainly one of the attractions of staging *Company* for both Chabert, who initiated the project, and me was that it is among the most textually androgynous of Beckett's narratives, written at a time when Beckett seemed consciously to be exploring the common or overlapping ground of fiction and theatre, immediately after *A Piece of Monologue*, the most narrative of his dramas. *Company* thus forms a striking complement to *A Piece of Monologue* and may be the most *dramatic* or performative of Beckett's prose narratives, one that works at least as well on stage as on the page. But even with such overlap, staging had its pitfalls, as Beckett never stopped warning potential adapters of his prose. The most fundamental issue about staging a narrative like *Company* was determining the stage image, which had to be both compelling and minimal. It was clear from the beginning that several fundamental flaws of previous adaptations needed to be addressed and avoided. Staging should not become a textual alternative to nor an attempt to *illustrate* the text. I would resist *dramatising* the stories of the second-person voice, for instance, or depicting and so literalising the image of the speaker as described, that is, the speaker must *not* be lying on his back since speaker and spoken are less congruent than disjunctive. And even if the speaking voice goes through a process of hypothesising very like the process a writer, like Beckett, might go through in creating his imaginative figments, the stage image should not overtly suggest that Figure is a writer at work: no desk, no bookshelves, no writerly appurtenances, no appurtenances of any sort, just a seated figure in a circle of light.

Theoretically, then, what was clear was that theatre ought not to function as the stepchild of fiction, that adaptation ought not to strive fundamentally to *literalise* or even necessarily to *concretise* (which is always a limitation) a prose text. Theatre may have its roots in just such a theory of adaptation – tales of Dionysus illustrated, biblical tales or cultural myths *performed* for the illiterate – but what is most valuable and lasting in theatre, in Beckett's theatre, at least, stands in inverse ratio to such illustrative function, the narrative thread and stage image opposed, incongruent, askew.

The image we settled on then was something *between* the twin dangers of adaptation, illustrating the episodes, and a mere reading of the narrative: a sole figure seated in a chair, which was all but occluded. Such an image would keep the emphasis on *words* and images and so avoid the pitfalls of other adaptations which in order to render concretely the illusive imagery of the fiction, resorted to a variety of highly technical machinations, which often became ends in themselves. E. T. Kirby's production of *Molloy* was supplemented by slides and film, for instance. Joseph Dunn's *Unnamable* was a nine-foot by nine-foot cylinder with a large oval window in which a barely perceptible light rotated – presumably the 'eye/I'. The Mabou Mines production of *Company* featured huge satellite dishes – presumably receivers of the interstellar voice. For us, the central figure in *Company*, that is, the figure we hear or see on stage, may himself be imagined, a figment, and such an ambiguity, a presence less re-presented than de-presented, ought to remain so in production. The vignettes of the second person may also be imaginative renderings and so trying to dramatise them on stage or on film, say, would only alter if not destroy their irresolution. Language is primary in *Company* on page and stage, and Figure's phrasing, the often baroque, inverted, elliptical, poetic syntax of both voices, its rhythms, is as much a source of company as the actual hypothesised vignettes, and I wanted to retain as much linguistic emphasis and imagistic ambiguity as possible and still stage a drama. In short, I was limiting the range of theatrical sign systems at work with or against language to transmit the theatrical image and its consequent affect. Such impoverishment of the traditional means of theatrical communication and expression (i.e., reduction of the body, voice, costume, props, lights, etc.) is what I deemed characteristic of Beckett's own drama and stagings, on the principle, as he has said on multiple occasions, that less is often more.

One advantage I did have as a director, which no other director has had in adapting Beckett's prose, was to watch and learn
from Beckett's comments in rehearsals and from the missteps of
the French production. Chabert's initial conception, to minimise
the speaker's corporeality by creating essentially a floating head,
was stunningly creative and in keeping with much of Beckett's
French fiction. The spirit of Chabert's conception seemed right: to
play against the concreteness of theatre. He decided to mask the
source of light on stage and so created a black box large enough
to accommodate and mask the lighting and most of the figure
sitting on a black chair within the box. Wearing a black cassock
the actor's body would be barely visible save for the head lit by
apparently sourceless light. In addition, the huge wooden box was
mounted on rubber wheels that would move so slowly and silently
across the stage that its movement was not consciously perceptible. The 'machine', as the crew called it, was designed as an invisible frame to mask the source of theatrical light and to subvert the
audience's faith in its own perception. Within the black box, Pierre
Dux (an institution in the French theatre), dressed in a black, neck-
high cassock, would sit on the black chair, and the machine would
move his speaking head imperceptibly across the stage. At some
point during performance the audience would suddenly discern
that the head had moved, was in fact at the opposite end of the
stage, although no movement, no sound, no change in the intensity
or source of light was perceptible. The machine was an ingenious
theatrical contraption that had swallowed up the corporeality of
the actor as well as two thirds of the production budget. But it
would create stunning theatrical effects, a levitated, speaking head
illuminated by sourceless light.

One week before the announced opening of *Companie* everyone
knew that Beckett would attend the afternoon run-through. He
had come to earlier rehearsals, had discussed this adaptation of
his novella with director Pierre Chabert and actor Pierre Dux
over coffee and whiskey, but he had not returned for three weeks
and had not seen 'the machine'. Even I, who had been watching
rehearsals as a less than disinterested party in preparation for
directing the English-language premiere at what was then the Los
Angeles Actors' Theater, was nervous.

Beckett arrived precisely at the appointed time, 4 p.m., at the
back of the Petite Salle of the Jean-Louis Barrault/Madeleine
Renaud Théâtre du Rond-Point, pulled a copy of *Companie* from

the pocket of his greatcoat, and sat inconspicuously at the make-shift desk at the back of the theatre. He exchanged a few words with Chabert who then muttered into his headset and turned on the masked reading lamp as the house lights began to fade. His wire-rimmed glasses perched on his forehead, Beckett followed the text with his finger, his nose nearly touching the page.

The run-through seemed flawless, if mysterious and eerie. The lights faded and came up to total silence. It was theatre in a vacuum, a ghost performance, the only kind Beckett attends. Beckett sat silently with his head bowed, rubbing thumb and forefinger so deeply into his eyes that his sockets had to be as empty as those of Rodin's Balzac. He was massaging his brain directly. Still no comment. He rose and began to make his way towards the stage, but his eyes which were failing him regularly now at seventy-eight were slow to adjust to the light change, and he stumbled on the stairs. He recovered, moved to the edge of the stage and stared at the floor. Silence. Finally, hesitantly, shaking his head: perhaps the narrative could not be staged at all. Four weeks into rehears-als, the advertised opening night a week away, Beckett was having second thoughts. It was all his fault for consenting to the adapta-tion. It was too complicated, too theatrical. Beckett had been reluc-tant to attend rehearsals from the first. It was, after all, Chabert's production. Chabert persisted, and persisting, incurred obligations.

Beckett's theatrical vision is unsparing; making concessions to audience, friendship, even finally to himself, is an alien notion. Theatre like politics is an art of compromise, but somehow Beckett found it unnecessary to make any – and succeeded nonetheless. He somehow resisted the collaborative nature of theatrical pro-duction. Perhaps, if the character were fully lit and his costume simplified, Beckett resumed, looking down at the floor – just a bathrobe, say. Perhaps, if the 'machine' were discarded. Perhaps, if Pierre Dux's moving lips could be masked during the second-person, listening phase of the narrative. Perhaps, if Dux were sur-prised by the second-person voice, which he spoke but which was amplified through speakers at the rear of the theatre. Dux ought not anticipate the voice and so he must begin speaking with his head still bowed and raise it to search out the source of the sound. There was no insistence on Beckett's part; his suggestions were made reluctantly, almost whispered. The cast and director, eager for imprimatur, agreed (as did the visiting American director). In good spirits despite a substantial restaging if not a rewrite a week before opening, the cast and crew withdrew to the bar room for drinks. A cheerful Pierre Dux was buying, so we followed his lead, whiskey neat all around. Everyone relaxed. At least they had a show! Beckett bought a second round and left.

I met Beckett the following morning at the pricey tourist hotel he favoured for its convenience to his Boulevard St-Jacques apartment, and we discussed changes for the American production. Why weren't the second-person narratives taped, I asked? That would be preferable, Beckett responded, but Dux insisted on reciting the whole text. Should the American text follow the cuts in the French text exactly (I wanted to restore some of the deleted material)? Not necessarily. He was unusually forthcoming today. He was obviously leaving me some working room, and so I grew a bit bolder. What is the relationship between the two voices? The third-person voice, he explained, was 'erecting a series of hypotheses, each of which is false'. The second-person voice was 'trying to create a history, a past for the third person'. We had spent an hour over one *double express*, and I had gathered enough clues for my staging. But I retained reservations about my role. Would it be *my* staging of *Beckett's* play? Working with Beckett forces one to rethink the nature not only of the director's role but of the nature of genre itself. Where is the theatre work, anyway? Whose work is it? It's Beckett's text, but whose theatre work?

What was clear once rehearsals had started was that even as a prose work *Company* already contained a fundamental dramatic structure, a tension between second- and third-person voices, and Beckett's characterisation of the two voices reflected the contrapuntal relationship not only between each section of the text but within it as well, and the issues were as ontological as theatrical or performative. The stage adaptation was designed to develop as many of those contrapuntal elements as possible.

The first change I made for the English-language production of *Company* was that instead of having the Figure speak both voices as Pierre Dux had, I would tape the second-person segments, as Beckett had suggested. This immediately solved a number of production problems and opened up additional staging possibilities. For one, the Figure could now truly be a listener, and I was freed from trying to mask his moving lips, a lighting problem which plagued the French production and was never adequately solved in Paris. More important, I could establish two separate modes of stage action. A speaking or hypothesising mode, and a listening or

Alan Mandell in *Company*

searching mode, and play the one against the other visually and aurally.

In the hypothesising mode Figure could move and speak normally in his chair. Here he existed in real time. The listening mode would, however, be highly stylised. As listener, Figure would move in slow, balletic motion quizzically seeking the source of Voice, one source at each of the two far corners of the theatre and one directly overhead. The Voice could be slow, deliberate, almost flat, and the effect generally would be to suggest that time too had slowed. Further, taping the second-person voice also allowed me to manipulate the sense of theatre space. I was working in a very small, intimate black-box theatre to begin with, and the initial effect created was claustrophobic. By varying the amount of echo and reverberation on each taped segment, I could open up theatre space, create the illusion in the dark that Voice was coming not only from a variety of sources but from varying distances, some from very far off, others whispers in his ear. I divided the second-person segments among the three speakers so that the figure's head moved slowly, almost painfully, to search out the source of the voice; the pattern of complex light changes (almost 100 light cues in sixty-five minutes, and most of those during the listening mode) enhanced that balletic motion by creating a series of silent facial sculptures. Taping the second-person voice then allowed for an additional series of counterpoints. Normal time could be played against slowed time, normal motion against slowed motion, hypothesising voice against the flat voice of memory and/ or imagination, the full light of the speaking head against the varying chiaroscuro of the listening head, rejection of the voice against acceptance of the voice: in short, light against dark, movement against stasis, sound against silence. As Beckett suggested, the lighting in *Company* should have 'musical possibilities'. That is, it should not only illuminate and as such reinforce the metaphor of imagination, but the light should also control the rhythm and pace of the drama, punctuating each paragraph into discrete segments and enhancing the fugal nature of the performance.

The production was designed to explore and reflect two fundamental and contradictory themes of the work: first, the strength and potential solace of the imagination as company, and second, the weakness and failure of the imagination as company, that is, its failure finally to alleviate humanity's most fundamental condition, isolation, loneliness. Unlike Chabert's production that was staged on a proscenium stage in a 250-seat theatre, the original Los Angeles *Company* was staged environmentally in a set beautifully conceived by designer Timiam Alsaker. The Half-stage was converted into a black box, no stage, no rake to audience seating. Audience shared Figure's space. The theatre's sixty seats were reduced to thirty, arranged in an irregular pattern so that each spectator would have clear sight lines but would not have the comfort of sitting next to anyone. As a precaution against spectators moving their chairs seeking whatever security proximity offers, the seats were bolted to the floor and covered in black floor-length felt. 'Most funereal thing', Krapp might have said (*CDW* 219).[5]

Once the basic contrapuntal, fugal relationship between modes was established, between second- and third-person voices, which do not comprise or add up to a first person, an 'I', say, the next step was to establish the relationship of the perceived Figure to voice. Almost all of the incidents that emanate from voice seem painful to Figure yet he seeks out their source. They suggest a loveless childhood where the child was rebuked or derided by his parents for his comment on the perception of the sun (*Company* 10–11), or for his report of being able to see the mountains of Wales from his 'nook in the gorse' (25) in the Wicklow Hills. There is the lovelessness of parents 'stooping over cradle' (47), the lack of parental concern for a child in desperate need of attention who throws himself from 'the top of a great fir' (21), or the embarrassment of the child's being on exhibition, standing naked at 'the tip of a high board' before the 'many eyes' of his father's cronies as he is urged to 'Be a brave boy' (18) and dive into the always frigid Irish Sea. The child in the memories seems never to have been the boy or the man his parents wanted. He kept busy, even in those days, developing the light of his imagination, one of *Company*'s dominant metaphors. Voice also recounts some embarrassing and

naive incidents: the boy who believes he can play God by intervening in the life of an ill hedgehog, the child who can look out the
summer-house window to see that 'all without is rosy' (39), or the
young adult who believes that his path (literal and metaphorical)
is straight, 'a beeline' (35), and looks back astonished one morning
to see the helicoidal pattern in the fresh snow, 'Withershins' (38).
The incident is wryly comic even as it also suggests the plight of
humanity living the pattern of the sinistral spiral of Dante's hell.
Even the sensual moments are finally painful. The erotic episode
of the young man's feeling the 'fringe of her long black hair' (48)
is intimately connected to the story of the lover's pregnancy, with
its pun about her being late. The episode's concluding line hints at
the disastrous end to this love affair, 'All dead still' (42).

Figure resists, indeed denies that voice for numerous reasons.
The memories are, of course, painful, for the most part, but he also
resists the simplified notion that a sum of memories (or stories)
will add up to a history, and so to a life. And even if the voice
recounts incidents from what might be his past, more or less accurately, memories are never historical but fictive, figments, selected,
re-ordered, re-emphasised versions, that is, alterations of past incidents. Philosophically, the separation of Voice and Figure allows
for the dramatisation of a phenomenological theme. In order to
be perceived, Voice needs to be separated from perceiver and so
the voice must always be something other than a self, and hence
cannot be accepted as part of the I. In fact, both the figments
Figure creates, the figure of one lying on his back in the dark and
the voice he hears, have been objectified and thereby separated
from a perceiving entity or being, a self, say; thus, they are not I,
as the narrative Mouth in *Not I* insists, no story I tell about myself
can be me. I am not what I am conscious of, Figure suggests to
us throughout the play, for consciousness entails objectification.
That dichotomy, moreover, also destabilises the perceiver since, as
Sartre develops in *Being in Nothingness*, only the known can *be*,
the perceiver, the knower, the Figure is *nothing*. The perceiver is
the opposite of what is perceived, what is known, the *en soi*, being,
and so the perceiver is a nothing to the perceived's being. What
Figure recoils from at the mention of the 'I' when he says 'quick
leave him' (followed each time in production by a blackout) is the
confrontation not only with the nothingness of his self per se, but
self's objectification once it has been perceived and the infinite
regress of nothingness that a self-reflexive consciousness entails.

Figure resists accepting the voice as part of himself as soon as he hears it, as soon as it is objectified and 'known', which process simultaneously nullifies the knower. The play explores once again the difficulties and paradoxes entailed in being and consciousness. Consciousness, or the *pour-soi*, Sartre tells us, 'is always something other than what could be said about it' (1956: 439).

And yet Voice is appealing. Despite the pain and embarrassment evoked by it, 'little by little as he lies [in both senses] the craving for company revives [. . .] The need to hear that voice again' (*Company* 55). The craving not only suggests that Voice helps to pass the time, is a companion through the long *nuits blanches*, but that it is also the fountainhead of creativity, the source of the art we witness on stage. And so the fugal quality of *Company*, its betweenness, suggests an aesthetics. Art is a counterpoint, a series of negating tensions, a perpetual dialectic between formalist hypothesising and the subconscious or projected voices from a past – someone's past. *Company*, drama and prose text, is precisely that sort of fugue. Dux's speaking both parts suggests a more or less simple interiority to the performance, a unity that Beckett was resisting. In production the formalist aesthetics implicit in the text was made explicit by recapitulating at the conclusion all the lighting patterns, visual imagery and sound variations used throughout the play.

As the audience entered the dimly lit black box with the strange arrangement of chairs, they had little hint of what the visual theatrical image might look like. The dim lights faded to dark and after a protracted pause the spectators heard, 'A voice comes to one in the dark. Imagine.' At the command 'imagine' lights faded up on a dishevelled figure in a grey bathrobe and pyjamas sitting on a black nondescript chair, an echo of the black chairs on which the audience sat. Figure appeared noiselessly, materialised, created by the audience's imagination. For some sixty-five minutes Figure hypothesised and listened amid, within, the audience, on intimate terms with it. Then as Voice asserted that despite the solace of imagination, the pleasures of mathematical calculations, the contemplation of formal symmetries, and the companionship of hypothesising, Figure was as he always was (fade to black, pause, lights up), 'Alone', the text's final word and perhaps Beckett's final word on the human condition. Lights fade to black and Figure silently disappears, dematerialises, as silently as he appeared. Dim house lights return, and the audience is, as it always was, alone. A curtain call would only have dispelled that moment of intimacy, intensity and bewilderment. And audiences were bewildered. The usual theatrical signs of completion had been withheld. Audiences generally didn't know whether or not the play was over, whether or not to applaud (most did not), whether or not just to leave the theatre. Even after the door was opened, spectators sat still, unsure what to do next.

The theatre piece *Company*, then, is in many respects a development of, a conception beyond, a translation of the prose text into the language (or sign system) of theatre. The novel posited a duality between a 'he' voice and a 'you' voice, while the narrator remained an irresolute conjunction or nexus of them. In this translation of *Company* to the stage, then, the narrator was our principal (if illusive or ghostly) icon, mediating the two pronouns, the you and the he, sharing characteristics of both but refusing to identify with either. That is, to the character sitting in his room, neither the creature he creates lying on his back, an extension of his imagination, nor the voices that he hears in the night, another extension of his imagination, are essentially part of the 'I' sitting in the chair, because both figments and Voice have been objectified and thereby separated from the perceiving self. And yet he is connected to both through the phenomenon, the phenomenological act of perception.

In the play we find a narrator, sitting in a room listening to voices very like but not coeval with his own memories and creating a figure of one lying on his back in darkness. But consciousness can also perceive itself sitting in a chair perceiving memories. The hypothesiser himself, the Figure we see on stage, is not a stable, core reality, not a transcendental creator, ego or stable sign or signifier. He keeps an eye not only on his creations, his figments, but over his shoulder as well, wondering not only about his created figment but whether he too is only figment, created creature, imaginative construct, *en soi* to another *pour soi*, *en soi* to his own *pour soi*. And so, finally, he is, for he is not an actual hypothesiser, Beckett continually reminds us linguistically, but an actor, a Figure in an art work created by a particular set of biological and cultural forces that for convenience we call Samuel Beckett. But this Samuel Beckett too is often glancing over his shoulder, wondering if he too has been written. One characteristic of consciousness Sartre notes is that it is capable of being conscious of itself being conscious. Sartre, however, rejected the possibility of an infinite regress, positing, phenomenologically, a transcendental ego; Beckett, in turn, rejects Sartre's rejection and entertains the fictive possibilities of the infinite regress by suggesting an infinite series of devisers: 'Devised deviser devising it all for company' (46). A transcendental unity is always arbitrary, for one can always ask, 'Who asks in the end, Who asks? . . . And adds long after to himself, Unless another still' (25).

From its opening theatrical image, then, *Company* emphasised a point Beckett was exploring at least in the late plays, that one source of dramatic action and conflict is a tension created by playing narrative against visual imagery, ear against eye, the story we hear against what we think we see. The play opens with precisely such a displacement – a figure in a chair recounting the story of a figure on his back; a figure perceiving voices and hence negating his own being; the spectator perceiving the voices, negating himself. *Company* is not merely a set of visual images in concord with the text, with dialogue, but a set of disharmonies. The iconography of stage image and the syntax of language, in short what we see and what we hear are as often in conflict with one another as in concord, and the drama, more often than not, resides precisely in that tension, that displacement of one by the other. Much of Beckett's drama, certainly the late drama, resides in such displacement. Fiction always entails absence. As Freud suggests, writing is the representation of an absent one. Theatre, on the other hand, has been the genre of presence. The audience is *present* at a certain time; actors present themselves to that audience for a pre-arranged period. One of Beckett's most startling literary innovations is to create a *theatre of absence* – either the present absence (in the form of writing) or the absent present (in the form of characters who may not exist, finally).

As a drama, then, *Company* shares characteristics with Beckett's early plays. The figure in *Company* is passing the time as Didi and Gogo are in *Waiting for Godot* or as Winnie is in *Happy Days*. His means are to create fictions as does Hamm with his chronicle, his narrative in *Endgame*. And much of the imagery of the voice, the 'you' portion of the text, suggests movement, but like the action in *Godot* and in *Mercier and Camier*, the movement is heading 'nowhere in particular' (23). But *Company* is more strikingly of a piece with Beckett's late, ghostly plays, plays during which we question our own perception, we question the validity, the existence of the images we see before us on stage, as we do in

Footfalls, *That Time, A Piece of Monologue, Ohio Impromptu* and *Rockaby*. *Company* is certainly part of Beckett's late Theatre of Absence. Figure himself, the image we see before us on stage, is the confluence of memory and imagination, and exists in fact as the tension between those forces, as does the figure lying on his back in the dark, as does the work we witness before us on the stage. In many respects the text acquires resonances through its translation into stage language. When Figure wonders whether or not another may be with him in the dark, he is invoking the ritual we call theatre, which is always fiction for company.

In April of 1986 I found myself back in Paris preparing to stage another of Beckett's plays. In June of 1985 Beckett had been in Germany directing a television version of his play *What Where*. In the process he had rewritten the text, filmed it, and offered the rewritten version to Chabert to stage in Paris. I was offered the English version, and would as usual attend Paris rehearsals in preparation for the American staging. Beckett was again preoccupied with simplifying the visual imagery and his dialogue. In the original stage version, the voice of Bam was represented by a hanging megaphone, and this is the version still published in all major editions of the play. For his television version, however, he substituted an enlarged, diffuse image of a face. Such an oversized face was not possible on the stage according to Chabert – at least on short notice – so Beckett suggested just the outline of a skull, a ring of diffuse light, an image with almost angelic overtones. Again we met after rehearsals, but in the deserted restaurant of the Théâtre du Rond-Point. I suggested that I thought I could create a hologram to serve as the image of Bam. That would be preferable, he suggested. Could we not restore the opening 'mime' as well, the wordless pattern of appearance and disappearance early in the play? The Paris version seemed over-cut. Yes, of course, if I wished.

I staged the revised *What Where* at the Magic Theater in San Francisco as *Visions of Beckett: A Quartet of One-acts*, and it was filmed for television by John Reilly of Global Village, who then took the tape to Paris to show Beckett. This would be the first production of mine that Beckett would actually see. He had of course seen photographs, listened to audio tapes of the *Company* performance, and the like, but that was all. He watched the tape of *Rough for Theatre I* in a hotel room rented for the purpose, and, as he later disclosed, had seen this work staged for the first time, ever, and he watched my production of *Ohio Impromptu*, and then *What Where*, about which he had most to say. Yes, yes, Beckett said, that's fine, but perhaps the lips could move when Bam speaks – difficult to arrange for a hologram. And perhaps the other characters, Bim, Bem and Bom, could be positioned differently. John Reilly, who was producing the piece for Global Village, returned to New York, and through the magic of computerised editing repositioned the images according to Beckett's instructions. He hired another actor, filmed his lips miming the dialogue, and electronically grafted those lips onto the computer-created face of Bam. He brought the videotape back to Beckett. Yes, yes, Beckett said, that's fine . . . but perhaps Bam's voice could have less echo. And so John returned to San Francisco to re-tape the voice with me and actor Tom Luce. To be safe we taped several versions of the dialogue and so brought Beckett several choices. The *What Where* production was finally published in 1992 as *Peephole Art: Beckett for Television*, which included productions of *Not I* and *Quad I & II*, as part of 'The Beckett Project' and a documentary, *Waiting for Beckett*, which included footage of Beckett discussing my production of *What Where*, which remains the only staging of Beckett's revised text of the play in English. (Evidently, the *Not I* and *Quad I & II* productions that form part of *Peephole Art* were never shown to Beckett for his comments.)

Not all actors and theatre professionals were willing to work so closely with Beckett, however, offering the playwright such authority over production, sharing his vision of theatre. In the winter of 1989 I was delighted to be asked to stage Beckett's revised text of *Endgame* at the Magic Theater in San Francisco with an actor who had a long, distinguished and finally tempestuous theatrical career, R. G. Davis, who in 1959 founded the R. G. Davis Mime Troupe as an offshoot from the San Francisco Actor's Workshop, and which finally became the world-famous San Francisco Mime Troupe. The *Endgame* project was part of my own extended enterprise of working through Beckett in that I was determined to stage all those plays which Beckett himself worked through by staging his revised texts. I had just finished working with Beckett on the final revised script of *Endgame* for publication by his British publisher Faber & Faber and by his American publisher Grove Press in their joint series, *The*

Theatrical Notebooks of Samuel Beckett. Again the revised text was based on Beckett's having directed *Endgame* twice, once at the Schiller Theater in September 1967 and once with the San Quentin Drama Workshop in May 1980. After I had transcribed, translated and annotated Beckett's German and English notebooks, and established a new text of the play based on Beckett's revisions for the German and English productions, I submitted the text – of the entire book in fact, complete with my 'Introduction' – to Beckett for his final corrections, emendations and additions, which he judiciously made. In 1989, then, I approached rehearsals of *Endgame* better prepared than I have for any production I ever staged, having spent two years poring over Beckett's German and English notebooks, interviewing actors and actresses he directed and reconstructing the German and English texts. In San Francisco, however, the actor playing Clov resisted Beckett's changes, arguing, much like the critic Colin Duckworth, that he liked the original text better. Davis argued at first that since the play was about progressive deterioration, Clov too must be going blind, and he should enter, therefore, always hugging the walls or crawling on the floor. Next he decided that since many of the exchanges between him and Hamm made little sense, to Davis, at any rate, Clov must therefore be insane, and he should suggest this by having Clov bang his head against the wall throughout the play, especially during Hamm's monologues. He was vehement about breaking down the fourth wall structure of the presentation, and the other three walls with his head, apparently. And he wanted to restore the scene which Beckett cut, particularly where Clov turns the telescope onto the auditorium: 'I see . . . a multitude . . . in transports . . . of joy' – and follows that with 'That's what I call a magnifier' (*Endgame* 29). This was one of Beckett's major revisions to 'simplify' the play; Davis, however, argued for the essential theatricality of the scene.

Moreover, why shouldn't the play represent the political realities of the period of its composition, Davis argued, the Algerian and Indochinese crises, for instance? The glib answer to these questions was that we were performing the play that Beckett wrote and then re-wrote in productions, not the play that Ronnie Davis might have written. But Davis's questions were not frivolous, or rather were not all frivolous. They represent a search for the art of the actor in Beckett's theatre. When Beckett is done paring down his texts, how much creative space remains for other artists: actors, designers and director? Or is there only a single artist in Beckett's theatre? Beckett's contributions to theatrical performance have been extraordinary. He has shorn the theatre of theatricality, reintroduced metaphysics and indeterminacy into the confident, plastic art of theatre, and reasserted the primacy of language, of narrative and poetry, of the playwright himself, even as the capacities of writer and narrative are simultaneously diminished and subverted. Beckett had thus both extended the primacy of the playwright, and so of authorial power, to an unprecedented extent while simultaneously proclaiming authorial impotence, a diminished author-ity. That creates an ideological and aesthetic vacuum which many a director and actor is all too willing to fill. It is a vacuum, however, that Beckett expects no one to fill, that, in fact, defines Beckettian performance, separates it from that of Others. If an actor or director fills that space, Beckett becomes Ibsen.

These differences with the actor led to his dramatic resignation on opening night. The headline in the *San Francisco Examiner* the following morning (Friday, 3 February 1989) read 'Angry Actor Quits Magic's "Endgame"'. The newspaper reported that Davis left 'in a contract dispute with the theater', 'but he also differed with Gontarski on matters of interpretation and approach to the play. "I didn't believe in the show"', he told reporters. There followed an angry exchange of letters in the Theater Bay Area publication *Callboard*, where Davis argued,

> I had always thought one could interpret [*Endgame*] in a progressive way, and I could turn Clov into more than a generalised slave. I could play Clov as one of the oppressed peoples, a third worlder – specifically, a representative [as opposed to a generalised, I guess] Algerian while Hamm would be a representative French colon[ial]. The play opened in France in the '50s and reflected much of the European colonial malaise.[6]

The resulting staging had Clov marching across the stage with the gaff over his shoulder like a rifle, presenting arms to Hamm when asked for the gaff. Less than subtle stuff! 'As may well be expected', Davis continued in his extended analysis in *Callboard*, 'we disagreed. He viewed the play as a series of "ambiguities" which I interpreted as metaphysical relativism, while my view was materialist and anti-imperialist'. My reply in the same issue of the same publication took issue with the interpretation:

The support for [Davis's Algerian interpretation] is that the play was written in the '50s. Such an analysis not only ignores Nagg and Nell, but suggests that while Beckett was really writing about this French colonial conflict, he seems not to have been able to do so directly and that he needed Ronnie Davis to help make his point directly, at least to American audiences.[7]

Such high-concept versions of Beckett's work are no doubt developments of the dominant mode of theatre today: a director's theatre, where text often becomes a pretext for a high-concept presentation. That high concept, the degree to which the director and actors alter the author's text, is a major measure of theatrical creativity. In Beckett's theatre at least, we somehow need to raise serious questions about devaluing the text or the author and thereby limiting the play's possibilities. There is no shortage of conspicuous concepts that could have been brought to bear on *Endgame*. And the play fundamentally would have survived them – most of them, at any rate. The play could have been racially mixed in what is generally called colour-blind casting. Clov might have been black and Hamm white, or in a more interesting postcolonial reversal, the other way around. The same games could have been played with gender. Why not cast a woman as Clov, or even as Hamm, as Caryl Churchill might suggest, to challenge our expectations about gender? And why not a masked *Endgame*: in Greek masks, in African masks, in versions of Marcel Janco's child-like paper masks or in some other neo-Dada junk masks made from cardboard cartons with egg-carton eyes? Or why not change the shelter, the refuge. The set might be made from discarded cardboard, chain link fencing and rusting sheets of tin to suggest the plight of the contemporary homeless, as André Gregory did in his 1973 production, which Beckett, prodded by Alan Schneider, tried to stop. Or the play might be set in a New York City abandoned subway car, as JoAnne Akalaitis did for her 1984 American Repertory Theater production, which Beckett again tried legal action to stop, unsuccessfully. Or we might put bars on the windows and so make the prison motif explicit. The same high-concept updating or particularisation could be done for other plays. Why not do *Happy Days* with a man playing Winnie, in drag? Willie too could be a man so that we could problematise gender or deal directly with homophobia. Why not have our drag Winnie in a mound not of sand or grass but of contemporary junk, trapping Winnie in a more contemporary culture? The simple answer to these questions is that such productions can work, and work well, but there is also something enormous to be gained by working through Beckett.

What Ronnie Davis calls 'metaphysical relativism' was simply an attempt to retain all of these interpretations at once, and one does that by working through Beckett, not by establishing oneself as the arbiter of Beckett's decisions. There are playwrights in the modern world whose vision is worth understanding and finally trusting. Davis's comment that the scene with Clov's turning his telescope on the audience was theatrically right gets to the heart of the matter. The problem with the scene was its very theatricality. Colin Duckworth has complained that Beckett's 'textual vandalism' has eliminated 'the most magical moments of the play' is also exactly on point, and there's also a point that Davis and Duckworth miss. Beckett had been working to detheatricalise theatre even before *Godot*, and of *All That Fall*, he wrote to Barney Rosset on 27 August 1957, of a planned stage reading of the radio play by *Godot* director Herbert Berghof:

> I am absolutely opposed to any form of adaptation with the view of its conversion into 'theatre'. It is no more theatre than *End-Game* is radio and to act it is to kill it. Even the reduced visual dimension it will receive from the simplest and most static of readings [. . .] will be destructive of whatever quality it may have and which depends on the whole thing *coming out of the dark*. [. . .] frankly the thought of *All that Fall* on a stage, however discreetly, is intolerable to me. (*Letters 3* 63–4, see also note 2 below)

Davis and Duckworth were struggling to retheatricalise a work that Beckett was struggling to detheatricalise. If we measure Beckett's theatre against traditional criteria – even against what has become the tradition of the avant-garde – we as critics, performers and audience will inevitably come up short. So much of what we have called Beckett's contribution to the modern theatre has been this steadfast detheatricalisation of theatre and his divorce of Voice (or voice) from body, voices separated from Figure or any discernible, corporeal, material speaker, voice, instead coming out of the dark. Duckworth's is a plaintive plea to retain what he calls 'some of the most magical moments of the play'. But it is precisely those 'magical moments' which needed to be cut. This is not a shift in aesthetic criteria, the fumblings of an artist in his dotage, but an artist continuing to develop his aesthetics into his mature years. Beckett is among those fortunate artists, like Matisse and less so Picasso, who manage late in life to enjoy another creative burst. In Matisse's life it took a brush with death for him to develop his late paper cut-outs. In Beckett's case it was a fate almost as bad, a major dose of practical theatre.

Notes

1. Correspondence between Samuel Beckett and Barney Rosset/Judith Schmidt from Barney Rosset/Grove Press Archives, George Arents Research Library, Syracuse University, and John J. Burns Library, Boston College. Quotations with permission of the principals.
2. Cited in Cohn 1989: 207. See also the final section of the chapter 'Jumping Beckett's Genres' for an account of the Kirby, Dunn and the first of the Mabou Mines adaptations, pp. 219–29. Matters have changed considerably of late, however, as Estate-sanctioned productions of *Eh Joe*, *Embers* and *All that Fall* are now regularly performed on the world's stages.
3. See www.nytimes.com/1986/09/12/theater/stage-worstward-ho-a-beckett-monologue.html (last accessed June 2016).
4. See www.maboumines.org/productions/cascando (last accessed June 2016).
5. The adaptation it resembles most in this regard is the Mabou Mines version of *The Lost Ones*, which was at first intended only as a reading and demonstration. Once the notion of reading was abandoned, designer Thom Cathcart conceived the idea of seating the audience within a black, foam rubber-lined cylinder.
6. 'Letterbox', *Callboard*, the monthly theatre news magazine published by Theatre Bay Area, May 1989, p. 13.
7. Ibid. p. 17.

References

Cohn, Ruby (1980) *Just Play: Beckett's Theater*, Princeton: Princeton University Press.

Gontarski, S. E. (1985) *The Intent of Undoing in Samuel Beckett's Dramatic Texts*, Bloomington: Indiana University Press.

Sartre, Jean-Paul (1956) *Being and Nothingness*, trans. Hazel E. Barnes, New York: Philosophical Library.

Beckett and the 'Idea' of Theatre: Performance Through Artaud and Deleuze

How could I write, sign, countersign performatively texts which 'respond' to Beckett? [. . .] I was able to risk linguistic compromise with Artaud, who also has his way of loving and violating, of loving violating a certain French language of its language. But in Artaud (who is paradoxically more distant, more foreign for me than Beckett) there are texts which have permitted me writing transactions. [. . .] That wasn't possible for me with Beckett, whom I will thus have 'avoided' as though I had always already read him and understood him too well. (Jacques Derrida, 'This Strange Institution We Call Literature'[1])

One mustn't let in too much literature. (Antonin Artaud, *The Nerve Meter*)

Through Artaud

At the entrance to the smaller, downstairs space of the Théâtre du Rond-Point, two oversized and dominating photographs hung in the 1980s, one of Antonin Artaud, the other of Samuel Beckett. From 1958 the theatre was directed by Jean-Louis Barrault (1910–94), from which post he was dismissed by the Gaullist culture minister André Malraux during the student uprising in the spring of 1968, even as the Théâtre du Rond-Point under Barrault's direction was one of the theatres in Paris where the Compagnie Renault-Barrault introduced Parisians to what was then European avant-garde performance and included the work of Samuel Beckett.

The Artaud/Beckett conjunction or contrast was dear to Barrault and formative to his sensibility, but the two influences seemed to represent very different, if not diametrically opposed strains in the emergence and development of twentieth-century, European, avant-garde theatre. On the one hand, Artaud advocated a performance-based theatre only loosely respectful of texts, which, he thought, tended to limit, even stifle the dynamics, the energy, the motion of performance, advocating instead an infectious theatricality, one that should be uncontained and spread like contamination, like a plague, and feature what he called 'cruelty', intense emotions too often avoided or masked by polite, boulevard or bourgeois theatre. On the other hand, Samuel Beckett, a literary if not lapidary playwright, heir both to Samuel Johnson and James Joyce, protective of his theatrical texts to the point of brooking no deviations from printed or typescript versions, and as a consultant or director, of his own work in particular, limiting displays of emotion. His most famous and frequent comment if not admonition to favoured actress Billie Whitelaw during rehearsals of *Footfalls* was, 'Too much colour, Billie. Too much colour.'[2] Barrault managed, at least personally, to reconcile such aesthetic tensions, as he did other antinomies like working both at the house of Molière, the somewhat staid Comédie Française, and at a trio of more experimental national theatres that not only featured Beckett's work but where Beckett himself would serve something like an early apprenticeship in his development as a man of the theatre: Théâtre du Rond-Point, Théâtre Marigny and the Théâtre de l'Odéon; that is, Beckett grew to become a theatre practitioner through his interactions with such French avant-garde artists and theatres, artists who were nourished and sustained by the little theatre movement in France. As Wallace Fowlie has noted, 'Such a [little] theater will allow a new dramatic poet, when he arises, to impose his own mode of interpretation, his own dramatic form' (1959: 644), in Beckett's case to redefine the dramatic as he became, finally, a prominent director in his own right who saw in theatre a process of becoming and multiplicity that he had already discovered and accepted for his fiction, at least from *Watt* forward, and where the dominant mode of expression was not story *per se*, not plot, but idea and image.

Beckett's initial theatrical contact would be through the original director of *En attendant Godot*, Roger Blin, but Blin's influences grew to be Beckett's as well: Artaud, Copeau of Vieux Colombier, and Barrault. Early, the American director Herbert Blau saw the connection among Blin, Artaud and Beckett thus:

According to Beckett (though, of what I know of Blin, this is not quite accurate), Blin considered himself a disciple of Artaud, who – having observed that Western actors have forgotten how to scream – denounced the theatre as we know it because it could never be cruel enough. Whether or not it was sufficient became a subject of disagreement between the two [. . .] when Blin later directed *Endgame* [. . .]. Certainly Blin admired Artaud [James Knowlson calls them 'close friends' (Knowlson 1996: 348)], and so did Beckett, though he didn't approve the enraptured ethic of ritual violence, with its sacrificial actor signaling through the flames, as if the apotheosis of theatre – its naked, sonorous, streaming realization, reimagined from the Orphic mysteries – were nothing but a scream. (Blau 2000: 14)

Of Blin in 1950, Beckett wrote to Georges Duthuit on 27 February as follows: 'I have seen Blin. He wants, sorry, would like to put on Godot. [. . .] Nice fellow. Very Montparnasse. I know him well by sight, great friend of Artaud, on whom he is going to do a Brod, in three volumes. But a bit embarrassed all the same.' In a gloss to Beckett's comment, the *Letters* editors explain that 'SB believes [*sic*] that Blin is intending to champion his [Artaud's] work, as Max Brod – in his case quite unapologetically – did for that of Franz Kafka, perhaps by publishing hitherto unknown works by Artaud, or his papers and letters (of which Blin is reported as possessing an abundance)' (*Letters* 2 184).

Beckett's idea of performance has, finally, more than a little in common with Artaud's call for a new theatre and his vision of the performing body. Susan Sontag has noted that Artaud's sense of the body was decidedly Gnostic. In a review of her essay collection, *Under the Sign of Saturn*, for the *New York Times* (23 November 1980), David Bromwich undercuts that insight, however: 'in her essay on Artaud, Miss Sontag describes Gnosticism as "a sensibility," and by doing so goes some way toward domesticating it'. Certainly Blau was interested neither in a domesticated Artaud, nor a domesticated theatre, and neither was Beckett, quite the contrary. Beckett's intent ran counter to aestheticising or domesticating agony, or anything else, for that matter. Such a scream as Artaud sought, with or without an actor's signalling through the flames, is how Blau saw Beckett's undomesticated theatre, and he cites an anecdote from Beckett's meeting with Harold Pinter. Beckett told the English playwright about a visit to a cancer ward and a man dying from throat cancer: 'I could hear his screams continually in the night [. . .] That's the only kind of form my work has' (Blau 2000: 14). That apparently was, or is, sufficient; even as what screams Beckett's theatre generates may be muffled, internalised, they remain central to the work's affect, even as he underplayed his relationship with Artaud. Asked by his American publisher, Barney Rosset, for a comment on Grove Press's newly translated edition of *The Theatre and Its Double*, Beckett declined so direct an association in a letter of 10 March 1958: 'Afraid I have nothing to say on the subject of the Artaud book. I'm sorry to be so eternally unsatisfactory' (*Letters 3* 116). But the editors of *Letters 3* note in their 'Chronology 1964' that Beckett attended '*Theatre of Cruelty* [workshop] productions organised by Charles Marowitz and Peter Brook, at LAMDA [London Academy of Music and Dramatic Art]', the date given as 29 January 1964, confirmed in a letter to Barbara Bray of 28 January, Beckett attending with Max Frisch, whose *Andorra* was in rehearsals at the Old Vic (*Letters 3* 587, 592–3). James Knowlson says little of the *Theatre of Cruelty* workshop production itself but reports,

> [Edward] Albee was in town for rehearsals [of *Who's Afraid of Virginia Woolf?*, directed by Alan Schneider] and remembered going for drinks with Beckett, Harold Pinter and Patrick Magee, who was about to play in Peter Brook's Royal Shakespeare production of Peter Weiss's play *Marat/Sade*, when they all sat around in the pub enthusiastically discussing the Marquis de Sade. (Knowlson 1996: 458)

While not prepared to share Artaud's agenda to disestablish authorship, although he was prepared to destabilise it, and not ready to discredit literature like Artaud, 'All writing is garbage' (Sontag 1988: 85–7), but quite ready to downplay literariness. As a theatre artist Beckett would grow less tied to the idea of permanent, inviolable, even sacred texts than to performance as a plane of research, a space of continuous process, of movement and flow, and so, finally, of change; and as he grew to be a committed man of theatre himself, such process, such flow came to be associated with the lived feel of existence, of which art was an image, its impact affect. Beckett's swerve towards the performative at very least redefines the idea of texts and textuality, and so of literature. In *What Is Philosophy?*, Gilles Deleuze and Félix Guattari would see such movement in Heraclitus, and then in Spinoza, Nietzsche and Bergson, as a plane of immanence and a mode of becoming, and, further, they found in Artaud's *The Peyote Dance* (Sontag 1988: 382–91) a link between a 'plane of consciousness' and 'a limitless plane of immanence', which, however, 'also engenders hallucinations, erroneous perceptions, bad feelings' (Deleuze and Guattari 1994: 49).[3] These are among Artaud's cruel emotions, based on 'thoughts [. . .] that begin to exhibit snarls, screams, stammers; it talks in tongues and leads it to create, or to try to' (Deleuze and Guattari 1994: 55). Artaud and finally Deleuze would celebrate such 'hallucinations', such 'snarls, screams' and 'erroneous perceptions', as the work of a madman, an idiot, or even a schizophrenic. For Beckett such fits and stammerings were not simply a gloss on Lucky's speech in *En attendant Godot*, but a way of doing theatre, a line of theatrical development that Deleuze calls immanent, a perspective, an emphasis, or an aesthetics, even, a process of thought and motion that would bring Beckett closer to (but never coeval with) the radical performativity that Artaud advocated and that finds much of its fulfilment in Beckett's late plays, stuttering works like *Not I* and *Play*, for example, or 'hallucinatory' works like *What Where*, *That Time* and *Footfalls*. Beckett was not prepared to reduce all art to or to subsume all art under the rubric of performance as a or the total art form, but he did share Artaud's principle that theatre should be pared down, that the theatrical experience should be as little mediated as possible and that performance should address neither mind nor body but the audience's total existence, at its nerve ends. Theatre may not be the means of unifying mind and body, but Beckett was prepared to share some of Artaud's Modernist delirium.

Sontag's assessment of Artaud and the body and her emphasis on his Gnosticism do stress Artaud's quest for reconciliation, at least of mind and body, what Bromwich calls 'domestication', and which Artaud thought for a time surrealism might offer. But the body as nerve centre is also what Artaud called a body without organs, as he wrote in his poem *To Have Done Away with the Judgment of God*: 'The body is the body / it is alone / it has no need of organs'. This is not a body *lacking* organs, but a pre-organic, undifferentiated body: 'no mouth / no tongue / no teeth / no larynx / no stomach / no anus / I will reconstruct the man that I am'. Deleuze will build a philosophy around such an image of the body without organs, and such an image might help suggest Beckett's post-humanism. Julia Walker assesses Sontag's position on the Gnostic body thus: 'Sontag maps Artaud's varied career onto four stages of Gnosticism – the affirmation of the body, the revulsion from the body, the wish to transcend the body, the quest to redeem the body' (Walker 2009: 132). Beckett may have little interest either in the affirmation or the redemption of the body, but Artaud's two central preoccupations certainly do map a territory that Beckett explored for much of his creative career.

Barrault's rapport, his rapprochement, his own version of aesthetic Gnosticism, that is, his working between these dominant twentieth-century figures, was shared with his audiences in the outsized, totemic photographs its members passed between as they entered the theatre. Such devaluation, the desacralisation of text is evident in Beckett's own rapprochement with performativity, with an art that hesitates and stutters, theatre, as often as not, an interruption in a continuity of mutterings and stutterings most clearly evident in *Not I*. Such a performative turn is much in evidence in his communication with publishers as well, since they constitute something of a liminal space between stasis and flow, between literature and performance. Writing as early as 18 May 1961 to Judith Schmidt of Grove Press about *Happy Days* (which he was translating almost simultaneously into German and Italian so that he was juggling at least three versions of the play): 'I should prefer the text not to appear in any form before production and not in book form until I have seen some rehearsals in London [to be directed by Donald McWhinnie, but after Alan Schneider's New York premiere]. It can't be definitive without actual work in the theatre.'[4] Or writing to Rosset about *Not I* on 7 August 1972, Beckett again foregrounds the creative function of performance: 'With regard to publication I prefer to hold it back for the sake of whatever light N.Y. and London rehearsals may shed. I have not yet sent the text to Faber.' Faber would publish *Not I* as a standalone volume featuring Billie Whitelaw's Mouth in 1973; Grove, in the miscellaneous collection, *First Love and Other Shorts*, in 1974.

But 'definitive' became less transcendent than immanent as Beckett worked more directly in and with theatre. Even after the appearance of the 'definitive' text from Grove Press and Faber & Faber, for example, Beckett turned his attention to the work afresh on two subsequent and separate occasions when he approached it as its director: *Glückliche Tage*, the *Happy Days* he directed in German in 1971 at the Werkstatt of Berlin's famed Schiller Theater and for which he kept a *Regiebuch*, that is, a detailed director's notebook which amounted to a rewriting; and the more famous production, his 1979 direction of Billie Whitelaw at London's Royal Court Theatre for which he also kept a detailed production notebook that James Knowlson edited and annotated as *'Happy Days': The Production Notebook of Samuel Beckett*, which appeared 1985.

Much of Beckett's transition, a career shift, really, may have been unplanned and came through total theatrical immersion in the 1960s as he found it difficult to escape the demands of performance. He seems to have slipped into a directing career like Krapp on his banana peel, by accident, by default, and even to relish at times the socialising that accompanied what amounted to almost a public creation of his art. Although Roger Blin acknowledged Beckett's increased involvement in performance from *En attendant Godot* to *Fin de partie*, Chabert may have witnessed something like the transformation, a conversion, an epiphanic moment for Beckett as he explains rehearsals for a Pinget play:

> Originally I had agreed to direct *Hypothesis*, a play with a single character. But faced with the daunting problems of this production, Pinget appealed to Beckett to attend rehearsals and to help us. Beckett came to a run-though of *Hypothesis* in the dance studio of the Scola Cantorum. After the run-through he made no comment except that he was willing to work on it, but first he had to find an 'idea' that would make the play more theatrical. In fact his mind was already working on this 'idea', and without another word he left as he had arrived. (Chabert 1986: 117–18)

What Beckett observed in the rehearsals of *L'Hypothèse* was a character, Mortin, himself rehearsing hypotheses from a text alleged to have been destroyed, and in conversation with it or between it and a projected image of some version of himself on a screen. What Beckett saw then was a theatre of dispersed or multiple character images; or character (an actor), the projected series of images, and the textual manifestation of Mortin. Chabert made the inevitable comparison to Beckett's earlier work in which he played the lead under Beckett's direction as well:

> In *Krapp* [*Krapp's Last Tape*], the protagonist, throughout the duration, talks to another version of himself, his recorded voice from thirty years earlier, thanks to a tape recording. In *Hypothesis*, Mortin

encounters, not the ghost of his father, [. . .] but his own image reflected
as in a mirror, an image which never ceases to haunt and invade him
– a dialogue made possible thanks to another technical medium, a
moving film. (1986: 118)

The text itself, a typescript sitting on a desk, becomes a character
in this performance, as was physically manifest in Krapp's archive
of tapes, as it had been implicitly in Hamm's chronicles in *Fin de
partie* but which will be featured materially again as a text in *Ohio
Impromptu*. In *L'Hypothèse*, text, tapes and narratives become
thus another mirror, or rather another set of branching, multiple
or doubling images. And again Chabert phrases this relationship
thus:

> The manuscript demonstrates the relationship between Mortin and
> the writing, Mortin and his work, because without the manuscript, the
> author is 'practically non-existent'. Mortin has an umbilical attach-
> ment to his work. [. . .] The relationship between the character and the
> manuscript is a physical and visceral one. There is a sensual one, even
> in the contact. [. . .] The manuscript is an object, *a being*, a relation, *a
> body*. (1986: 122; emphasis added)

One might quibble some with Chabert's phrasing, which is hier-
archical as it focuses on '*the* character' as the primary entity and
so subordinating other manifestations as, say, reflections of an
original, but, as the sole actor in the performance under Beckett's
direction, he can be forgiven for seeing himself as the focal point,
as a principal being, in traditional terms a character embodied by
a live actor. In performance, however, being itself may finally be
elusive, dispersed, evade confinement and slip into becoming, that
is, the movement, flow or interchange between the live actor, the
projected images and the leaves of the text, which are gradually
discarded to cover the stage and are finally burned.

This visceral relationship with the text appears to have been 'the
idea' that Beckett brought to the production, like that of Krapp
with his tapes, and the voice of the projected image, unlike that in
Krapp, Chabert reminds us, is intrusive, 'it breaks into his universe
and its presence alone is a form of aggression. [. . .] It also makes
it clear that he is himself the subject, the author about whom he is
talking. [. . .] The form in which the image appears by surprise has
a shattering effect in its filmic doubling of the character' (1986:

123). Such an intrusive voice, projected as if exterior, a voice between interior and exterior, would feature in Beckett's own teleplay that he was writing at almost the same moment that he was reconceiving *L'Hypothèse – Eh Joe*, begun in earnest at Ussy on 13 April 1965. *L'Hypothèse* itself then enacts images, the devaluing of the text in the performing of it, replaces the material text with its performance, even as its function is raised to that of material character: Artaud, thus, simultaneously embraced and distanced, if not rejected.

Through Deleuze

If the conjunction between Beckett and Artaud seems, at casual glance, unlikely, another such might be that between Beckett and Gilles Deleuze, whom Beckett doubtless never read. Deleuze was, nevertheless, the apostle, after Nietzsche, of betweenness, which we might define, after Beckett, as neitherness, that is, neither wholly of one nor of another, but partly of both, which, most simply, is Bergson's definition of the image itself, neither wholly physical nor wholly metaphysical, or as material as it is immaterial. In his assessment of French cinéaste Jean-Luc Godard, for instance, Deleuze stresses such in betweenness, between sound and vision, between television and cinema, between image and text. This is Deleuze's critique of post-war cinema as a 'time image', which offers the perspective of a disinterested, bodiless perceiver and which, at its best, presents the pure flow of time, becoming. Deleuze's in betweenness, admittedly, owes much to what French metaphysician Henri Bergson would call *durée*, and whose formulation of the image Deleuze essentially follows as something between matter and memory, as much material as immanence. As Deleuze reminds us in his essay on Beckett's teleplays, 'The Exhausted', an image is neither representation nor thing, but a process, a constant becoming, which, as it creates affect is the ultimate impact of art, not only in cinema but in other arts as well. Such an emphasis on process, flow and becoming, a perpetual in betweenness, between stasis and movement, between text and image, suggests an incipient theory of theatre as well. Beckett's colour pallet, excepting *Quad*, which is startling in its exceptionality, is restricted to grey, not a blend of white and black, nor a 'light black', as Clov would have it, but close to Clov's vision of 'light dying', a twilight, perhaps, a light between white and black, a paleness associated with, connected to both, embracing neither. Certainly, in Beckett's work, particularly his late work for theatre and television in which we find a preponderance of spectral, grey figures, ghosts, what appears on stage or screen as a something, a material entity, an object, is not always fully present, something not quite wholly material, nor quite immaterial or ethereal either, something in between presence and absence, sound and image, or text and image, between the real and surreal, an image between inner and outer, matter and mind, Beckett himself thus an artist in between, neither wholly of his time nor wholly of ours, say, fully neither, even as he is always, if partly, both.

The pacing May of *Footfalls* is a case in point: apparently a physical, material entity on stage, or at least we as audience perceive an image in motion, she may not be there at all, or not fully there, as the final short scene of the stage without her figure suggests. Spirit become light, say, as the assailing voice of *Eh Joe* echoes her fellow victim. Beckett's theatre is thus not about something, not a simulation or representation of a known or knowable world; the image or images of the artistic creation are not images of something outside the work; they are *'that something itself'*, as he famously quipped as early as 1929 in reference to James Joyce's then-titled *Work in Progress* (*Disjecta* 27). Beckett's move into television reemphasised the imagistic nature of performance with bodiless narrators' voices offering narratives contrary to images we see on screen, voices performing narrative dislocations. Such a disembodied narrator of *What Where* tells us, for instance, that 'This is Bam', Bam thus already an object other than the narrating voice of Bam, who apparently is himself plural already, a multiplicity. 'We are the last five', he tells us, the grammar sliding from singular, Bam, to the multiple, a voice that is a 'We' (Beckett 2006: 153). At best, however, images of four characters appear, identified as the barely distinguishable Bam, Bim, Bom and Bem, the mysterious fifth, apparently 'Bum' if we follow through on the vowel sequence, only incipient or already dispatched. 'In the present as were we still', the voice continues, the subjunctive tense or mood signalling the fact that this statement is contrary to fact (153). These are characters not there, voices from beyond the grave, the pattern of images coming and going, moving to and fro, to an off-stage not empty but fraught with possibility, to receive 'the works'.

Such images with their narrative and visual dislocations disrupt expected continuity and are part of or give an insight into the pure

flow of time, what Deleuze calls the Plane of Immanence, perceptions always on the verge of becoming, that is, becoming other,
something else, unsettling the received, that which we expect;
they are thus a material bridge that generates affect, an emotional
response not always specifiable or describable. The classical artist
assumes an omnipotence and 'raises himself artificially out of Time
in order to give relief to his chronology and causality to his development', as Beckett phrased it in his treatise on Marcel Proust
(1957: 81). Art is the pure expression of pure feeling, he noted in
Proust, to present a 'non-logical statement of phenomena in the
order and exactitude of their perception, before they have been
distorted into intelligibility in order to be forced into a chain of
cause and effect' (86). Such a non-logical statement of phenomena
is difficult to achieve through language, and Beckett recognises the
fact: 'At that level you break up words to diminish shame. Painting
and music have so much better a chance', he admitted to Lawrence
Harvey (1970: 249). Billie Whitelaw describes her performance in
Footfalls thus: 'Sometimes I felt as if he were a sculptor and I a
piece of clay [. . .]. Sometimes I felt as though I were modeling for
a painter or working with a musician. The movements started to
feel like dance' (Whitelaw 1996: 144).

Such a world as Beckett achieved is thus a virtual world that
includes and commingles past and present, material figures, imagination and memory; off-stage or what appears to be empty space
is thus a virtual whole, a nothing full of possibilities, including all
possible actions and movements. In this regard Beckett's theatre
runs contrary to that described by Peter Brook in his famous theatrical treatise, *The Empty Space*; for Beckett the stage is never
empty. The fourth scene of *Footfalls* remains full of nothing, of
interpretive possibilities, opens those possibilities even further. It
is always replete, full of potential meanings and worlds, of all the
possibilities that theatre has to offer since it includes the whole
of the past as well as the full potential to create new worlds. The
space then is always already full; in short, it contains the process of
the virtual, part of Deleuze's Plane of Immanence. Beckett's plays
do not represent a world of actuality as we know it or as can be
known, a world outside themselves, do not, in fact, represent at
all, but offer images that make us feel, in their generated affect,
the movement of existence, its flow, becoming, *durée*. Possibilities
are not closed off by separating inside from outside, matter from
spirit, present from past.

What has too often frustrated readers or spectators is precisely this resistance to, this undermining of representation that characterises Beckett's art since most of us operate on the Plane of Transcendence that produces or alludes to an exterior to the art work, the world we know and try to represent in art. This is the world of what Beckett calls the classical artist (1957: 81). For Deleuze the perceiving mind of a doubting Cartesian subject is only a piece of ribbon that separates inside from outside, or is merely a membrane, as Beckett dubs it in *The Unnamable*, where the narrator calls himself a tympanum vibrating and in between, like the ribbon, neither inside nor out but both in relation to the other. The Plane of Transcendence, or what Foucault has called an 'ethics of knowledge', is the struggle for grounding, a search for ultimate truths, say, that we are driven to obey. Who is Godot? What information is being solicited in *What Where*? What are the secrets being exchanged in *Come and Go*? These are, we might venture, exactly the wrong questions to ask of these works. The right question is to ask how these performances work, what sorts of affect are they generating, what possible worlds have they unveiled and led us into? The series of plateaus, perhaps 1,000, that Deleuze critiques in the book of that title, is an assault against such groundings, the stability of language included, as is Beckett's art. Transcendence is a human disease that Deleuze calls 'interpretosis' and what the director of *Catastrophe* calls 'This craze for explicitation. Every I dotted to death. Little gag. For God's sake!' (*CDW* 459). 'We're not beginning to . . . to . . . mean something', asks Hamm. 'Mean something!' responds Clov, 'You and I mean something? Ah, that's a good one' (*Endgame* 22), and they share a communal laugh over the possibility of transcendence, that they might be representative, part of a greater system, or a greater truth beyond images of themselves in process, in performance. The alternative to transcendence is to accept, to embrace, even to love, simply what is; Deleuze's term like Foucault's is also an ethics, but, after Nietzsche, an 'ethics of the *amor fati*', the love of fate as necessity, or simply of what is.

One anecdote that Hamm tells has often been cited by critics but less than satisfactorily critiqued. The 'madman' that Hamm visits in the asylum is shown the beauty of an exterior, the corn, the herring fleet, from which the madman turns away appalled. Hamm's conclusion is that 'He [the madman] alone had been spared' (41). Critics may point out the likely reference here to the visionary poet

William Blake, but what or how the 'madman' has been spared is seldom parsed. One possibility is that he has been spared preoccupation with the requirements of a transcendent world; he has doffed what Deleuze will call the illusion of transcendence, an illusion that will close and explain experience. Hamm's 'madman', this 'idiot', is thinking 'other', possible, alternative worlds. It may indeed be those alternative worlds that Hamm keeps asking Clov to find beyond the shelter. In Act II of *Waiting for Godot* the issue is put thus: 'We are all born mad. Some remain so' (Beckett 1954: 77). Perhaps those are the saved, the parallel to the one thief on the cross. Hamm's gesture is, evidently, to pull the madman back from the end of the world. Hamm's position, his attitude (yes, seated) would resist the flow of alternatives, becomings, *durée*. Later a wearier Hamm concludes the prayer scene with an overt rejection of such transcendence, such 'ethics of knowledge'. Of a transcendental reality, God, he says, 'The bastard. He doesn't exist' (*Endgame* 34), a line Beckett deemed indispensable to his play in his battle with Britain's Lord Chamberlain. Perhaps Hamm too has been or might be spared, saved.

In his playlet of 1968 that Beckett designated as images of motion, *Come and Go*, we are denied access to information that would, if disclosed, shut down the process of thinking. Without that knowledge, without those revelations, the process, the thinking, the generation of possibilities, alternatives, parallels the flow of movement on stage. Language is not so much devalued among the 128 (or so) words in this dramaticule since much of it is elegant, musical and poetic. What is resisted is knowledge that would still movement and flow, freeze it, and end a process that Deleuze calls thinking or philosophy.

When the American actress Jessica Tandy complained, first to director Alan Schneider and then, bypassing him, directly to Beckett, that *Not I*'s suggested running time of twenty-three minutes rendered the work unintelligible to audiences, Beckett telegraphed back his now famous but oft misconstrued injunction, 'I'm not unduly concerned with intelligibility. I hope the piece may work on the nerves of the audience, not its intellect' (cited in Brater 1974: 200). If we take Beckett at his word and do not simply treat this comment as a dismissal of the actress or an admonition that she listen to her director, through whom, as he told her, he would henceforth communicate, he is suggesting a theoretical position, a theory of theatre. Evidence for the latter may be found in his attitude towards *Play*, which, similarly, should be staged at incomprehensible speed. Admittedly, many a director, Alan Schneider among them, has resisted, or at least complied with other theatrical forces. Beckett's instructions to Schneider were that '*Play* was to be played through twice without interruption and at a very fast pace, each time taking no longer than nine minutes' (Schneider 1986: 341); that is, eighteen minutes overall. The producers of the New York premiere, Richard Barr, Clinton Wilder and, of all people, Edward Albee, threatened to drop the play from the programme if Schneider followed Beckett's instructions. Schneider capitulated, and wrote to Beckett for permission to slow the pace and to eliminate the *da capo*: 'For the first and last time in my long relationship with Sam, I did something I despised myself for doing. I wrote to him, asking if we could try having his text spoken only once, more slowly. Instead of telling me to blast off, Sam offered us his reluctant permission' (1986: 341).

What then are we to make of such a neural approach to theatre that seems to put the emphasis on what Deleuze, writing *after* Beckett, will call 'pure affect' (Deleuze and Guattari 1994: 96). We can resist Beckett here, as Schneider's producers and, finally, Schneider himself did, or take him at his word; that is, this is how theatre works, not dealing with overall truths, not outlining a compelling story, but by demonstrating process and change, life as immanence even as it is materially rooted. 'Make sense who may', Beckett would conclude his final work for the theatre, *What Where*.

In these shorter plays Beckett's most radical artistic vision, his most revolutionary theories of theatre, emerge. This brings us, moreover, to one of the most contentious questions in Beckett studies, the degree to which Beckett's work is representational at all, or, on the contrary, whether its persistent preoccupation is with resisting or breaking though representation, or rather focusing, putting the spotlight on how slippery and artificial representations are as they are played amid the Plane of Immanence, the perpetual flow of becoming. That is, Beckett's art on stage or page is not a stand-in for another reality; it is that reality itself and more often than not 'virtual' in the Deleuzean sense of that term. Beckett's theatre is always a theatre of becoming, a decomposition moving towards recomposition, itself decomposing, a deterritorialisation resisting reterritorialisation. It is a theatre of perpetual movement or flow, all comings and goings, a pulse that generates affect, even as the affect itself may be indescribable. Even as it often appears stationary or static, even amid the famous Beckettian pauses, images dominate, move, flow, become other, not representing a world that we already know, but perpetually creating new worlds. Bergson would call this *durée*, Deleuze 'becoming', Beckett simply art, or theatre. It is a theatre struggling to resist the world as we know it, struggling to resist conceptualising our world and the condition of being since those are mere snapshots and not the process, becoming.

Such an approach begins to suggest something of an Artaudian, Deleuzean, Beckettian line of performativity, which Barrault was able to sense, intuit and use, creating a theatrical rapport even amid differences.

Notes

1. Derrida 1991: 60–1.
2. 'When we rehearsed eyeball to eyeball, he opened up in me whatever there was to open up . . . I can still hear him saying "Too much colour, Billie, too much colour." That was his way of saying "Don't act." He wanted the essence of you to come out.' See http://theconversation.com/billie-whitelaw-was-one-of-becketts-greatest-actors-she-suffered-for-her-art-35776 (last accessed June 2016).
3. Artaud in fact wrote to Barrault from Mexico City on 10 July 1936 asking for money to help 'carry out a mission in connection with the old races of Indians [the Tarahumara]. This mission has to do with discovering and reviving the vestiges of the ancient Solar culture' (Sontag 1988: 374–5).
4. Beckett's letter to Grove Press of 18 May 1961 (not included in *Letters 3*, cited from the Rosset Archive) opens as follows: 'I shall soon begin to type final text of *Happy Days*. It will go off to you towards end of month. At the same time as to you I shall give copies to McWhinnie, who is to direct London production probably at Royal Court, and to Tophoven for German translation. Copies must also go as soon as possible to Suhrkamp and [Editore] Einaudi. I am not satisfied with it, but cannot bring it any further. I think and hope it is understood that Grove has world rights to this play.' Beckett would 'bring it [. . .] further' by working directly on stage, and such theatrical testing before publication became his preferred pattern for work written for theatre (see also Gontarski 1999).

References

Ackerley, C. J. and S. E. Gontarski (2006) *The Grove Companion to Samuel Beckett: A Reader's Guide to His Works, Life, and Thought*, New York: Grove Press.

Beckett, Samuel (1954) *Waiting for Godot*, New York: Grove Press.

Beckett, Samuel (1957) *Proust*, New York: Grove.

Beckett, Samuel (2006) *Krapp's Last Tape and Other Shorter Plays*, ed. S. E. Gontarski, London: Faber & Faber.

Blau, Herbert (2000) *Sails of the Herring Fleet: Essays on Beckett*, Ann Arbor, MI: University of Michigan Press.

Brater, Enoch (1974) 'The "I" in Beckett's *Not I*', *Twentieth Century Literature* 20:3 (July), pp. 189–200.

Bromwich, David (1980) 'Under the Sign of Saturn', *New York Times*, 23 November, at www.nytimes.com/1980/11/23/books/booksspecial/sontag-saturn.html?_r=0

Brook, Peter (1985) [1968] *The Empty Space: A Book About Theatre*, New York: Touchstone Reprints.

Chabert, Pierre (1986) 'Rehearsing Pinget's *Hypothesis* with Beckett', in *As No Other Dare Fail: For Samuel Beckett on His 80th Birthday by His Friends and Admirers*, trans. and ed. John Calder, London: John Calder, pp. 117–32.

Deleuze, Gilles (1995) 'The Exhausted', trans. Anthony Uhlmann, *Substance* 24:3, Issue 78, pp. 3–28.

Deleuze, Gilles and Félix Guattari (1994) *What Is Philosophy?*, trans. Hugh Tomlinson and Graham Burchell, New York: Columbia University Press.

Derrida, Jacques (1991) 'This Strange Institution We Call Literature', in *Acts of Literature*, ed. Derek Attridge, New York: Routledge.

Fowlie, Wallace (1959) 'The New French Theatre: Artaud, Beckett, Genet, Ionesco', *The Sewanee Review* 67:4, pp. 643–57.

Gontarski, S. E. (1999) 'Beckett's *Play*, in extenso', *Modern Drama* 42:3, pp. 442–55.

Harvey, Lawrence E. (1970) *Samuel Beckett: Poet and Critic*, Princeton: Princeton University Press.

Knowlson, James (1996) *Damned to Fame: The Life of Samuel Beckett*, London: Bloomsbury.

Schneider, Alan (1986) *Entrances: An American Director's Journey*, New York: Viking Press.

Sontag, Susan (1988) *Antonin Artaud: Selected Writings*, Berkeley: University of California Press.

Walker, Julia A. (2009) 'Sontag on Theater', in *The Scandal of Susan Sontag*, ed. Barbara Ching and Jennifer A. Wagner-Lawlor, New York: Columbia University Press.

Whitelaw, Billie (1996) *Billie Whitelaw ... Who He?*, New York: St Martin's Press.

13

Greying the Canon: Beckett in Performance, Beckett as Performance

Samuel Beckett's resistance to self-refection, to a public meta-text, to theorising his own theatre was legendary, and yet his personal letters and notebooks, his intimate, occasionally 'uncautious' conversations with directors and actors, were replete with just such reflections and revelations. While he told the critic Colin Duckworth in 1965, 'I'd be quite incapable of writing a critical introduction to my work' (Duckworth 1966: xxiv), his own musings – recorded in manuscripts and typescripts, in theatrical notebooks, in letters to directors, publishers, friends and confidants – constitute, collectively, just such critical insights.

The disparity suggests something of a multiplicity of voices, diction and contra-diction, a plural, at times a dialogic relation with his work. In one voice private discourse echoed public posture as it outlined a resistance to and incapacity for self-reflection. In a letter of 18 October 1954 to his American publisher, Barney Rosset, Beckett expressed a sense of diminished authority of authorship soon after translating *Waiting for Godot*.[1] In a London meeting with Ralph Richardson, Beckett 'told him that all I knew about Pozzo was in the text, that if I had known more I would have put it in the text, and that this was true also of the other characters' (*Letters 2* 507).

The position bordered on the obsessive and Beckett restated it to his American director Alan Schneider nearly a decade and a half later, on 16 October 1972, looping back again to the Richardson incident. This time the offending 'stars' were the legendary American theatrical couple, Hume Cronin and Jessica Tandy, the play in question, *Not I*:

This is the old business of the author's *supposed privileged informa-tion* as when Richardson wanted the lowdown on Pozzo's background before he could consider the part. I no more know where she is [in this case Mouth in *Not I*] or why than she does. All I know is in the text. 'She' is purely a stage entity, part of a stage image and purveyor of a stage text. The rest is Ibsen. (Harmon 1998: 283; emphasis added)

To Duckworth he termed that 'stage entity' merely 'an object': 'I produce an object. What people make of it is not my concern' (Duckworth 1966: xxiv).

Such resistance to self-reflection is sprinkled throughout not only Beckett's letters but also in newspaper articles and those limited interviews that Beckett granted. On 26 October 1957, he wrote to Schneider, 'Sorry I was not of more help about the play [*Endgame*] but the less I speak about my work the better' (Harmon 1998: 17). When Schneider and Rosset decided to publish what amounted to evidence to the contrary – excerpts from Beckett's letters published in *The Village Voice* to help advertise *Endgame* and make it more accessible to its American audience – they did so without sufficient clearances. Beckett was furious. He wrote to Rosset adamantly on 8 January 1958: 'I am disturbed by the letter montage. You don't say what it's for. I suppose the programme. I dislike the ventilation of private documents. They [the *Endgame* letters] shed no light on my work' (*Letters 3* 92). He repeated the admonition to Schneider the following day, 'I received from Barney yesterday jacket of book and extracts from our letters, with no indication of what the latter was for. This disturbed me as I do not like the publication of letters' (*Letters 3* 93). Even as he became his own theatrical director (some might say his own best interpreter), much of that public posture remained intact. Asked by Michael Haerdter, his assistant during rehearsals of *Endspiel* (*Endgame*) in 1967, 'Are you of the opinion that the author should have a solution for the riddle at hand?', Beckett replied curtly, 'Not the author of this play' (cited in McMillan and Fehsenfeld 1988: 14). When Ruby Cohn came to edit Beckett's *Miscellaneous Writings* in 1984 under Beckett's suggested title *Disjecta*, that is, *disiecta membra*, or scattered fragments, limbs or remains, she included the *Endgame* letters that Beckett disparaged to Rosset and Schneider to no objection, so that they have since become part of the official pronouncements on the play, an extension of the play itself, and thus part of Beckett's *oeuvre*.

Such extension of the canon is precisely what Beckett sought to resist, evidently, the traditional presumption of authorial authority, what he called the 'supposed' privilege of authorship. While he may have recoiled from the role of omniscient author, creating and proffering instead an image of authorial impoverishment, indigence and impotence, a diminished author-ity, he nonetheless simultaneously extended such authority, insisting on the primacy of text and the author throughout the process of performance, and so projecting authorial presence into the theatrical process (in what was otherwise an age of the director) to an unprecedented extent. The public posture of diminished authority often became a useful strategy of deflection, itself something of a performance, a powerful creation that resonated with the public and thus inseparable from the theatricality of the work itself. As the Beckett canon is extended into the palimpsest that Gerard Genette calls 'paratexts', that is, as more of the peripheral, secondary, or what we might call the grey canon comes to light, is made public (letters, notebooks, manuscripts, and the like), and is cited repeatedly by scholars, it is thus folded into the official texts; it inevitably interacts with and re-shapes, re-defines, even from the margins (or especially from the margins), the white canon or the traditional canon, and the more apparent it becomes that Beckett's voice was as plural if not as contradictory as that of his (other) characters. That is, Beckett had at least a second alternate or counter voice regarding his work. He had, in short, a great deal more insight into his creations and their circumstances than is apparent (at least directly) in his texts, despite protestations to the contrary. The voice of Beckett we hear as a commentator on his work might best be read as fictive, the creation of his own imago, an ideal reader or spectator.

As the grey canon has expanded, then, it sounds another, a counter voice. Schneider himself heard that voice more than most. On 21 November 1957, Beckett would be more open or 'uncautious' to his American director about the relationship of the boy in Hamm's story to the young Clov than he would be to Cluchey in 1980. What *Hamm evokes* in his 'chronicles', he told Schneider, are 'events leading up to Clov's arrival, alone presumably, the father having fallen by the way'. He further confided to Schneider that 'Clov's "perception" [the word in quotation marks suggests Clov's fabrication, Clov's own narrative] of boy at end [is] to be interpreted as [a] *vision* of himself *on last lap to "shelter"*' (Harmon 1998: 23; emphasis added). Beckett's observation is a stunning detail, and with such direct revelations to Schneider,

Beckett affirmed that *both* Hamm and Clov are, amid their dreams and visions, telling stories, chronicles, that take as their subject Clov's early years and his arrival at the shelter. That is, Beckett's comments finally form something like traditional exposition, more Ibsen than he would like to acknowledge. As more letters and notebooks emerge and are made available, the more apparent it becomes that Beckett had a counter voice regarding his work; that is, he had a great deal more insight into his characters and their circumstances than he revealed (at least directly) in his texts. Why else did a small circle of directors incessantly seek his council? Beckett may have been repelled by the thought of 'writing a critical introduction' to his work, but his consultations with directors, on paper and in person, and his self- conversations in preparation for his own productions recorded in *The Theatrical Notebooks of Samuel Beckett* series, nearly constitute that abhorred introduction (if not a theatrical manifesto).

Unsurprisingly, Beckett resisted the transition to the public role of self-interpreter or self-commentator that directing entailed. As he wrote to Schneider on 7 July 1967:

> Have undertaken like an imbecile to direct *Endgame* for the Schiller (Werkstatt). Five weeks beginning Aug. 16. Schröder (whom I don't know) and Bollmann (whom I do and like) Hamm & Clov. Latter apparently miscast. But a tubby Clov will be a change. Set by Matias. That shd. about finish me if all goes well. (Harmon 1998: 211)

Rather than finish him, directing *Endspiel* launched an official directing career that would include some twenty-two productions in three languages and would last until his own *Schwanengesang*, *Was Wo (What Where)*, at Süddeutscher Rundfunk, Stuttgart, in 1985. Such a project would leave a residue, an extraordinary collection of notebooks documenting that self-collaboration, the director in intimate conversation with the author, that dominated the last two decades of his creative life.

In 1967, then, after almost a full year of non-stop theatre, advising and mostly uncredited directing ('Forget what writing is about', he wrote to Rosset), Beckett accepted the invitation from the Schiller Theater to direct a play; he chose *Endspiel* (*Endgame*), the 'favourite of my plays', he confessed to Haerdter in Berlin, or as he put it to Tom Bishop, 'I suppose the one I dislike least is *Endgame*' (McMillan and Fehsenfeld 1988: 163). As he approached the Schiller *Endspiel* he rethought his play on paper in a *Regiebuch*, a meticulous director's notebook. Such notes would thenceforth characterise his approach to directing, and directing would in turn liberate the counter voice. One understands very quickly reading the notebooks, reading Beckett on Beckett, that the apparently disconnected dialogue of his plays is on the contrary linked by a strong, almost traditional subtext. On the one hand, in Berlin he resisted intellectualising his text with his actors ('I don't want to talk about my play, it has to be taken purely dramatically, to take shape on the stage. [. . .] Here the only interest of the play is as dramatic material' [*TN* 2 xxi]); that is, the 'stage entity' he spoke of to Schneider or the 'object' to Duckworth. But Beckett also and astonishingly suggested to his cast that 'the play is to be acted as though there were a fourth wall where the footlights are'. While, on occasion, he would reject cogent connections ('Here it oughtn't to be played logically'), more often he would offer just such connections. He cautioned Schneider in 1957, 'Don't seek deep motivation everywhere', but he went on almost immediately to explain the logic of the apparently illogical red faces of Hamm and Clov, as opposed to the very white faces of Nagg and Nell, although its function is finally formal: 'Actually illogical that H and C, living in confinement, should have red faces. Scenically it serves to stress the couples and keep them apart' (Harmon 1998: 29).

Beckett had regularly revealed what he called 'uncautious' and privileged information to Schneider ('I never talked so unrestrainedly and uncautiously as with you', he wrote to his director on 11 January 1956 [Harmon 1998: 8]), and such connections were a lifeline to the oft-perplexed American director (as they were to many other directors). While he told Schneider on 29 December 1957, 'I simply can't write about my work, or occasional stuff of any kind' (Harmon 1998: 24), by 10 January 1958 he was doing just that. He explained to Schneider that after Hamm's second 'What'll I do!', Clov's enigmatic 'Pity' suggests the hostility between them: 'pity you don't give me the opportunity of saying "There are no more lozenges"' (*CDW* 127). Such comments sound very like what used to be called 'subtext' in the theatre. Beckett outlined several of the key themes for Schneider. Hamm snarls '*Your* light!' (*CDW* 98) because 'Every man has his own light. Hamm is blind, in the dark, his light has died. What he means is: "Think of me in my black world and don't come whining to me because yours is fading"' (Harmon 1988: 29). Hamm's need for light drives his tour around the room and is manifest in his preoccupation with the colour white: 'It seems they've [my eyes] have gone all white' (94); 'He's [the black dog] white, isn't he?' (111); 'Am I very white . . . I'm asking you if I'm very white!' (123). Schneider was puzzled by Hamm's final soliloquy and especially Hamm's line as he discards his paraphernalia, 'A few more squirms like that and I'll call' (33). Beckett explains that 'to call' means here 'to call out' – for Clov and his father, terrestrial and celestial, apparently. Beckett elaborates: 'This time he feels that Clov will not "come running" and that his father will not answer. But he cannot be *absolutely* certain until he has whistled and called in vain' (Harmon 1998: 30). In Beckett's outline to Schneider, the dramatic line of *Endgame* is almost conventional: Hamm and Clov take refuge from their misery not only in the shelter but in their dreams and visions as well. Beckett directly linked such preoccupation to a biblical quotation from Acts 2:17: 'And it shall come to pass in the last days, saith God, I will pour out of my Spirit upon all flesh, and your sons and your daughters shall prophesy, and your young men see visions, and your old men shall dream dreams.' Hamm and Clov endure their existence, their '"thing" by projecting away from it', he explained, 'Clov outwards towards going, Hamm inwards towards abiding. When Clov admits to having his visions less it means that his escape mechanism is breaking down. Dramatically this allows his perception of life (the boy) at the end and of course of the rat to be construed as hallucination' (Harmon 1998: 22–31). That is, the breakdown of Clov's *vision* of escape forces him to create an alternative, another cycle to life in the shelter with his playing Hamm and another boy's playing Clov. But their escape mechanisms resurface on occasion: Hamm, 'Let's go from here the two of us, South!' (*CDW* 109); 'But beyond the hills? Eh? Perhaps it's still green' (111). To Hamm's story of the young 'brat', Clov responds: 'He would have climbed the trees' (122). This dialogue associated with dreams and visions, the residuum of pastoralism, Beckett suggested, should be presented with a lyrical tone, in a 'life-voice' he told his German cast (McMillan and Fehsenfeld 1988: 221).

Rather than close off or ossify the play, such 'uncautious' revelations expose the richness of interpretive possibilities. In his revelations to actors and directors and especially through his own direction, Beckett taught us not only to look more closely at his work but to look for patterns, echoes and symmetries. Once we understand that Clov's opening monologue is already an echo, a repetition – that what appears to be Clov's voice is that of another, or that of others – the source of the voice we hear when characters (apparently) speak becomes of central concern; that is, who is echoing or speaking through whom becomes a central structural and thematic feature. Clov's opening, 'Finished, it's finished, nearly finished, it must be nearly finished' (*CDW* 93), not only announces the end of a play (or a day) barely begun, a paradox with which Beckett plays throughout this drama of endings and games, but is already an echo of Christ's Parthian shaft, his final words on the cross, as recorded by the author of John 19:30: 'When Jesus therefore had received the vinegar, he said, It is finished: and he bowed his head, and gave up the ghost', that is, became incorporeal or inhuman again. Among the play's play of echoes, Hamm reiterates these words near the play's end to announce his own demise, his own giving up the ghost, but Hamm's concluding remark, his echo of Christ, is already anticipated in Clov's opening because, as Hamm reminds us, the 'end is in the beginning' (126). With Hamm's final utterance, what is disclosed is perhaps a greater fear: the beginning may be in the end.

Clov's initial pronouncement of ending might reasonably lead to a critique of what exactly is finished: the morning ritual, the day itself (apparently just begun, if days begin or end at all in this world, with Hamm's unveiling, though he wants to go back to sleep and so apparently end the day at its inception), their lives, together or severally, or life itself, that is, more apocalyptically, does Clov announce (or dream) an end to existence, as he or they know it? The subaltern, Clov, has no language of his own, however, and so the subaltern is from the first already a colonial echo. Had he a language, he might offer an alternative version (or vision) of life in the shelter. Instead, he can only perform or re-play Hamm's script: 'Grain upon grain, one by one, and one day, suddenly, there's a heap, a little heap, the impossible heap' (93). The allusion is admittedly arcane; nonetheless, it generates much of the impetus, force and structure of their play. The apparent paradox is that as the end approaches, the more impossible the end is to achieve. The solution that Clov reiterates, knowingly or not, is that the part is already, illogically, paradoxically, the whole, the single grain already the heap, the instant already a life. In the conundrum, Clov (or Hamm, or 'the Old Greek', or Zeno, or Protagoras, or whomever Protagoras is echoing) asks at what point does one discrete grain and another discrete grain constitute a unit, a singularity we might call a heap? Or at what point do separate dramatic incidents or moments add up to a unit we might call a play, or an entity we might call a life. Beckett glossed the allusion to Schneider on 21 November 1957, 'the Heap and the Bald Head (which hair falling produces baldness)' (Harmon 1998: 23). Otherwise put, at what point can one define baldness? Is someone who loses a single hair bald? A second? A third? How many lost hairs does it take before we can say that person is bald. The difference between baldness and its opposite is finally but a single hair. 'One purpose of the image throughout the play', Beckett continues, 'is to suggest the impossibility logically, i.e., eristically, of the thing ever coming to an end [and he quotes himself]. "The end is in the beginning and yet we go on". In other words the impossibility of catastrophe. Ended at its inception, and at every subsequent instant, it continues, ergo can never end' (Harmon 1998: 23). Hamm returns to the paradox in terms of ontology as he contemplates the point at which separate instants of existence become or add up to the heap we call a life: 'all life long you wait for that to mount up to a life' (*CDW* 70). That existential, ontological conception (not just figurative, nor metonymic, nor synecdochic, the part for the whole, say, but more radically and literally the part *as* always already the whole) will inform much of Beckett's late, apparently metonymic but strongly imagistic theatre. All one ever has is the part, the fragment, the image, in life, in art.

Hamm's repetition of the paradox at the end of the play, then, reminds us that Clov's initial monologue is already a loop, a repetition among repetitions, an echo among echoes. When the nature of language itself arises in their conversation, Clov snaps at Hamm, 'I use the words you taught me. If they don't mean anything any more, teach me others. Or let me be silent' (44). Clov here is again an echo, this time of Caliban's malediction to Prospero in *The Tempest*, or in general the colonial's (even the Irish colonial's) complaint to his overlord:

> You taught me language; and my profit on't
> Is, I know how to curse: The red plague rid you
> For learning me your language!' (I.ii.365–7)

Being already an echo, Clov apparently has no substance, and so no character, no language of his own. What there is of what we might call character is a reflection, an echo of Hamm. 'The play is full of echoes', Beckett reminded his German cast in 1967, 'they all answer each other'. Much of that contrapuntal, dialectical structure of this game of endings emerges only in the performance, in the theatre, as Beckett became his own best interpreter in 1967 with his direction of *Endspiel* at the Schiller Theater (Werkstatt) – and subsequently with the echo of performance, the expansion of the grey canon with the publication of his notebooks and fully revised, rewritten texts.

Directing then allowed Beckett the luxury of approaching his work from multiple perspectives, using, dramatically, a plurality of voices, to be finally as 'uncautious' with his audience as he had been with Schneider. As director and author Beckett could approach his play from inside and outside simultaneously. Such luxury was afforded to him some fifteen times on stage and another seven times in the television studio; during each of those self-confrontations, he seized opportunities to play multiple roles, both self and other, and that multiplicity is reflected in the plurality of voices he used to discuss his work. He spoke differently as a director (or to directors) and as an author. On one level then, directing was liberating, allowing the 'director' to refine, if not re-define, the play's creative vision, to continue to discover latent possibilities in the texts, to demonstrate afresh his commitment to, if not preoccupation with, the form, the aesthetic shape of his work, even in the midst of its continual reshaping. Beckett had thus created his own ideal director, and so his own ideal spectator or reader.

In those conversations with himself that constitute his theatrical notebooks Beckett would explain to himself Clov's initial perplexity: 'For opening discover Cl [Clov] in perplexed position – then he looks' (*TN* 2 44–5, 195, 197); that is, he inspects the room before beginning a series of disclosures, unveilings, moving only his head, in the usual clockwise, circular order: Hamm, Nagg and Nell, sea window, earth window. Who is writing these notes, the author or director? And to whom are they directed? Can the author not already know this? Can these be simple self-reminders for rehearsals? But the notebooks were never used, never referred to in rehearsals. Do they constitute an extension of the text itself? Were they used to perform the work for the *mise en scène* of the mind, Beckett's only ideal theatre, one where he could play all the parts.

After Clov's initial inspection, Beckett notes to himself: 'Head bowed in perplexity before going for steps' (*TN* 2 195, 197). All seems to be in order, and yet Clov is uneasy; something has changed. As Beckett put it: 'C perplexed. All seemingly in order, yet a change. Fatal grain added to form impossible heap. *Ratio ruentis acetvi*' (195). The question of the audience for such 'uncautious remarks' pertains again. Beckett's note refers to Horace's argument in the *Epistle* to Augustus, where he uses the logical puzzle called *sorites* or 'heap' (*acervus*) to ask how many individual grains it might take to constitute a heap. By the play's end Hamm is already echoing the full complexity of Horace's conceit. In his inspection of the room, then, Clov senses the impossible, an almost imperceptible change to this day, the single extra grain 'needed to make the heap – the last straw', according to Beckett, and that sense of change, that almost imperceptible alteration, a change of degree that becomes a change of kind, provides the dramatic impetus for the rest of the day – and play. At the onset, then, Clov begins a series of what Beckett called unveilings, each of which mimics the opening of the theatre curtain. Clov parts the curtains on the windows, then unveils the twin bins, and finally unveils the central figure in a chair. Curtain up! After expressing the logical paradox, and so his anxiety about this day, Clov returns to the safety, the seclusion and the harmony of his kitchen, 'ten feet by ten feet', to contemplate the paradox of the fatal grain and to await his being called to attend to Hamm.

In the play's fifth unveiling, Hamm removes his 'old stancher', that is, the handkerchief he uses to staunch his bleeding – probably from a cerebral haemorrhage of some sort, or an aneurysm perhaps. His opening comment suggests the beginning of a game of chess: 'Me to play'. Beckett commented that Hamm is King in a game lost from the start, making senseless moves that only postpone the inevitable defeat, like a poor player unwilling to concede. Delaying the inevitable, Hamm resists defeat in an endgame lost from the first move. Such resistance might have been heroic in an earlier age, his fall, then, tragic, if not tragedy. He persists, even trying to invoke some tragic dignity from his futile and degenerated position. 'Can there be misery [. . .] loftier than mine?' he intones, and answers his own question: 'No doubt. Formerly' (*CDW* 93). During an age of tragic heroes, dignity in the misery of a fallen king might have been possible. But Hamm inhabits a world of the fundamentally unheroic. In Beckett's world such struggle, such resistance, is only clownish (hence the original red faces, perhaps).

Hamm's inflated oratory, the set pieces he repeats, revises and rehearses daily, begin to sound like the bombast of a 'ham' actor more than that of a tragic hero. His pains are rehearsed, his grief theatricalised, his misery aestheticised. His resistance to an inevitable end, or action of any sort, begins to sound like the rationalisations of the English theatre's great procrastinator, Hamlet; on the one hand, resolve, 'Enough, it's time it ended, in the refuge too'; on the other, dissolution of resolve, 'And yet I hesitate, I hesitate to . . . to end', and finally impasse, 'Yes, there it is, it's time it ended and yet I hesitate to . . . to end' (*CDW* 93). Except perhaps on this fatal day.

With the introductory themes established in the first scene, with the dumb show and the twin, almost symmetrical opening monologues and the sequence of five unveilings, the play moves into its dramatic conflict, the tempo of which Beckett described to his actors: 'There must be maximum aggression between them from the first exchange of words onward. Their war is the nucleus of the play' (McMillan and Fehsenfeld 1988: 205). One trope Beckett used to express this war is a hammer (Hamm) driving three nails: Clov (from the French *clou*), Nagg (from the German *Nagel*), and Nell (from the English nail). Asked directly by his cast if *Endgame* is a play for a hammer and three nails, Beckett responded in his circumspect voice, 'If you like'. Mother Pegg, whose light, like Hamm's, has died, might constitute yet a fourth nail. Furthermore, hammer and nails inevitably suggest the passion, the nailing of Christ to the wooden cross. Throughout the play, then, all the banging – including Hamm's tapping on the wall, Nagg's tapping on Nell's bin lid, Clov's tramping his booted feet – echoes the crucifixion theme. Another day Beckett explained the Hamm-Clov relationship with another metaphor, in terms of fire and ashes or embers, one character agitating the other, and from that stirring flames flare. Clov's goal throughout these conflicts is retreat, escape: to his visions, to his kitchen at least, but on this day (which appears to be different from the others because the grains of sand may have reached a critical mass, their impossible heapness, or the seconds of human existence may have accumulated to constitute a life, the lineaments of which are evident only in retrospect, that is, only at its end) Clov's larger goal is, finally, to escape the shelter. But Hamm warns him, 'outside of here it's death' (*CDW* 96). Hamm's goal, then, is to detain, and thereby retain his lackey, and so like the characters in *Waiting for Godot*, Hamm and Clov are ti-ed to this spot and to each other, and, faced with the prospect of filling time, they abuse each other. As Beckett said to the original Clov, Jean Martin, 'You must realize that Hamm and Clov are Didi and Gogo at a later date, at the end of their lives' (McMillan and Fehsenfeld 1988: 163).

Hamm has another means of filling the time. 'It's time for my story' (*CDW* 115), he announces. In Beckett's notebooks it is clear that Hamm's chronicle is already a repetition, a set piece, a performance with four distinct voices. Beckett explains to himself as if to another: 'First Hamm carries on a monologue, second, he speaks to the beggar he is imagining lying at his feet, third, he lends the latter his own voice, and he uses the fourth to recite the epic, linking text of his own story. Each voice corresponds to a distinct attitude [that is, position]' (*TN* 2 61). Hamm changes his posture to address the beggar lying at his feet, but his theatrical bending is difficult and painful. 'Hamm is fenced in', said Beckett; he is 'crippled; it is an effort for him to bend forward, to reach out his arm' (*TN* 2 61).

The theatrical nature of Hamm's chronicle and his need for an audience to witness the performance and so validate him and his story, brings to the fore the overriding theatrical metaphor for the entire play. *Endgame* is, after all, a play about play, or about *a* play. Hamm is always in need of an 'other', an audience. Even as a child, he needed fictional others, a Clov-like factotum, perhaps. Alone as a child he confesses to turning 'himself into children', that is, to creating an audience for himself. Beckett returned to this paradoxical image of creativity, unity in division, some two decades later in *That Time* where the protagonist of narrative A describes hiding as a child, 'making up talk breaking up two or more talking to himself being together that way' (*CDW* 390, 393). Such comments could gloss his own theatrical notebooks where in the safety of his study he created another with whom to converse, with whom to be 'uncautious' about his work. The repetitions of dialogue and action suggest that the characters are caught in a play, in a Mobius strip of narrative, in a chamber where sound is only echo. Clov threatens departure with the phrase: 'What's there to keep me here?' Hamm answers, 'The dialogue', then prompts Clov to the next performance: 'I've got on with my story' (*CDW* 121). Clov is needed as an audience as much as a domestic. Nagg and Nell, aged parents living without their 'shanks' in separate dustbins, Hamm's 'accursed progenitors', evidently, have little function in life (hence their relegation to dustbins) *except* that on occasion they form an audience for Hamm's performances and so act to witnesses him, his being, and the performance of his dying. The endgame is not Hamm's dying, but his performance of dying, a play. And Nagg's music hall story of the Tailor, complete with multiple voices, needs Nell's audition and so echoes Hamm's need for an audience, Nagg losing his audience on this day.

On this extraordinary day, in a world where nothing is left to change, where everything has run out, especially pain-killer (a palliative mentioned seventeen times in the play), something *has* perhaps changed, as Clov had observed from, or even before, the raising of the curtain: Nell dies and a flea appears; one life replaces another, perhaps. The lowly flea then terrifies Hamm as he shouts, 'But humanity might start from there all over again' (108). Terrified of ending, Hamm has a corresponding fear, not ending, that is, of a cyclical, recurrent, repetitious existence. Critics have long noted the anti-creation or anti-re-creation themes in *Endgame*. Hamm, an echo of Ham, the cursed son of Noah, fears that the whole cycle of humanity might restart from the flea, and so all this suffering – his own and humanity's – may have come to naught but a repetition, his suffering a rehearsal for another performance on another day. And the setting, the shelter, takes on qualities of Noah's ark, from which, according to Christian mythology, all earthly life began again, was repeated. In the earlier, discarded, two-act version of the play, the Clov-like character read aloud the portion of the book of Genesis requested by the Hamm-like character. Genesis 8:21–2 and 11:14–19 are specified, the story of Noah, as Beckett reportedly reread those passages during the play's composition. The threat of cyclical existence is echoed in the play's chess imagery, since even in the endgame the alternative to checkmate is stalemate. And in the theatre, of course, action resumes in almost exact repetition, that is, in an echo, the following night. The final irony of the *play* (in both senses of that term) is that while Hamm has been resisting the end, he is finally coming to terms with finality, ready to say 'yes' to the nothingness, accept the 'no' of existence, by the end of the play as he prepares his own re-veiling for a new performance. The gesture is belied, betrayed, by Clov's silent, unresponsive presence, his witness to Hamm's performed ending, a persistence that suggests at least one more turn to the wheel. If Hamm comes finally to accept that 'All's Well that Ends', well or ill, he may be deceived yet again. Clov may have outplayed him in this 'endgame'. It is Clov's best joke, one that can and must be shared (doubled) with an audience watching Clov watching Hamm – all at the expense of Hamm's dignity.

Or is the joke on Clov, Hamm's reveiling a signal of the conclusion, 'just play', that will resume, da capo, the next day with Clov's performed perplexity and his dramatic unveilings? The retreat from the physical world into the shelter may echo a solipsistic retreat (perhaps of an artist) into the recesses of the mind, only to find that it proves no retreat since consciousness itself is a conflicted, warring entity rather than a serene, coherent unity and so a refuge, an asylum, a favourite paradox of Beckett since the word suggests both haven and incarceration.

At some point Beckett learned to perform himself, in rehearsals, which almost always included an audience and so a public: friends, actors, critics, fellow authors, whom Beckett would permit, encourage, sometimes invite, to watch the show, even this author. His feigned ignorance to Rick Cluchey was doubtless a circumstantial expedient, and his response to Gudrun Genest, playing Nell in Berlin, was as playful. When she asked directly, 'Nell, doesn't she die, after all?' Beckett responded coyly, 'so it seems, but no one knows' (McMillan and Fehsenfeld 1988: 212). More often Beckett's self-stagings demystified his plays as more of the subtext was disclosed and more paratext revealed. Much of the unveiling that Beckett performed in his 'uncautious' notebooks resulted from a drama of self-conversation. As a director Beckett seems to have performed his plays to himself, for himself, on paper, before he could perform before his actors, before they could perform before their audience. Critics have on occasion raised the issue of privileging Beckett's own direction of his work. Why, some might ask, are Beckett's productions not treated like those of any other director? The simple answer is that Beckett was not 'any other director'. He was another director to himself. The texts on stage are fuller, more complete in Beckett's self-stagings, since much of the grey canon that he often struggled to suppress and to communicate only reluctantly, or as necessary to other directors and actors, is folded into those productions. It is the role Beckett played in the theatre in contradistinction to the one he played to the public at large. Beckett's stagings are not definitive, not the only ways to mount his plays, but they are the fullest expressions of the texts themselves. Texts augmented, they become the soundest argument for performance as the principal text in theatre.

Beckett may not always have been directly revelatory as a director, but his productions were always direct revelations, because he always performed them.

Note

1. Unless otherwise noted all letters to and from Barney Rosset and the Grove Press staff are from the Barney Rosset/Grove Press Archives. Material used with the permission of the principals.

References

Duckworth, Colin, ed. (1966) *En attendant Godot*, London: George G. Harrap & Co.

Harmon, Maurice, ed. (1998) '*No Author Better Served': The Correspondence of Samuel Beckett and Alan Schneider*, Cambridge, MA: Harvard University Press.

McMillan, Dougald and Martha Fehsenfeld (1988) *Beckett in the Theatre*, London: John Calder.

'I think this does call for a firm stand': Beckett at the Royal Court

> Ours is not to be a producer's theatre, nor an actor's theatre; it is to be a writer's theatre. (George Devine, 1956)

> I have always regarded the Court as you and our understanding as essentially a personal one between you and me rather than with the Society. The theatre will never be the same for me with you gone. (Beckett to Devine, 7 March 1965)

> To work on a Beckett play with Sam directing is an experience never to be forgotten. (Jocelyn Herbert)

Samuel Beckett's working relationship with the Royal Court Theatre, where some of his most stunning English-language productions were staged and where his most protracted aesthetic and cultural battles were fought, was unprecedented in British theatre history. But the Royal Court meant for Beckett less a building, a playhouse, a Society, a stage, than a collection of people, especially those associated with the English Stage Company, particularly George Devine and Jocelyn Herbert. At the Royal Court, particularly during the Devine years, Beckett was playwright and shadow director and so simultaneously both tutor and tutee, master and apprentice, and, as Martin Esslin has noted, 'In fact the Royal Court was the home of Beckett' (Doty 1990: 208). In 1956 the English Stage Company declared itself 'A Writers Theatre', and, at a conference in 1981, Esslin went on to laud such emphasis as the Royal Court maintained: 'this is a theatre that really does have respect for the writers and doesn't go in for one of the great diseases of the theatre of our period, namely, the so called director's theatre where the director has some concept which he imposes and thinks the script is little more than raw material' (Doty 1990:

205). Over his career in the theatre Beckett would be extraordinarily fortunate to find producers and directors who 'have respect for the writer': Roger Blin in Paris, Alan Schneider in the United States, and, perhaps chief among them, George Devine in the UK.

Devine had been interested in Samuel Beckett's work at least since he developed the English Stage Company at the Royal Court in 1957. Almost immediately thereafter Devine was in touch with Beckett about staging Beckett's first mime and was negotiating the English-language rights for what would be Beckett's second produced play, *Fin de partie*. When he heard that the Théâtre de l'Oeuvre had backed out of or postponed its commitment to stage the play, Devine rushed to Paris to offer the Royal Court Theatre as a venue for the premiere in French as part of what he conceived as a 'French Fortnight' in London. Thus Beckett's second major play would have its French and subsequently its English-language premieres in London at the Royal Court, beginning on 3 April 1957 in French, the production accompanied by Deryk Mendel in *Act sans parole*. 'The Court agreed to pay production costs, budgeted at 760 Pounds, and running expenses for one week', according to Terry W. Browne; even more importantly, something of a *quid pro quo* was established: 'As part of the agreement Beckett [. . . would] translate *Fin de partie* into English and give the English Stage Company the option to mount its own production at a later date *using the original sets*' (Browne 1975: 32, emphasis added), which it did, finally, opening, not without substantial resistance, on 28 October 1958 and running for a respectable thirty-eight performances (if only at 40 per cent capacity, according to Browne [1975: 114]). Although the French production ran for only six performances it opened with a gala, the French Ambassador in attendance. Beckett would attend rehearsals for the Blin production, but from what he saw he deemed the London production 'not very satisfactory. But I am told the première went much better' (*Letters 3* 40). From its short Royal Court run, the production went to the Studio des Champs-Elysées in Paris where it opened on 26 April, and where, as Beckett wrote to A. J. 'Con' Leventhal in a letter of 28 April, 'Blin has made enormous progress since London and gives now a quite extraordinary performance. The play gains greatly by the smallness and intimacy of the Studio' (45).

This was a watershed moment for Beckett not only because it established his working relationship with Devine and the Royal

Court, but also because he agreed to translate *Fin de partie* for the Court, a play he deemed almost untranslatable, or at least, as he wrote to his American publisher, Barney Rosset, on 6 April 1957, 'the French is at least 20% undecantable into English and will forfeit that much of whatever edge and tension it may have' (*Letters 3* 38). Rosset too was among those who had gained Beckett's confidence as a publisher, and Beckett now decided to expand Rosset's dossier; he would transfer the American performance rights from his English theatrical agent, Curtis Brown, and offer them to Rosset, even as this decision 'would bring down, from Covent Garden and I suppose from [*Godot*'s American producer, Michael] Myerberg, thunderbolts upon my head' (39).[1] Equally important was Beckett's decision to sell the English publication rights of this new play to his American publisher: 'When Faber offered to advance me money on the Fin de partie translation I replied I was selling it to you, and I prefer it that way. [. . .] I do not think there is anything in my contract with the Royal Court that infirms the above' (38); with that decision there would be no opportunity for Faber & Faber to publish an edited, truncated or censored version of *Endgame* as it had for the first publication of *Waiting for Godot*, which Beckett deemed mutilated.[2]

But the Lord Chamberlain would make the staging of Beckett's second play at least as difficult as he had his first. The French-language production, however, gained its licence with little interference, and the French production was even recorded in studio on 5 April for national broadcast (2 May 1957) on the BBC's Third Programme, which had broadcast *All That Fall* on 13 January 1957.[3] The English-language premiere of *Endgame*, on the other hand, was initially refused its performance licence. As Terry Browne put the matter:

When *Fin de partie* received its world première, in French at the Royal Court [. . .] no objections were raised to it by the Lord Chamberlain. However, when the play was submitted to him a year later in English, he found parts of it blasphemous and insisted upon alterations. Beckett agreed to some changes, but to others he was obdurate. After six months of negotiations the main point was resolved – to the satisfaction of the Lord Chamberlain, if not entirely satisfying to the English Stage Company or Beckett. In the scene in which Hamm, Clov, and Nagg all pray to God and then give up, Hamm was forbidden to say, 'The bastard! He doesn't exist.' Instead the Lord Chamberlain accepted, 'The swine!' as somehow or other less offensive. (Browne 1975: 58)

The conflict with the Lord Chamberlain's office ran even deeper than Browne suggests as representatives of the Lord Chamberlain seemed particularly hostile to Beckett during this procedure. Assistant Examiner, Sir Vincent Troubridge, writing to the Lord Chamberlain on 14 December 1957, put the matter thus:

> This is the English version of '*Fin de Partie*', the ridiculous, despairing, meaningless play by Samuel Beckett (author of *Waiting for Godot*) that I read in French before its production earlier this year. It is a play about an old blind man who confines his father and mother in two dust bins and talks interminably. I refer the Lord Chamberlain to my report on the French version for at least the sequence of actual events, if not what it all means, which is Mr Beckett's secret.[4]

Beckett's replacements in a letter of 26 December 1957 that answered Devine's letter of 21 December were in fact as follows, Beckett listing the changes that he considered 'easy' compared to a replacement of 'the bastard':

> 1. Replace 'balls' by 'botch' and, four lines later, 'botches by 'ballockses'. Or, if they object to 'ballockses', simply replace 'balls' by 'hames'.
> 2. Replace 'pee' by 'urinate' or, if they object to 'urinate', by 'relieve myself'.
> 3. Replace 'pee' by 'urination' or, if they object to 'urination', by 'relief'.
> 5. [*sic*] It is a pity to lose 'arses' because of its consonance with 'ashes'. 'Rumps' I suppose would be the next best. (*Letters* 3 81)[5]

The Lord Chamberlain's office at first accepted the following excisions or changes:

1. 'balls of the fly' replaced by 'botch of the fly'
2. 'I'd like to pee' replaced by 'I want to relieve myself'
3. 'What about that pee' replaced by 'What about that relieving yourself'
4. 'bastard' replaced by 'swine'
5. 'arses' replaced by 'rumps'

The Lord Chamberlain then went further, asking for the elimination of all the lines except number four above, which replacement was agreed, finally. On 22 January 1958, a defensive Assistant Comptroller wrote to the Lord Chamberlain to suggest a strategy for dealing with what might have been a public outcry:

> I stress that the Lord Chamberlain has not banned the play, but only required a small alteration which could be made with no detriment to the play if its author was not a conceited ass.
>
> If they put it about that the play has been banned we should do our best to prove them liars.[6]

One compromise that Devine had offered was to play the offending prayer scene, from 'Let us pray to God' to 'he doesn't exist' (*Endgame* 54–5), in French, a version the Lord Chamberlain had already accepted, but Beckett demurred in his letter to Devine on 26 December 1957:

> I am afraid I simply cannot accept omission or modification of the prayer passage which appears to me indispensable as it stands. And to play it in French would amount to an omission, for nine tenths of the audience. I think this does call for a firm stand. It is no more blasphemous than 'My God, my god, why hast Thou forsaken me?' (*Letters* 3 81)

Beckett further noted that he had already made some changes for publication: 'I have made a few inoffensive changes (including as it happens "ballockses" for "botches") when correcting proofs' (81).

By 3 January 1958, the Lord Chamberlain seemed to be compromising to some extent in a letter to Devine from Sir Norman Gwatkin, suggesting the elimination of 'God' or the mumbling of much of the speech and finally accepting Beckett's suggestion and substituting 'the swine' for 'the bastard' (*Letters* 3 89n1). Beckett, on the other hand, hardened his position on the centrality of the prayer scene in a letter to Devine of 5 January 1958: 'I am obliged to maintain the prayer scene as I wrote it' (*Letters* 3 89n1). At this point, then, or rather by February 1958, a licence for *Endgame* had been refused by the Lord Chamberlain (see note 6 below). Six months on, 7 July 1958, Beckett was still adamant:

It is quite impossible for me to consent to a weakening of this passage.

If the position is that the Lord Chamberlain, having taken his stand against 'bastard', is now committed to its removal, but would accept a different term of more or less equal force, then a compromise is still possible.

I could accept, for example, 'The swine, he doesn't exist'. (*Letters 3* 157)

At this point Beckett was headed to 'Jugoslavia' (which he called 'Titonia' after its dictator Marshall Tito) so further communication on the issue would not be possible. On his return on 28 July 1958, he wrote to Devine as follows: 'There are no alternatives to "bastard" agreeable to me. Nevertheless I have offered them "swine" in its place. This is definitely and finally as far as I'll go' (165).

In the same letter of 28 July, Beckett demonstrated his gratitude for the protracted battle that Devine was waging on his behalf: 'I should like to assure you, whatever course you adopt, and to mark in a small way my gratitude to you personally and to the Royal Court theatre, that I undertake here and now to offer you the first option on UK rights of my next play, in the unlikely event of my ever writing another' (165–6).

Endgame was delayed to the point that it would finally appear on a double bill with the world premiere of the promised next play, *Krapp's Last Tape*, on 28 October 1958, the latter conceived for Patrick Magee whose work Beckett had known from the previous year's BBC production of *All That Fall*. *Endgame* of 1958 would feature Devine himself as Hamm and the actor many consider Beckett's favourite, Jack MacGowran, as Clov. In fact Faber & Faber in its 1958 hardcover edition of *Endgame* would feature Devine as Hamm, hands folded in the disputed prayer scene.

For Krapp the first prospect would be Alec Guinness, but he declined the role (*Letters 3* 124); Magee then would be perfectly acceptable to Beckett, who, as usual with his Royal Court productions, oversaw rehearsals closely and made some changes to his text in the process, namely that he originally wanted the voice of Krapp to come directly from the tape recorder itself but that proved impractical and risky in production: 'This is probably too obvious to be worth saying, but when writing the thing I actually thought of the voice as coming from the visible machine!' (124).

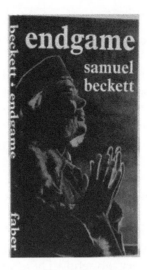

Moreover, after writing *Krapp's Last Tape* Beckett worried about productions outside of his oversight, particularly its American performance. He wrote to Rosset on 1 April 1958 to say of its premiere, 'I'd hate it to be made a balls of at the outset and that's why I question it's [*sic*] being let out to small groups beyond our controp [*sic*] before we get it done more or less right and set a standard of fidelity at least' (123). On 10 April 1958 Beckett wrote to Rosset that he was grateful for Rosset's withdrawing *Krapp* from Mary Manning's The Poet's Theatre of Cambridge, MA, noting to Manning that he did not want the play 'rushed into production in the States' (128n2), thus giving priority not only to the Royal Court production but to his oversight of the same as well, noting to Rosset that he was off to London to oversee the Devine production, 'where I hope to get the mechanics of it right' (127).[7]

That next play at the Royal Court would be *Happy Days* (already premiered in New York by Alan Schneider, it opened at the Cherry Lane Theatre on 17 September 1961 with Ruth White as Winnie) and would again involve the Royal Court's set designer Jocelyn Herbert, whose 'excellent sketches' Beckett approved of, particularly the one

> (where Winnie has her head on the mound). I like it very much and if this effect can be obtained when the set is lit I think it is just about right. The sky might perhaps be a little hotter (slightly more orange at the top only). Blue sky I'm afraid simply won't work – tant pis for the word in the text. (*Letters 3* 498)[8]

The *Happy Days* production was not otherwise going well, as Beckett noted to Patrick Magee on 17 September 1962:

> Things are in such a mess at the Court – no Winnie decided on yet [Beckett had suggested the American Ruth White on Schneider's recommendation but finally Brenda Bruce was Devine's choice], and opening scheduled for Oct. 18th! – that it may not come off at all. I shall know this week one way or another. If it does come off I shall be there for rehearsals this day week. (501)

And he wrote to Tom MacGreevy on 30 September 1962, 'I go to London tomorrow week for rehearsals of <u>Happy Days</u> and will be there till the opening on Nov. 1st' (*Letters 3* 501). By October 9, the production was looking promising: 'After two days' rehearsing I'm very hopeful. There are some good things about her. It had started off badly – voice and inflexions all wrong. Now much better', as she put on a 'Half Scots half Cockney' accent, 'amazing what an improvement it makes. [. . .] If she goes on progressing at the same rate it should be really quite something' (507). But to Barbara Bray he admitted on 11 October 1962:

> Poor rehearsal today, B.B. [Brenda Bruce] quite lost in text & business. When I went to theatre this morning George asked me (nicely) to let them work alone today. I seem to be upsetting her. That is, failing in what I came to do. I'll let them get on without me now & then, <u>every</u> now & then. [. . .] George rang me after <u>sine me</u> rehearsals to tell me how it had gone, obviously upset at having to dismiss me. In a burst of maximanimity I suggested I shd. leave them in peace on Monday again & only renew intrusion on the Tuesday. (507–8)

Beckett remained cordial with Devine, however, spending weekends 'Down here [in Long Sutton, near Basingstoke, Hampshire] with George & Jocelyn & divers children since yesterday till tomorrow' (509), but he continued to complain to Bray about rehearsals which had not gone well in his absence:

> Saw Bruce again Friday. She went through [the text]. Disastrous. [I] Stuttered a few groans and fled. Shall have it out here with G.[eorge] today. But fear nothing to be done. He has her back on her puke English – only dead flat – if you know what I mean. I shall get the

Scots back or perish in the attempt. [. . .] Haven't suffered & sweated so much for decades. (509–10)

Despite such overt tensions as *Happy Days* generated, Beckett's relationship with Devine remained exceptional; by November of 1962 Beckett offered him first option on all his theatre work, beginning with *Play*. Writing to Alan Schneider on 7 November, Beckett notes:

What I should like to know from you and Barney [Rosset] is whether or not I am free to make arrangements in London & Europe. I mean, do you want the world première or merely the new world? I have given the script to Devine. I have decided to give Royal Court first option on all my work in the future, this applying both to revivals & to new work. Devine is the nicest and most decent man one could meet and this is very important to me. He is not a great director, but most conscientious and painstaking and *will always let me be in on production*. Happy Days opened Nov 1, with Brenda Bruce & Peter Duguid. I don't think she carries the guns for the part, but she has done well and got – I am told – great praise. Excellent set by Jocelyn Herbert. I haven't read the critics and don't intend to read any more notices of my work. Friendly or not it's all misunderstanding. [Harold] Hobson for as usual, [Kenneth] Tynan as usual against. (*Letters 3* 513; emphasis added)

Beckett wrote to Herbert on 8 November, praising her set and confirming his decision to offer the Royal Court options on all of his theatre work: 'I wrote to [John] Barber [of Curtis Brown] to tell him what I told George that evening in Chelsea, viz. first option on everything, revival or new, to Royal Court in future. I feel happy about this' (515).

By July 1963 a fledgling National Theatre, then at The Old Vic, approached Devine 'with a suggestion he should produce [i.e., direct] PLAY for them next Spring, with a Sophocles play [*Philoctetes*]. I like the idea and have asked for further details. *I wd. of course be there for those rehearsals*' (565; emphasis added). *Play* would open 7 April 1964, but not without protracted battles that threatened the production since the work seems, in many respects, to be an all-out assault on theatre itself – as, in fact, *Eleutheria* and *Godot* had been a decade earlier – drama playing against itself, theatre against the very idea of theatre. If *Godot* eliminated 'action' from the stage, *Play* all but eliminated motion. If *Godot* eliminated intelligible causality, *Play* all but eliminated intelligibility itself. Beckett at first modified his stage directions on tempo from the 'whole movement as rapid as possible' in Typescript 5 to the final 'Rapid tempo throughout' (*TN* 4 307), but he evidently urged the former to Devine, much to the chagrin of the National Theatre's Literary Manager and general Beckett foe Tynan. Rehearsals of *Play*, even without the Lord Chamberlain involved, seemed to generate a whole new set of conflicts between producers and directors, or rather between those who understood and accepted Beckett's aesthetic shifts and those who could not. As Billie Whitelaw, who was introduced to Beckett's work through this production, recalls 'Rows between Sir Laurence Olivier and Ken Tynan turning up at rehearsals and saying "you cannot possibly go as quickly as this" and everyone keeping very quiet, as George Devine had no intention of going any slower – and neither had Beckett' (Whitelaw quoted in Knowlson 1978: 85). Tynan, in fact, attacked Beckett's presence at rehearsals, finding his influence finally intrusive and detrimental, as he noted in an acrimonious exchange of letters with the play's director:

> Before Beckett arrived at rehearsals, *Play* was recognizably a work we all liked and were eager to do. The delivery of the lines was (rightly) puppet-like and mechanical, but not wholly dehumanized. [. . .] It seems that Beckett's advice on the production has changed all that – the lines are chanted in a breakneck monotone with no inflections, and I'm not alone in fearing that many of them will be simply inaudible. [. . .] The point is that we are not putting on *Play* to satisfy Samuel Beckett alone. [. . .] I trust the play completely, and trust your production of it. What I don't trust is Beckett as co-director. If you could see your way to re-humanizing the text a little, I'll bet the actors and the audience will thank you – even if Samuel Beckett doesn't. (Tynan 1994: 84–5)

Devine (ever the Beckett loyalist) retorted:

> The presence of Beckett was a great help to me, and to the actors. [. . .] To play the play as you indicate would be to demolish its dramatic purpose and turn it into *literature*. [. . .] I certainly would never have leased the play to the National Theatre if I had thought the intention was to turn it into something it isn't, to please the majority. (Devine quoted in Wardle 1978: 208; emphasis added)

The critic Bamber Gascoigne, however, shared Tynan's reservations and complained of the English premiere, 'The words are to be gabbled so fast that we can't understand them (we may seem to catch them the second time round but not in such a way as to appreciate them).'[9]

Undeterred by such charges, Beckett would go on to write yet another 'unintelligible' play, *Not I*. American actress Jessica Tandy complained that the twenty-three-minute running time rendered the work unintelligible. Beckett responded with his now famous if oft misconstrued injunction: 'I'm not unduly concerned with intelligibility. I hope the piece may work on the nerves of the audience not its intellect' (quoted in Brater 1974: 200). The play certainly worked on the nerves of at least its actress, Billie Whitelaw: '*Not I* came through the letter-box. I opened it, read it and burst into tears, floods of tears. It had a tremendous emotional impact on me. I knew then that it had to go at great speed' (Knowlson 1978: 86). For Whitelaw, the work on *Play* nearly a decade earlier had thoroughly prepared her for the extraordinary ordeal of *Not I*. The experience was finally nerve-wracking for her. Blindfolded with yet another hood secured over her face, she suffered sensory deprivation in performance. 'The very first time I did it, I went to pieces. I felt I had no body; I could not relate to where I was; and, going at that speed, I was becoming very dizzy and felt like an astronaut tumbling into space . . . I swore to God I was falling' (Knowlson 1978: 87).

From *Play* onward and despite the Tynans of British theatre, Beckett's stage images would grow increasingly dehumanised, reified and metonymic, featuring dismembered or incorporeal creatures as Beckett's became a theatre of body parts and spectres, a theatre striving for transparency rather than solidity, a theatre, finally, trying to undo itself. And as plot and character dissipated, the playing space grew more delimited, circumscribed, controlled. The proscenium arch, however, is indispensable for such works, framing a playing space. The works from *Play* onward make little sense performed on modern, thrust stages or in the round. In his programme notes to the English premiere, Devine, clearly echoing Beckett on the subject, sounds prophetic:

> very often in Beckett words are not used for their intellectual content or their emotional impact. This is especially so in 'Play', where 'story and dialogue' are of a deliberately banal order. Here the words are

used more as sounds, as 'dramatic ammunition', to quote Beckett's own phrase, and they take equal place with the visual action but do not dominate it. (University of Reading Samuel Beckett Archive ms. 1581/15)

Despite Devine's implication that the anti-literary nature of Beckett's dialogue – or rather the three monologues – in *Play* is characteristic of Beckett's theatre work, his comments fit the original texts and productions of *Godot*, *Endgame*, *Krapp's Last Tape* or *Happy Days* poorly; but it is precisely the aesthetic perspective Beckett was to bring to revising these works. Devine's observation presages not only the theatre Beckett would write from *Play* onward, it also anticipated Beckett's need to revise and even to reconstitute all his theatre works through an aesthetics that percolated through *Play*.

Waiting for Godot would finally come to the Royal Court in Anthony Page's direction with Jack MacGowran as Estragon and Nicol Williamson as Vladimir in December of 1964, a production, as was his custom at the Royal Court, that Beckett oversaw with Page's blessing. Page would revive his staging in New York in 2009 for the Roundabout Theatre Company at the legendary, if not infamous, Studio 54, with Nathan Lane, Bill Irwin and John Goodman. The set, unfortunately, was disastrous, simulating a ring of stone, the constrictions of which, finally, did little more than limit the ability of the actors to move about the stage. In an educational programme supplement, Page noted 'I directed it formerly in '65 with Beckett there most of the time. So I still had the confidence, more or less, that I knew what he was after.'[10] Page would work under Beckett's close supervision again on the 1973 Royal Court Theatre production of *Not I* with Billie Whitelaw cited above.

Shortly after Devine's second 'firm stand' on behalf of Beckett's theatrical vision, he retired from day to day activities at the Royal Court. Beckett wrote to Devine on 7 March 1965 about a request from Peter Hall that Beckett's work become a permanent part of the Royal Shakespeare Company's repertory. A young Hall had become Artistic Director of the RSC in 1960 (and remained until 1968), and in addition to turning it into a year-round company and establishing a London base for it, mostly for transfers of successful productions from Stratford-upon-Avon, the ambitious Hall wanted to expand the RSC's repertory to contemporary work from home and abroad, precisely the aegis that Devine had set for himself and for the English Stage Company at the Royal Court. Hall had directed *Waiting for Godot* for its London premiere at the Arts Theatre in August of 1955, and so had done battle with the Lord Chamberlain on Beckett's behalf as well, and this just at the time that Devine was establishing the credibility of the English Stage Company. Hall had, moreover, recently produced *Endgame* with the RSC at the Aldwych Theatre, the first of the group's London bases, in July 1964, with essentially what might be deemed a Royal Court cast. The RSC *Playbill* for that production carried the following credit:

> *Endgame* (*Fin de Partie*) was given its world première by a company from Paris at the Royal Court Theatre, London, on April 2nd, 1957. It later opened in Paris. The following year an English version was seen at the Royal Court. The play was very successfully revived in Paris recently [i.e., February] with an English cast and two of the cast of the Paris revival now appear at the Aldwych: Patrick Magee (as Hamm) and Jack MacGowran (as Clov which he also acted at the Royal Court in 1958). The Aldwych production opened on July 9th, 1964.[11]

Beckett replied to Devine as follows:

> He [Hall] knows of my commitment to the Court. I have always regarded the Court as you and our understanding as essentially a personal one between you and me rather than with the Society [i.e. the earlier incarnation of the English Stage Company as the English Stage Society Ltd.]. The theatre will never be the same for me with you gone and quite frankly I am not interested in maintaining its priority in your absence. If you agree with this view I shall be free to consider whether or not to accept Hall's offer. If on the other hand you ask me to maintain the priority after your departure I shall bow to that view and reply to Hall accordingly. (*Letters 3* 663)

Devine was understandably suspicious about what he may have deemed a threat to his legacy, his reservations suggested by his response to Beckett on 17 March 1965: 'I personally feel that it would be a pity if you were to give Hall an exclusive right to produce your plays. [. . .] I know that Gaskill, who is taking over here in September, will want to do your work' (664n3). Beckett, who generally consulted any number of friends on such occasions, wrote to his British publisher John Calder on 9 April to say, 'After correspondence with George and Peter Hall I have decided that my commitment to the former ends in September when he leaves and not to commit myself to the Royal Shakespeare, though welcoming any proposal from them' (664n3).

The Aldwych *Endgame*, then, had actually opened in Paris first with essentially the same cast, and Beckett wrote to Rosset's assistant, Judith Schmidt, on 7 February 1964: 'Rehearsals of *Endgame* with Pat Magee and Jack MacGowran very exciting. They are both marvellous. We open at the Studio des C.E. [Champs-Elysses] Monday the 17th [of February] for a month's run.'[12] Writing to Alan Schneider on 11 April 1964 Beckett lamented his exhausting theatre schedule: 'Have been rehearsing practically continuously since Jan. and shall be on again in London in June-July for Aldwych *Endgame* with Jack & Pat. After that simply must go into retirement for a long spell' (Harmon 1998: 155); and on 31 May, Beckett continued, 'I am going to London June 29 to rehearse ENDGAME. We open July 9 [in London]. From then on I am at your disposal' (157). Beckett then oversaw both Paris and London rehearsals.

On 7 August 1965 George Devine suffered a heart attack followed shortly thereafter by a stroke. Beckett responded with a short but touching, comforting, and very personal note ending, 'I send you my deeply affectionate thoughts. In my old head I have your hand in both of mine' (*Letters 3* 672), and on 15 September he answered a letter from Herbert, 'distressed that the news is not better. [. . .] You know what's in my heart for you and George, so I needn't try and say it. But you do, to you both, from me. You're with me here and I'm wishing for you hard. All loving thoughts, dear George and Jocelyn' (673–4). Devine would never recover, and he passed away on 20 January 1966, but Beckett remained close with Herbert for the next twenty-three years.

In the post-Devine era, the Royal Court would maintain its emphasis on new British and European theatre, paying particular attention to Beckett's work, especially under Devine's successor as Artistic Director, William Gaskill (1965–72, with Anthony Page as co-AD from 1969–72), the theatre hosting the Compagnie Renaud-Barrault in Blin's direction of *Oh les beaux jours* with Madeleine Renaud in September of 1969, to the evening of shorts, 'Beckett / 3', featuring *Come and Go*, *Cascando* and *Play* in March of 1970, to Anthony Page's twin bill, *Krapp's Last Tape* and *Not I*, the former with Albert Finney, the latter with Billie Whitelaw, in January of 1973, to Anthony Page's revival of *Not I* with Billie Whitelaw in January of 1975, to the Beckett season of 1976 celebrating, if that is the word, Beckett's seventieth birthday, featuring Beckett's self direction of the Schiller Theater *Warten auf Godot* in April, a revival of *Endgame* in May, *Play*, *That Time* and *Footfalls*, the first two directed by Donald McWhinnie, the last Beckett's landmark self-direction of the play written for and performed by Billie Whitelaw in May, to what is perhaps his crowning achievement, *Happy Days* again with Billie Whitelaw in June of 1979.[13] In May 2013, forty years after the landmark 1973 Whitelaw world premiere under Beckett's direction, *Not I* returned to the Royal Court with a performance by Lisa Dwan, who was 'tutored in the role by Billie Whitelaw', as the Royal Court's press release and the post-performance video interview describe it. Dwan's iteration was first performed at Battersea Arts Centre in 2005, at the Southbank Centre in 2009 and at the inaugural International Festival of Beckett in Enniskillen in 2012. The role was reprised at the Court in January 2014 in an evening of plays for women, including *Footfalls* and *Rockaby*, all three featuring Dwan, the latter two directed by long-time Beckett associate Walter Asmus. Through them all the spirit of Beckett as a complete and committed man of the theatre, as a playwright and practising director, has remained a central thread of the Royal Court.

Notes

1. In a letter to Rosset of 2 April 1957, Jérôme Lindon suggested that it was he who suggested that Rosset handle American performance rights (*Letters 3* 41n4).

2. See Beckett's letter to Rosica Colin 'after' 18 January 1957: 'But I shall not authorize a bowdlerized edition [of *Endgame*]. If I had known that Faber were going to bring out Godot in the Lord Chamberlain's text I should have refused my auth[orisation]. But they did this without consulting me. If it can only be published in England in an expurgated form, I prefer not to be published there at all' (*Letters 3* 16).

3. According to the *Radio Times* issue 1746, 26 April 1957, p. 47; at http://genome.ch.bbc.co.uk/cc7443ffcc744aa0b71d1c64a4ce5456 (last accessed June 2016).

4. Material throughout from the Lord Chamberlain's archives at the British Library, particularly the correspondence files as follows: LCP CORR 28 December 1957/578 and LCP CORR February 1958/215. The analysis of *Waiting for Godot* that Troubridge refers to and in which he calls for the 'elimination of words of Joycean grossness' is found in LCP CORR July 1954/6597.

5. The Beckett published letters included '[*sic*]' after the number 5 as quoted above, indicating that Beckett had mis-numbered the sequence, but the inclusion of '[*sic*]' is itself an editing error since Beckett was responding to the five principal objections from the Lord Chamberlain as cited by Devine. The missing number 4 is what would become the 'the swine' for 'the bastard' exchange that Beckett at this point had no 'easy' answer for so it was omitted.

6. Such defensiveness from the Lord Chamberlain's office is belied by the file card in the LCP archive that is marked in red ink 'Refused February 1958', amended in pencil to the side 'Later passed'.

7. It would be Alan Schneider who set the 'standard of fidelity' for the American *Krapp's Last Tape*.

8. See further, McMullan 2014, and the website 'Jocelyn Herbert and Samuel Beckett: An Exhibition', at http://blogs.reading.ac.uk/staging-beckett (last accessed June 2016).

9. *The Observer*, 12 April 1964. Michaël Lonsdale, who played M in Serreau's French premiere, notes of Beckett's instructions, 'Il voulait qu'on parle à une vitesse de mitrailleuse' (He would like it spoken with the speed of a machine gun) (Auclair-Tamaroff 1986: 75).

10. See roundabouttheatre.org/upstage/godot.pdf

11. We should note at this point that the excisions and alterations called for by the Lord Chamberlain in 1958 were still in effect when the RSC petitioned to license the play for a London revival for the 1964 season at the Aldwych, where it planned to stage *Endgame* in repertory with Pinter's *The Birthday Party*. Michael Hallifax, writing to director Donald McWhinnie on 1 July 1964, proposed 'bunch' for 'botch', 'leak' for 'relieve myself', and to reinstate 'arses'. 'Swine' in reference to the deity was to be retained. Unsigned notes on the correspondence are as follows: 'I think we had better let this one go – it is a replacement although it is still rude'; and in response, 'yes, it's still offensive but in this sort of play I suppose it will pass'. The RSC Aldwych would continue to become something of a competing venue to the Royal Court in the post-Devine years, hosting: Roger Blin's Théâtre de France production of *Oh les beaux jours* on 3 April 1965; Beckett's staging for the Schiller Theater, Berlin, of *Das*

Letze Band on 29 April 1970; and the following year a Schiller twin bill, Beckett's stagings of *Endspiel* and *Das Letze Band* from 29 April to 1 May 1971, these in addition to the MacGowran-Magee *Endgame* that the RSC opened on 9 July 1964 in the Devine era and is cited above (see also the University of Reading 'Beckett in the UK' performance webpage: www.reading.ac.uk/staging-beckett/Venues. aspx?p=pspace-1567137020, last accessed June 2016).

12. Rosset/Grove Press Archive, Florida State University Special Collections.

13. Beckett's manuscript notebook prepared for his production of *Happy Days* at the Royal Court Theatre in June 1979 has been edited by James Knowlson and published by Faber & Faber, London, and Grove Press, New York (1985). A full account of Beckett's *Happy Days* rehearsals at the Royal Court is included in McMillan and Fehsenfeld 1988. See also Knowlson 1987. Beckett's work with *Footfalls* at the Royal Court is discussed in detail in Beckett 1999.

References

Auclair-Tamaroff É., et Barthélémy (1986) *Jean-Marie Serreau Decouvreur de Theatres*, Paris: L'Arbre Verdoyant Éditeur.

Beckett, Samuel, Correspondence of Samuel Beckett and Jocelyn Herbert (1962–89), Beckett International Foundation, Reading University Library (RUL MS 5200) [access and citation restricted].

Beckett, Samuel (1999) *The Theatrical Notebooks of Samuel Beckett, Vol. 4, The Shorter Plays*, ed. S. E. Gontarski, London: Faber & Faber; New York: Grove Press.

Brater, Enoch (1974) 'The "I" in Beckett's *Not I*', *Twentieth Century Literature* 20:3 (July), pp. 189–200.

Browne, Terry W. (1975) *Playwrights' Theatre: The English Stage Company at the Royal Court Theatre*, London: Pitman Publishing Ltd.

Doty, G. A. and B. J. Harbin (1990) *Inside the Royal Court Theatre, 1956–1981: Artists Talk*, Baton Rouge, LA: Louisiana State University Press.

Harmon, Maurice, ed. (1998) *No Author Better Served: The Correspondence of Samuel Beckett and Alan Schneider*, Cambridge, MA: Harvard University Press.

Knowlson, James (1978) 'Practical Aspects of Theatre, Radio, and Television: Extracts from an Unscripted Interview with Billie Whitelaw', *Journal of Beckett Studies* 3, pp. 85–91.

Knowlson, James (1987) 'Beckett as Director: The Manuscript Production

Notebooks and Critical Interpretation', *Modern Drama* 30:4, pp. 451–65.

McMillan, Dougald and Martha Fehsenfeld (1988) *Beckett in the Theatre*, London: John Calder.

McMullan, A. (2014) 'Designing Beckett: Jocelyn Herbert's Contribution to Samuel Beckett's Theatrical Aesthetics', in S. E. Gontarski, ed., *The Edinburgh Companion to Samuel Beckett and the Arts*, Edinburgh: Edinburgh University Press, pp. 409–22.

Tynan, Kenneth (1994) 'Life and Letters: Between the Acts', *The New Yorker*, 31 October 1994, pp. 82–5 (excerpts from *Kenneth Tynan: Letters*, ed. Kathleen Tynan, London: Weidenfeld & Nicolson, 1994).

Wardle, Irving (1978) *The Theatre of George Devine*, London: Jonathan Cape.

Index